AF271589

Poland's Foreign Policy Library

edited by

Karina Paulina Marczuk, University of Warsaw
Dariusz Popławski, University of Warsaw

Volume 1

Andrzej Wierzbicki

Polish-Belarusian Relations

Between a Common Past and the Future

Translated from the Polish by
Anthony Sloan

Reviewed by
Prof. Józef Tymanowski, University of Warsaw
Prof. Svetlana Kozhirova, Academy of Public Administration under the President of the
Republic of Kazakhstan

The Deutsche Nationalbibliothek lists this publication in the
Deutsche Nationalbibliografie; detailed bibliographic data
are available on the Internet at http://dnb.d-nb.de

ISBN   978-3-8487-4749-8 (Print)
        978-3-8452-9114-7 (ePDF)

British Library Cataloguing-in-Publication Data
A catalogue record for this book is available from the British Library.

ISBN   978-3-8487-4749-8 (Print)
        978-3-8452-9114-7 (ePDF)

Library of Congress Cataloging-in-Publication Data
Wierzbicki, Andrzej
Polish-Belarusian Relations
Between a Common Past and the Future
Andrzej Wierzbicki
204 p.
Includes bibliographic references and index.

ISBN   978-3-8487-4749-8 (Print)
        978-3-8452-9114-7 (ePDF)

1st Edition 2018
© Nomos Verlagsgesellschaft, Baden-Baden, Germany 2018. Printed and bound in Germany.

This work is subject to copyright. All rights reserved. No part of this publication may be
reproduced or transmitted in any form or by any means, electronic or mechanical,
including photocopying, recording, or any information storage or retrieval system,
without prior permission in writing from the publishers. Under § 54 of the German
Copyright Law where copies are made for other than private use a fee is payable to
"Verwertungsgesellschaft Wort", Munich.

No responsibility for loss caused to any individual or organization acting on or refraining
from action as a result of the material in this publication can be accepted by Nomos or
the author.

Contents

Contents

Introduction

Belarus is one of four states that arose on Poland's eastern border after the collapse of the USSR. Official contacts between Poland and Belarus were initiated in 1990 after the Belarusian Soviet Socialist Republic declared independence, and diplomatic relations between the Republic of Poland and the Republic of Belarus were established on 2 March 1992. Yet, the history of Polish-Belarusian relations dates from long before the beginning of the 1990s. It is important to remember that, for a very long time, Belarus and Poland were both part of the same state. As the Polish historian Marceli Kosman has written, those relations were therefore "very close, though not always idyllic" (Kosman, 1979, p. 6; Winnicki, 2015, p. 229-230). In turn, the Belarusian author Piotra Rudkoŭski has put it this way: "For Belarusians, Poland is something more than a neighbour. In the historical and cultural dimension, Belarus and Poland are Siamese twins" (Rudkoŭski, 2007, p. 185). Without undermining the sense of these arguments, an even bolder, unequivocal statement can be made – that, seen against Poland's relations with its other neighbours, Polish-Belarusian relations have involved the least conflict, and are virtually free of historically rooted mutual resentment and hatred. The memory of this common, relatively tranquil past is still very much alive in the consciousness of many Poles and Belarusians. It would seem, then, that nothing should stand in the way of continuing these healthy, relatively 'normal' relations – even today, when Belarus is an independent state. It is worth adding, after Andrzej Drawicz, that "it is difficult to consider relations between states in terms of the fault of either side. They always result from both objective factors and subjective conditions" (Bieleń, 1997, p. 17). If, then, there are no historical scores to be settled between sides, it shouldn't be difficult for them to exist as good neighbours.

This study is intended to provide answers to a basic research question, namely: Why can we not deem current Polish-Belarusian relations as "model" relations, but on the contrary, as relations featuring each side's suspicion and mistrust of the other's intentions? The cause of this state of affairs is to be found in the wider geopolitical context, which includes Poland's policy towards the east since the country's political transformation, including its policy towards Russia. On the one hand, then, we have

Poland's accession to NATO and the EU, and on the other hand Belarus's military alliance with Russia and its active participation in Eurasian integration projects. It would seem, however, that these should also pose no great obstacle to maintaining healthy, peaceful mutual relations. Participating in European integration need not lead to a conflict with states that are not involved (including, of course, with states that are interested in Eurasian integration), and vice versa. Unfortunately, however, with Poland and Belarus this is not the case. Polish-Belarusian relations are subordinate to Polish-Russian relations, including the current rivalry over the identity of Belarusians. This stems from a historical confrontation between the Polish and the Russian concepts of nationhood – mutually exclusive identities that intersect in Belarus. Poland's efforts are directed towards an occidentalisation of Belarusian consciousness, which would be furthered by the removal of Alexander Lukashenko from the power he has held since 1994. Certainly, Belarus finds itself in a border zone between the Byzantine-Orthodox and Latin civilizations. Disregarding this factor means a failure to understand the complex history of the country. It is worth emphasising that, in the above rivalry, it is the Russians who now have the advantage, mainly due to their shared past with the Belarusians, from the Rurik state, to religion (Orthodoxy under the jurisdiction of the Patriarch of Moscow) to ancestry, to language (the Russian language sphere, closeness of the Russian and Belarusian languages, and above all, the Cyrillic alphabet), to ethnic structure (a large Russian minority), to forms of authority and values – democracy and human rights are not what is most important to Belarusians. Russia also has the advantage of strong economies ties, and is seen as a guarantor of security since, until recently, Belarus saw NATO as its biggest threat. In favour of Poland, there are memories of an ancient, joint statehood, linguistic proximity (perhaps even greater than that between Belarusian and Russian) and influences of the Polish language, identification with the West and its higher standard of living (but with the requirements of democratization and the protection of human rights), and the perception of Poland as a representative of the European Union and the West as broadly understood.

Because, as stated above, Polish-Belarusian relations are a derivative of Polish-Russian relations, and because the perception of Russia as a "perpetual threat", as a state that is striving to re-subjugate Poland, has been a determining factor in Poland's policy towards the east since 1990, Polish-Belarusian relations are to a large extent a function of Belarusian-Russian relations. The closer the latter, the less congenial the former. Poland has not given up attempting to move Belarus's geopolitical orientation Westward, using for that purpose the ideology of "exporting democracy to the east" (Zięba, 2011, p. 69) – a mission of presenting freedom and Westernisation as a prerequisite for civilizational development. While for Belarus, its relations with Poland depend on whether and to what extent Poland tries to influence its internal political process, in line with the slogan "Don't try to teach us how to live". Belarus does not intend to withdraw from the process of Eurasian integration, yet is not against the idea of being a bridge between the European Union and the Russian Federation, and acknowledges the interests it has in common with Poland and other Central European countries: "Our objective strategic interests coincide to a large extent with the interests of Ukraine, to a significant extent with those of Poland and the Baltic States. All of those countries, though they belong to different groups, in the new stage will increasingly deal with the problem of securing their own interests, which differ from those of the superpowers, their allies and large countries. It is in this that we find an objective basis for our common interests" (Lukashenko, 2004). Here arises a certain asymmetry. By using its membership in the EU as an instrument for achieving its own goals and interests in its relations with Belarus, Poland also becomes a direct representative of the interests of that organisation, and even of other powers outside Europe, in the geopolitical rivalry over post-Soviet territory. While Belarus is politically oriented towards Russia, in its relations with Poland its strives to act as an autonomous entity, and not as an exponent of the interests of the Russian Federation – while this, of course, is not always properly understood.

It is in the Polish national interest to maintain friendly, neighbourly relations with all of its neighbouring states. Poland, as Andrzej Szeptycki writes, is "vitally interested in the adoption by its eastern neighbours of European standards (democracy, human rights, the rule of law, a free-market economy, respect for minority rights, etc.), wishes to develop cooperation between these countries and the Euro-Atlantic structures, and in the long run to expand those institutions, and finally, seems to be seeking to weaken Russia's position in the region" (Szeptycki, 2011, p. 294). At the same time, as noted by Stanisław Bieleń, "by its own choice, and partly under the influence of the expectations of certain Western states, particularly the United States, Poland took on the unrealistic role of the key actor working to weaken Russia's ambitions to retain and then rebuild its influence among the other CIS countries" (Bieleń, 2008, p. 24). Let us add, however, that such a view of Poland having an "international position as a 'middle-sized' state" is beyond its capability, and in a given situation may even harm Polish-Belarusian relations.

The nature of Polish-Belarusian relations, then, is determined by the following factors:

1) *the historical and cultural position* of the two countries situated at the point of contact between the Latin and Byzantine-Orthodox civilizations. Poland's affiliation in this respect has been aptly described by Jerzy Jedlicki: "…the West created a higher type of civilization whose values serve as a universal standard and will therefore radiate to ever more distant countries; Poland indisputably belongs to this civilization, but is backward and immature in relation to the West; on the other hand, it is the most Western Slavic nation, as a result of which it has the mission of transmitting the beam of Western light further to the East" (Jedlicki, 1988, p. 31). In the case of Belarus, its civilizational adherence is different than that of Poland, though the final character thereof is ambiguous. In a study that serves to interpret the internal and foreign policy of Belarus – *Foundations of the Ideology of the State of Belarus* – it is written that "Belarus never belonged to Western Europe ethnically or culturally, but developed as an ethno-cultural community and as a country in the bosom of Eastern Orthodox Christian civilization and in the Eurasian geopolitical sphere" (*Akademiia upravleniia pri prezidente Respubliki Belarus'*, 2004, p. 35). This does not question that Belarus belongs to Europe, but to Europe as broadly understood, not the European Union. The intention is to underscore that Belarus is specific and culturally separate, as the Belarusian President Lukashenko has pointed out: "We don't choose the East and the West, or the East or the West – we choose Belarus, which, because of its history, because of its geography, because of its culture and mentality, will be in the East, and in the West" (Lukashenko, 2004)

2) *identity*, formed on the one hand by the memory of the historical affiliation of Belarusians with the Polish state and nation, and on the other hand by Belarusians's strong feeling of unity with eastern Slavs, or adherence to the "Russian world"

3) *the geopolitical situation*, in which Poland and Belarus are each connected with powers vying for influence in the post-Soviet territories.

These factors show that, within this scope, the theory of international roles (Zając, 2015), the category of international identity (Bieleń, 2015) or, indirectly, the category of rivalry (Włodkowska-Bagan, 2015) can all be applied in various configurations.

In order to verify the research assumptions made, that is, to present the current state of Polish-Belarusian relations, this work consists of an introduction, five chapters, and a conclusion. The Introduction sets out the theoretical assumptions and the conditions of Polish-Belarusian relations. Chapter 1, *Historical and cultural conditions*, shows the cultural and historical foundations that have shaped relations between the two states, from the Grand Duchy of Lithuania to the present day. Chapter 2, *Polish-Belarusian relations from the perspective of Polish policy towards the east*, concerns the broader context in which those relations have developed, particularly Poland's policy towards the east. It also examines the systemic conditions of the foreign policy of each country, their geopolitical positions, and their social and economic potential. Chapter 3, *Political relations*, traces the evolution of Polish-Belarusian relations in the political dimension that has determined other fields of cooperation – from the promising contacts at the beginning of the transformation to the "critical dialogue" conditioned by the internal and foreign policies of Belarus, to the challenges arising out of Poland's accession to the European Union, up to the "reconstruction" brought on in part by recent events in Ukraine. Chapter 4, *Difficult issues*, concerns such mutual problems as the historical dialogue, ethnic minorities – Poles in Belarus and Belarusians in Poland – and bordering crossing and visa issues. Chapter 5, *Economic relations*, covers such issues as the legal and treaty foundations of economic cooperation, cross-border cooperation, energy, and other areas of, prospects for and barriers to cooperation. Finally, Chapter 6, *Cultural cooperation*, looks at mutual contacts in the fields of culture and education. The monograph concludes with a summary, conclusions and recommendations.

In preparing this work, use was made of the literature directly concerning the subject of research, and to works that were helpful in the broader context. Polish-Belarusian relations are not completely absent from Polish academic literature. Many works on the subject have been written in the last couple of decades. There is Helena Głogowska's monograph *Stosunki polsko-białoruskie w XX wieku. Od Imperium Rosyjskiego do Unii Europejskiej[Polish-Belarusian Relations in the 20th Century. From the Russian Empire to the European Union]* (Głogowska, 2012). Other publications are anthologies, to which belong: *Belarus' i Pol'shcha. Polska i Białoruś [Poland and Belarus]*, edited by Adam Eberhardt and Uładzimir Ułachowicz (Eberhardt and Ułachowicz, 2003), which contains contributions by both Polish and Belarusian authors; *Polska Białoruś. Problemy sąsiedztwa [Poland and Belarus. Problems of Neighbours]*, edited by Henryk Chałupczak and Elżbieta Michalik (Chałupczak and Michalik, 2005); the two-volume *Polish-Belarusian Relations* (vol. 1: *History and Politics*, vol. 2: *Society and Politics*), edited by Stanisław Jaczyński and Rafał Pęksa (Jaczyński and Pęksa, 2009); *Polska I Białoruś w współczesnej Europie [Poland and Belarus in Contemporary Europe]*, edited by Józef Tymanowski, Aleksandra Daniluk and Józef Bryll (Tymanowski, Daniluk and Bryll, 2015) with the participation of Belarusian and Polish authors. It also made sense to consider both monographs and anthologies concerning Belarusian foreign policy, or how the country is situated in international relations. These include Rafał Czachor's monograph *Polityka zagraniczna Republiki Białoruś w latach 1991-2011 [Foreign Policy of the Republic of Belarus 1991-2011]* (Czachor, 2011), Józef Tymanowski's *Rola i znaczenie Republiki Białoruś we współczesnej Europie [The Role and Significance of the Republic of Belarus in Contemporary Europe]* (Tymanowski, 2017), and the anthology *Białoruś w stosunkach międzynarodowych [Belarus in International Relations]*, edited by Ireneusz Topolski (Topolski, ed., 2009). Worthy of mention among foreign publications is an anthology by Latvian authors in English, edited by Andis Kudors: *Belarusian Foreign Policy: 360°* (Kudors, 2017). Yet, within this scope there is a palpable absence of works by Belarusian authors, apart from a collection in Belarusian of documents and maps concerning the period 1918-1989: *Belaruska-pol'skiia adnosiny 1918-1989* (Snapkoŭski, 2013). In these and other publications, various aspects of Polish-Belarusian relations are addressed.

Also worthy of mention among other sources are studies on the history of Belarus, which must inevitably touch on the period when Poles and Belarusians lived within a single state – the Republic. Such works include those by the Polish historians Marceli Kosman (Kosman, 1979) and Eugeniusz Mironowicz (Mironowicz, 2011), and by Belarusian historians such as Malinovskiĭ (Malinovskiĭ, 2003), Vladimir Picheta (Picheta, 2003), Hiennadź Sahanowicz (Sahanowicz, 2001) and Zachar Szybieka (Szybieka, 2002). On the subject of the conditioning of the culture and civilization of Belarus, the most important works are the monograph and other articles by Ryszard Radzik (Radzik, 2009; 2012) and, among Belarusian studies, the monograph by Anatoliĭ Lazarevich and Il'ia Leviash (Lazarevich and Leviash, 2014).

The theoretical and methodological foundation of this work derives from monographs and studies by Józef Kukułka (Kukułka, 1998): *Po-*

land's Foreign Policy in the 21st Century, edited by Stanisłąw Bieleń (Bieleń, ed., 2011) and *Teorie i podejścia w nauce o stosunkach międzynarodowych [Theories and Approaches in Research on International Relations]*, edited by Ryszard Zięba, Stanisław Bieleń and Justyna Zając (Zięba, Bieleń and Zając, eds., 2015).

The source materials comprise international treaties and agreements, documents, acts of law, monographs, scientific articles, reports, expert opinions, statistical data and press materials in Polish, Russian, English and Belarusian.

This work is distinctive in that it attempts approach the subject of Polish-Belarusian relations comprehensively, taking account of the latest processes and tendencies. The author does not aspire to the role of a 'dogmatist' who will not permit other views on the subject at hand. The research concept is original, and has not previously been employed in Polish academic literature. The author is aware of the monograph's shortcomings, but offers it in order to promote deeper reflection on the material it contains.

The author would like to express his sincere gratitude to Professors Karina Marczuk and Dariusz Popławski of the Institute of International Relations at the Faculty of Political Science and International Studies at Warsaw University for their initiative in making this publication possible, and for their academic and organizational support. Thanks also go to Professor Stanisław Sulowski – Dean of the Faculty of Political Science and International Studies, for his benevolence and financial support.

References

Akademiia upravleniia pri prezidente Respubliki Belarus', 2004. *Osnovy ideologii belarusskogo gosudarstva, 2004*. Minsk: Redakcionno-izdatel'skiĭ centr Akademii upravleniia pri Prezidente Respubliki Belarus'.

Bieleń, S., 1997. Długa droga do przyszłości. *Wiadomości Kulturalne*, 51-52 (187-188), p.17.

Bieleń, S., 2008. Deficyt realizmu w polskiej polityce zagranicznej. *Stosunki Międzynarodowe – International Relations*, 38(3-4), p. 24.

Bieleń S., ed., 2011. *Poland's Foreign Policy in the 21st Century*. Warsaw: Difin SA.

Bieleń, S., 2015. Tożsamość uczestników stosunków międzynarodowych. In: R. Zięba, S. Bieleń and J. Zając, eds. 2015. *Teorie i podejścia badawcze w nauce o stosunkach międzynarodowych*. Warsaw: Wydawnictwo Wydziału Dziennikarstwa i Nauk Politycznych Uniwersytet Warszawski, pp. 153-176.

Chałupczak, H. and Michalik, E. eds., 2006. *Mniejszości narodowe i etniczne w procesach transformacji oraz integracji*. Lublin: Wydawnictwo Uniwersytetu Marii Curie-Skłodowskiej.

Czachor, R., 2011. *Polityka zagraniczna Republiki Białoruś w latach 1991-2011. Studium politologiczne*. Polkowice: Wydawnictwo Dolnośląskiej Wyższej Szkoły Przedsiębiorczości i Techniki in Polkowice.

Eberhardt, A. and Ułachowicz, U. eds., 2003. *Belarus' i Pol'shcha. Polska i Białoruś*. Warsaw: Polski Instytut Spraw Międzynarodowych.

Głogowska, H., 2012. *Stosunki polsko-białoruskie w XX wieku. Od Imperium Rosyjskiego do Unii Europejskiej*. Białystok: Wydawnictwo Uniwersytetu in Białystok.

Jaczyński, S. and Pęksa, R., eds., 2009. *Stosunki polsko-białoruskie*. Siedlce: Wydawnictwo Akademii Podlaskiej, Vol.1 Historia i polityka, Vol.2. Społeczeństwo i polityka.

Jedlicki, J., 1988. *Jakiej cywilizacji Polacy potrzebują. Studia z dziejów idei i wyobraźni XIX wieku*. Warsaw: Państwowe Wydawnictwo Naukowe.

Kosman, M., 1979. *Historia Białorusi*. Wrocław-Warsaw-Kraków-Gdańsk: Zakład Narodowy imienia Ossolińskich.

Kudors A., ed., 2017. *Belarusian Foreign Policy: 360°*. Rīga: University of Latvia Press, The Centre for East European Policy Studies. Available at: <http://appc.lv/wp-content/uploads/2017/05/book_Belarusian_360-www-2.pdf> [Accessed 7 September 2017].

Kukułka, J., 1998. *Traktaty sąsiedzkie Polski odrodzonej*. Wrocław – Warsaw – Kraków: Zakład Narodowy Imienia Ossolińskich – Wydawnictwo.

Lazarevich, A. and Leviash, I., 2014. *Belarus': kul'turno-tsivilizatsionnyĭ vybor*. Minsk: Belarusskaia navuka.

Lukashenko, A.G., 2004. *Vystuplenie Prezidenta Respubliki Belarus A.G. Lukashenko „Vneshniaia politika Respubliki Belarus' v novom mire" na soveshchanii s rukovoditeliami zagranuchrezhdeniĭ Respubliki Belarus'*. [online] Available at: <http://president.gov.by/ru/news_ru/view/vystuplenie-prezidenta-respubliki-belarus-aglukashenko-vneshnjaja-politika-respubliki-belarus-v-novom-mire-na-5837/> [Accessed 10 April 2017].

Malinovskiĭ, V., 2003. *Istoriia belorusskoĭ gosudarstvennosti*. Minsk: Belarus'.

Mironowicz, E., 2001. *Historia Białorusi*. Białystok: Orthdruk.

Picheta, V., 2003. *Istoriia beloruskogo naroda*. Minsk: Izdatel'skiĭ centr BGU.

Radzik, R., 2009. Kulturowo-cywilizacyjna tożsamość społeczeństwa Białorusi. In: I. Topolski, eds. 2009. *Białoruś w stosunkach międzynarodowych*. Lublin: Wydawnictwo Uniwersytetu Marii Curie-Skłodowskiej, pp. 39-75.

Radzik, R., 2012. *Białoruś. Między Wschodem a Zachodem*. Lublin: Wydawnictwo Uniwersytetu Marii Curie-Skłodowskiej.

Rudkoŭski, P., 2007. *Paŭstan'nie Belarusi*. Vil'nia: Instytut belarusistyki.

Sahanowicz, H., 2001. *Historia Białorusi. Od czasów najdawniejszych do końca XVIII wieku*. Lublin: Instytut Europy Środkowo-Wschodniej.

Snapkoŭski, V., 2013. *Belaruska-pol'skiia adnosiny (1918-1989 gg.): dasledavanni, dokumenty, iliustratsi i karty.* Minsk: Èntsyklapedyks.

Szeptycki A., 2011. A new phase of Polish messianism in the East?. In: S. Bieleń, ed. 2011. *Poland's Foreign Policy in the 21st Century.* Warsaw: Difin SA., pp. 292-316.

Szybieka, Z., 2002. *Historia Białorusi 1795-2000.* Przeł. Hubert Łaszkiewicz. Lublin: Instytut Europy Środkowo-Wschodniej.

Topolski I., ed., 2009. *Białoruś w stosunkach międzynarodowych.* Lublin: Wydawnictwo Uniwersytetu Marii Curie-Skłodowskiej.

Tymanowski J, Daniluk, A. and Bryll. J. eds., 2015. *Polska i Białoruś we współczesnej Europie.* Warsaw: Wydział Dziennikarstwa i Nauk Politycznych.

Tymanowski, J., 2017. *Rola i znaczenie Republiki Białoruś we współczesnej Europie.* Toruń: Adam Marszałek.

Winnicki Z.J., 2015. Cywilizacyjno-kulturowe uwarunkowania współczesnych relacji polsko-białoruskich. In: J. Tymanowski, A. Daniluk, J. Bryll, eds. 2015. *Polska i Białoruś we współczesnej Europie.* Warszawa: Wydział Dziennikarstwa i Nauk Politycznych, pp. 227-257.

Włodkowska-Bagan, A., 2015. Kategoria rywalizacji. In: R. Zięba, S. Bieleń and J. Zając, eds. 2015. *Teorie i podejścia badawcze w nauce o stosunkach międzynarodowych.* Warszawa: Wydawnictwo Wydziału Dziennikarstwa i Nauk Politycznych Uniwersytetu Warszawskiego, pp. 241-259.

Zając J., 2015. Teoria ról międzynarodowych [Theory of International Roles]. In: R. Zięba, S. Bieleń, S. and J. Zając, eds. 2015. *Teorie i podejścia badawcze w nauce o stosunkach międzynarodowych.* Warsaw: Wydawnictwo Wydziału Dziennikarstwa i Nauk Politycznych Uniwersytet Warszawski, pp. 127-151.

Zięba R., 2011. The search for an international role for Poland: conceptualizing the role of a „middle-ranking" state. In: S. Bieleń, ed. 2011. *Poland's Foreign Policy in the 21st Century.* Warsaw: Difin SA. pp. 61-79.

Zięba R., Bieleń, S. and Zając, J. eds., 2015. *Teorie i podejścia badawcze w nauce o stosunkach międzynarodowych.* Warsaw: Wydawnictwo Wydziału Dziennikarstwa i Nauk Politycznych Uniwersytet Warszawski.

Chapter 1 Historical and cultural conditions

Belarus emerged as an entity taking part in international relations only in 1991. For this reason, institutional relations between Poland and Belarus as relations between two states only began to develop as from that point in time. Nevertheless, historically speaking, Polish-Belarusian relations as relations between two political and territorial groups – Poles and Belarusians – go back much further, despite the absence of a Belarusian state in the strict sense of the word. For centuries, the role of such a state was played by the Grand Duchy of Lithuania, though the name provides no indication of this.

It is not possible to properly identify Polish-Belarusian relations in time and space without first determining when the Belarusian nation was formed, and the Belarusian state established. This is especially true because one can say of Belarus that it is "a little-known country", both in Poland and elsewhere. For several centuries, Poland and Belarus had a shared history as part of a single state organism to which Belarus belonged as part of the Grand Duchy of Lithuania. Relations between Poland and the Eastern Slavs inhabiting the eastern parts of the Polish state, where the Belarusians formed a distinct group, were affected by their having a separate religion (which was used instrumentally in the geopolitical rivalry taking place in Eastern Europe). It was that religion which to a large extent laid out the lines of the ethnic division between the Poles and the Belarusians.

1. Name of the state, ethnogenesis, the state- and nation-building process, Belarusian identity

Belarus is one of Poland's neighbours to the east. Unlike Poland, it has no natural boundaries, and so it can be described as an open country, having no mountains or access to the sea, and is mainly flat, with some areas of marshland. The current name of the country was popularised within its current area only at the end of the 19th century. There is no full agreement among scholars as to the etymology of the name. The subject was first investigated in the 18th century[1]. The term "Biała Ruś" ["White Rus"], how-ever, first appeared in the 12th century; it referred to the Duchy of Ros-towsko-Suzdalski, situated in northeastern Rus. The phrase was meant to indicate a state that was "free, great and enlightened" and subordinate to no one, as opposed to "Black Rus", which was threatened with subjuga-tion by its neighbours[2]. After the Tatar and Mongolian invasion, the name "White Rus" shifted westward and was applied to the area of the Duchies of Vitebsk and Polotsk until these became part of the Grand Duchy of Lithuania. In Polish literature, the name "White Rus" first appears in the chronicle of Jan of Czarnków in connection with struggles among the Lithuanian dukes; in 1382, the chronicle states, Jagiełło's uncle had him imprisoned "in a certain stronghold in White Rus called Polotsk" (Łatys-zonek, 2010, p. 40). After a break of more than a century, the Italian hu-manist Filippo Buonaccorsi reintroduced "White Rus" to Polish literature, but without assigning the term to any particular geographical area. His conception was developed by the Polish geographer Jan of Stobnica, for whom "White Rus" covered all the Russian lands of the Grand Duchy of Lithuania to the Neman River and the Great Novgorod Republic. The final geographic form of "White Rus", which approximates Belarus's modern political borders, was provided in Polish literature by Marcin Kromer, in his work *Polska [Poland]*. He excluded Great Novgorod, Wołyń and Pod-lasie and, after the Union of Lublin, the region of Kiev. In the 16th and 17th centuries, "White Rus" (*Russia Alba*) covered the lands of Vitebsk and Mogilev. The inhabitants of Belarus who were the ancestors of today's Be-larusians had not previously known the term (Łatyszonek, 2010, p. 42). At the beginning of the 20th century, with the creation of the Belarusian Peo-ple's Republic and the Belarusian Soviet Socialist Republic, the toponym Belarus also acquired political significance, and finally stuck as the name of the area, with Belarusians as the name of its inhabitants (Vonsovich, 2005, p. 10).

---

1 The term "White" before the name "Rus" has many meanings. One group of re-searchers considers that it derives from the "abundant snowfalls in this northern land". Another group holds that the adjective "white" is connected with the pre-dominance of white-coloured clothing worn by the area's inhabitants, and with their fair hair.
2 The division of Rus into "White" and "Black" also has a religious context. "White" denoted the area that had been Christianised, and "Black" those lands that were still pagan.

Belarusians belong to the Eastern Slavic nations. Among Belarusian scholars, there is no agreement as to the origin and emergence of a Belarusian ethnos. In every existing concept of ethnogenesis, we can find arguments confirming and casting doubt on the subject. In the second half of the 19th century, the *Krivich theory* was formulated; it was disseminated in the early 20th century by the historian Vaclav Lastovski. The theory stated that the ethnic root and progenitor of the Belarusian nation was an East Slavic tribal association, the Kriviches (Evstigneev, 2005, pp. 25-26). Lastovski argued that the Kriviches were the most populous tribe inhabiting what is now Belarus and the surrounding areas, and proposed using the ethnonym Kriviches rather than Belarusians, and Krivia rather than Belarus. Another historian, Vladimir Picheta, held views close to this theory: he stated that the root of the Belarusian nation included not only the Krivichs, but also the East Slavic tribes of the Dregoviches, and partially, the Drevlians (Picheta, 2003, p. 17). The Polish historian Marceli Kosman also leans in this direction, writing that "the Kriviches... exerted influence over a considerable number of the Baltic peoples: the Latvians and frontier Lithuanians, as well as the small Finnish tribe of the Livonians" (Kosman, 1979, p. 38).

In the 19th century, the concept of *Old Russia* also arose, proposed by Mihail Koialovich, among other theorists. It states that Belarusians comprise one component of the *All-Russian nation*, alongside Russians (Velikorusov) and Ukrainians (Malorusov) that emerged from the Old Russian nation, that is, the community of East Slavs that inhabited the area of Kievan Rus. Nowadays, Belarusian historians such as, for example, Hienadź Sahanowicz, believe that at that time there was no ethnic and cultural unity among the Slavs, even though they comprised a single state and political organism (Sahanowicz, 2001, p. 39).

The most recent theory of the ethnogenesis of the Belarusians stems from around the beginning of the 1970s. Its name – *Baltic* – points to a synthesis of the Slavic and Baltic tribes as a result of which the Belarusian ethnos arose. During this process, the local Baltic and, to some extent, Finno-Ugric, peoples were assimilated into the incoming Slavic population. The Belarusian ethnos was formed in the basin of the Dnieper, Daugava and Neman rivers. One of the authors of this theory was the Russian archaeologist Valentin Sedov (Vonsovich, 2005, pp. 5-8).

Each of the above theories finds both supporters and critics. Our goal is not to evaluate their credibility, but only to point out their variety. We assume, after Vladimir Picheta, that the emergence of the Belarusian nation is related to what is known at the Lithuanian epoch, from the 13th century, when, as one Belarusian historian writes, Belarusians became detached from the other East Slavic tribes and incorporated into the state of Lithuania (Picheta, 2003, p. 17).

According to one concept of how nations originate, ethnogenesis, which results in the formation of an ethnic community, is deemed as the beginning of the process of the creation of a nation, that is, of social changes that are historical, cultural and political in nature. As a result of these, the ethnic community is transformed into a nation. As a rule, every national community has its own ethnic and cultural roots that are usually homogeneous, but may be heterogeneous. In accordance with constructivist thought, it is then that a nation arises as a conglomerate of various collectives in respect of which the ethnic community plays a consolidating role, and which takes on the form imagined on the basis of an invented tradition. In reality, the answer to the question of how nations, including the Belarusian nation, originate is ambiguous. To some extent, every nation is the result of both conscious activity and a natural process. From the political perspective, one determinant of the genesis of nations, regardless of the research approach accepted, is the state, which integrates the nation around a specific cultural root. Belarusians, one of the "small nations of Europe"[3], had no national statehood of their own for a very long time, and so the assumption that "the nation creates the state" as the crowning achievement of the process of nation-building does not apply to them. In relation to modern Belarus, it would seem more appropriate to assume that "the state creates the nation". If we accept the typology of the process of the formation of nations proposed by Miroslav Hroch, we find that the third, mass phase (Hroch, 2008, pp. 8-9) ending in the achievement of independence came for the Belarusians at the end of the 1980s, during the

---

3 A term introduced by Miroslav Hroch referring to the nature of the process of the creation of nations, and not to demographic potential. According to Hroch, the "small nations of Europe" are communities that during the 19th century – the period of the awakening of national consciousness – were weak, had been violated, had no tradition of high culture expressed in their own language, or, in the majority, had an incomplete social structure. Inhabiting areas of multi-ethnic monarchies (the Russian Empire in the case of the Belarusians), if they wanted to take part in society they had to accept the identity and language of the nation that controlled the state. Over time, some members of the intelligentsia began to convince the other members of the community that they are a fully-fledged nation, and demanded equal entitlement for their language and autonomy, and strove to create their own elites.

time of *perestroika* and *glasnost* in the USSR (Bukhovets, 2010, pp. 16-17; Radzik, 2012, p. 216). That event came as a surprise to many Belarusians. The emergence of an independent Belarus after the collapse of the USSR gave the Belarusian nation-building process a new impetus.

The preamble to the Constitution of the Republic of Belarus contains a reference to "the nation of the Republic of Belarus" and to the "centuries-long history of Belarusian statehood" (Konstitucia Respubliki Belarus', 1994). From the inception of post-soviet Belarus, two conceptions of the process of the creation of the state and the nation have competed with each other (Leshchenko, 2004). They are crucial to our subject. Up until the middle of the 1990s, a conception that can be described as *national* prevailed, while thereafter, the *soviet* tradition has been in force officially. Both argue that Belarusian statehood began in the 9th century in the Polotsk and Turov principalities. The Principality of Polotsk, centred around the city of Polotsk, occupied an area corresponding to the northern part of modern-day Belarus. To the south lay the Principality of Turov, the second most important political body within the area of Belarus, with its capital in Turov. Each of these two conceptions, however, assigns those principalities a different role. In the national conception, which nowadays finds itself in the opposition, the principalities are considered as "the first independent states within the territory of modern Belarus", and they are explained as Belarusian in that they were created by tribes that participated in the ethnogenesis of the Belarusians" (Sahanowicz, 2001, pp. 44, 60). Whereas the official narration emphasises that the principalities comprised parts of Kievan Rus, from which the conclusion should be drawn that "Belarusian statehood has Old Russian roots, and is strictly tied with the history of the statehood of the Russian and Ukrainian nations" (Vonsovich, 2005, p. 196).

The national conception also identifies itself with the Grand Duchy of Lithuania (GDL) and the Belarusian People's Republic. Particular emphasis is put on the role of the GDL in the history of Belarusians and Belarus due to its importance in this part of Europe. It is stressed that the Belarusian lands constituted a large part of the territory of that state, that the Old Belarusian language was an official language in which the most important documents were drawn up and literature created, and that, demographically, a significant part of the population were East Slavs – the Belarusian proto-nation. The Belarusian historian Vladimir Picheta, who lived in the late 19th and early 20th centuries, wrote on this subject expressly: "The Russian lands recognising the authority of the Duke of Lithuania retained their internal autonomy. The Lithuanian state was a federation of regions weakly connected to the centre. Within it, the Belarusian nationality dominated. Rus exerted considerable influence on Lithuania: the Orthodox faith was disseminated, Russian law and customs were absorbed, the Russian language became the language of the state" (Picheta, 2003, p. 25).

Yet, because there was no Belarusian nation state for almost the entire 20th century, the legacy of the GDL was practically absent from the consciousness of ordinary Belarusians (Kravtsevich, 2011, p. 84). The Belarusian People's Republic, which existed for just a few years after the fall of the Russian Empire, is perceived as a real form of Belarusian statehood, an alternative to Soviet Belarus, but awareness of it is limited today to opposition circles. Adherents of this conception, in accordance with the processes of the politicisation, ethnicity and ethnicisation of the state characteristic throughout the post-soviet territories, have sought to transform Belarus into a mono-ethnic state. Having influence on the authorities in the first half of the 1990s, they attempted to implement the belarusisation of the country. This policy was founded on an appeal to the European roots of Belarusian culture, and on the negation of its connections with Russia. The Russian language was presented as the language of a foreign power. Adherents claimed that those inhabitants of the country who supported the existence of an independent state but did not speak Belarusian should be denied citizenship. This led to a situation where, paradoxically, after those adherents fell from power, the Belarusian language became synonymous with the opposition, and using it in public is now looked on with disapproval by the authorities. Historians favouring this conception tried to date the Belarusian ethnos as far back as possible, at the same time idealising its past. This European consciousness and separateness from Russia, however, were limited to a small part of certain elites, and were simply not understood by most people, which led to the conviction among those elites that it was necessary to implement a pro-Western internal policy invoking liberal democratic and foreign values, oriented towards integration with the European Union and NATO.

The official conception of the process of the creation of the state and the nation that has been in force since the mid-1990s does not reject the existence of the GDL as a "proto-Belarusian" state, but identifies the sources of the current Belarusian state in the East Slavic legacy of Kievan Rus and accepts the symbols of socialist statehood from the period of the Belarusian Soviet Socialist Republic. The ethnic and cultural content of this conception is Russian in nature, and not Belarusian, as in the first conception, although it is not categorically stated that the Russian cultural identity of Belarusians is equal to Russian identity[4]. Russian culture is understood broadly in this case as the sovietised, urban lifestyle and the values and outlook it entails, rather than as those traditional Russian characteristics associated with folklore (Kosmarskaya, 2011)[5]. Another paradox contemporary Belarusians face is that their mother tongue – Belarusian – does not play a nation-building role. Yet Belarusians do maintain certain traits that attest to their ethnic and cultural distinctiveness, which the above ethnogenetic conceptions are said to prove.

The 'Russian' conception was consciously exploited by President Aleksander Lukashenko when he organised a referendum after his first election in 1994. On 14 May 1995, the citizens of Belarus voted in favour of recognising the Russian language as an official language alongside Belarusian (83.1% of votes), for new state symbols referring to Soviet symbols, for replacing those associated with the Grand Duchy of Lithuania (75.1% of votes), and for integration with Russia (83.3% of votes) (Wierzbicki, 2012, p. 110).

The ideological foundations of the Belarusian state contain the assertion that the value system of Belarusians was formed under the influence of both Eastern Slavic and Western cultures. Yet the justification of that assertion leaves no doubt about which culture the current authorities, headed by the President, consider those values closest to: "It [the value system] has a lot in common with the values of Russian [russkogo] society, pan-Slavic values. It features specific characteristics... such as collectivism, a striving for justice, and a communal-collectivist [Eurasian] orientation, not individualistic (Western European) values. For Belarusians, as for Russians and Ukrainians, the foundation is not the individual, but the collective – society with the ideals of brotherly love and solidarity. The formation of the spiritual values of the Belarusian nation is strongly connected with the influence of the Byzantine Orthodox spiritual legacy" (*Akademiia upravleniia pri Prezidente Respubliki Belarus'*, 2004, pp. 357, 362-364; Leshchenko, 2004).

There is no doubt that, in the case of Belarus, the phrase "between the East and the West" is a fact that remains current even today. Until the 13th

---

4 In the state and territorial context, Belarusians describe themselves as *Belorusy*, but in terms of cultural affinity, they describe themselves as *Russkie*, while calling inhabitants of Russia of Russian nationality *Rossiiane*.

5 Here, then, it is about Russian high culture (music, art, ballet, literature, cinema).

century, Byzantine influences predominated through the agency of the Orthodox Church. The acceptance thereof meant that the writing system that developed used the Cyrillic alphabet. There were also strong trade connections with Byzantium. In the 10th and 11th centuries, the lands of today's Belarus were also subject to influences from Scandinavia and Western Europe. The role of Western culture grew at the end of the 14th century due to political factors and an associated religious factor – the spread of Catholicism. An important role in transmitting Western culture to Belarus was played by its political and cultural connections with Poland. For a long time, the people within the area now comprising modern Belarus were subjected to polonisation, or russification when belonged to the Russian Empire and later the USSR. This hindered the development of a unique identity.

The most important characteristic of Belarusians today is their territorial identification with the independent state and, even more interestingly, with a model of economic transformation under which, in contrast to other post-soviet republics, Belarus is presented as an oasis of stability and relative prosperity within the CIS. In surveys conducted among the rural population of Belarus in which the target group was asked what it means to be a genuine Belarusian, the answers most frequently given were knowledge of Belarusian culture and history, and self-determination (Wyszyński, 2010, p. 229)[6]. The majority of the inhabitants of Belarus feel a connection with Russia. The average Belarusian, as the Polish sociologist Ryszard Radzik writes, identifies him or herself as Belarusian in folkloristic, ethnographic and linguistic categories, with a regional distinctiveness that is part of a greater whole formed together with the Russians, with whom Belarusians compare themselves – they do not compare themselves with the West (Radzik, 2009, p. 41).

In order to evaluate the degree of advancement made in the process of the creation of a nation in Belarus, essentially we must accept the hypothesis of Robert Wyszyński that, at present, we are dealing not with a Belarusian nation, but with a post-soviet Belarusian nation that identifies with Soviet, Russian, and to some extent folk Belarusian symbols and values (Wyszyński, 2010, p. 245). In Belarus, as in other areas of the post-soviet territories, an ethnicisation of the state is taking place. Paradoxically, however, it is an ethnicisation made not by means of Belarusian language and

---

6   A good command and use of the Belarusian language came only in fourth place.

culture, but through Russian language and culture. Properly speaking, then, Belarus is a state that has been de-ethnicised, if we understand ethnicisation as the appropriation of a state by a titular nation, that is, the appropriation of its language, culture or values (Kuzio, 2001). Post-sovietism and Belarus's strong ties with Russia constitute a powerful barrier to Belarusian national consciousness, although, paradoxically, it was the Belarusian Soviet Socialist Republic that was the first (not counting the short-lived BPR) real, if not sovereign, political organism that included the term "Belarusian" in its name.

But to return to the Middle Ages and the existence of the Grand Duchy of Lithuania – it is important to realise that, while Polish ethnic awareness already existed at that time, there was no such equivalent among the Belarusians. One the other hand, East Slavs comprised a majority of the population of the GDL, and the lands of today's Belarus constituted the territorial root of that state. It is fully justifiable, therefore, to consider the GDL as the beginning of Belarus's statehood and political system, and the cultural and religious conditions in its relations with the Crown of Poland as the very beginning of Polish-Belarusian relations. Using such a methodology, two milestones in those relations were the Union of Krewo between the Crown of Poland and the Grand Duchy of Lithuania in 1385, and the Union of Lublin almost two centuries later.

2. *The Union of Krewo and the Union of Lublin*

In the 14th century, and especially in the second half thereof, Poland and the Grand Duchy of Lithuania founds themselves in a difficult geopolitical situation in which both states were threatened by the expansion of the Teutonic Order. The idea arose, therefore, of joining forces for mutual benefit. The initiative for an alliance between the GDL and Poland came from the Lithuanian side. Apart from their struggle against a common enemy, the conclusion of a union was also beneficial economically: it opened up new possessions for the aristocracy and knights from those parts of the country that were considered congested, while for Russian merchants it provided an opportunity to expand their markets (Kosman, 1979, p. 70). The foundation of the agreement concluded in Krewo in 1385 was that Jagiełło, Grand Duke of Lithuania, would marry Jadwiga, Queen of Poland, and would take over the Polish throne. The joint struggle against the Teutonic Order and the possibility of Poland expanding into Rus were dependent on

Jagiełło accepting baptism in the Catholic faith and Christianising Lithuania, by Lithuania and Poland merging, etc. Those conditions were accepted only reluctantly in the GDL, for two reasons. Firstly, from a legal perspective, the Union of Krewo in fact meant that the Lithuanian-Rusian state was to be incorporated into the Crown of Poland, and this was not implemented at once. Secondly, it meant that conversion to Catholicism was also required of those dukes, boyars and populations that had accepted Orthodoxy. This also concerned Jagiełło himself, who, before accepting Catholicism, had been baptised and raised by his mother Julianna in the Orthodox tradition, so that what is known as the baptism of Jagiełło was in fact his conversion to Catholicism (Kappeler, 2015, p. 19; Mironowicz, 2001, p. 24).

The main objective of the Union was achieved. The amalgamated Polish, Lithuanian and Rusian forces triumphed over the armies of the Teutonic Order at the Battle of Grunwald in 1410. As M. Kosman points out, internally, the positions of Lithuania and Rus were strengthened, and under the Union of Horodło of 1413, the King of Poland remained equal to the Grand Duke of Lithuania as the "highest duke" (*supremum dux*), while the Grand Duchy of Lithuania retained its political autonomy, being joined with the Crown in the person of the ruler. The Union of Horodło granted Catholics exclusive entitlement to offices and titles, restricting the rights of the Orthodox population. Also, marriages between Orthodox and Catholic magnates were prohibited (Mironowicz, A., 2001, pp. 61-62). The dissemination of the Catholic faith within the GDL was the first step towards the cultural and political polonisation, though for the moment only among the upper spheres. Initially, Catholicism in the GDL affected almost solely Lithuanians, who had been pagans up to the time of the Union of Krewo. Converting to Christianity through baptism in the Catholic Church made it possible for them to assume high positions in the state. Through political discrimination against the Russian Orthodox elites, Catholic Lithuanians became the ruling class. Every attempt to upset this order met with the approval of Orthodox Belarusian feudal lords. As noted by Belarusian historian V. Picheta, in such a clash between two cultures – the Polish and the Russian – the victory goes to the culture with whom the authorities side. And in this case it was Polish culture, supported by the Catholic Lithuanian aristocracy, when 90% of the inhabitants were Orthodox Rusians (Picheta, 2003, p. 121).

The rivalry between Catholicism and Orthodoxy affected the lives of those living in the eastern lands of the Republic, including those inhabited by Belarusians. This was important enough for the Grand Duchy of Moscow to claim spiritual and political supremacy over the Rusians in the Republic. Understanding this challenge, in 1443 King Władysław III issued a privilege in Buda putting the Orthdox and Catholic Churches on an equal legal footing. This did not become binding law, however, but merely remained a royal declaration having little effect in reality. The death of King Władysław and the exile from Moscow of the Metropolitan Isidore, a supporter of an Orthodox-Catholic ecclesiastical union, sharpened the policy of the Polish rulers on Orthodoxy. In the Crown and in the Grand Duchy of Lithuania, it was realised that some of the Russian Orthodox elite sympathised with the idea propagated by the rulers of Moscow that the lands of Rus should be unified on the basis of their common faith. Even after the Muscovite Metropolitans waived the title of Metropolitan of Kiev, whose jurisdiction covered the Orthodox lands of the GDL, these fears did not abate.

Yet, the policy of the Polish rulers of the Jagiellonian dynasty towards Orthodoxy was full of contradictions. On the one hand, restrictions were introduced on the eligibility of members of the Orthodox Church for public office, while on the other hand, no barriers were erected against the overall development of Orthodoxy, including in respect of building new churches and establishing monasteries. The development of monastic life was also supported by the policy of the Lithuanian Rusian magnates, who gladly funded Orthodox monasteries in order to enhance their own prestige. These magnates, some of whom were Orthodox, sought greater independence, while the growing power of the Muscovite state ensured that the privileged position of Catholics and political discrimination against Rusians had no future. And so, Sigismund August lifted the last of the restrictions against Orthodox believers holding public office.

At the same time, the beginning of the Renaissance brought changes in the culture of the Belarusian lands and its gradual, but not complete, occidentalisation. This penetration of Western culture took place through the presence of the Catholic Church. Because of this religious element, that occidentalisation only affected the higher strata of society, the ruling class – those of the magnates and nobles who converted to Catholicism and became subject to cultural and linguistic polonisation. The local people retained their faith and, as a result, their language, culture and customs. Another source of the penetration of Western culture was direct contacts with the West through trade, particularly from the 15th century on. This was supported as well by a privilege of Kazimierz Jagiellończyk of 1447 permitted the nobility to travel freely abroad. After the fall of Byzantium, an increasing number of people, including Rusians from the Crown, travelled to Catholic Europe to study at its universities. Rusians also became a numerous group among the students of the Academy of Kraków, representing well-known families of magnates, but also families of nobles and townspeople (Sahanowicz, 2001, p. 176). Western influence on the lands of Belarus is also attested to by the Reformation, which gained support among the aristocratic families. Western culture, including the presence of Polish culture in Belarus, left lasting traces in the form of sacral and secular architecture.

Western influence was also exerted in Belarus through the Latin alphabet, which began to be used alongside the Cyrillic alphabet. In the 16th century, four different written languages were used in the area of today's Belarus. In addition to the traditional Christian-Slavonic and Old Belarusian languages, literary works also appeared in Latin and Polish. The development of literature in Old Belarusian – the official language of the GDL – was particularly intense. An invaluable contribution to this was made by Franciszek Skaryna, born in Polotsk, a graduate of the Academy of Kraków. First abroad, and later in Vilnius, he published religious writings in the Christian-Slavonic language (Belarusian editions) and secular works in Old Belarusian. In 1519, he published a Bible in Belarusian. Skaryna's work is one example of the positive, mutual interaction between the Western and Eastern cultural traditions, and of Polish and Belarusian peaceful co-existence. It also shows that Belarusians took an active part in the intellectual life of Europe, even though the East Slavic lands at the frontier of the Polish state were the "periphery of the periphery" of Western civilization.

In the Republic of the 16th-century, a nation of the nobility was developing that was polyethnic but held uniform political ideals. "To be a Pole" meant a political, not an ethnic, affiliation, as encapsulated in the phrase *gente Ruthenus, natione Polonus* (of Rusian descent, of the Polish nation). The idea that Polishness was dependent on ethnicity lost significance. Extending the privileges and status of the Polish nobility to the Rusian nobility (including the Belarusian nobility in the meaning of the time) increased the ethnic and religious component of the nation (Walicki, 2009, p. 42). In this way, Rusian nobles became polonised both politically and culturally, and often converted to Catholicism. The gap between them and that part of the non-Polish population of the eastern lands of the Republic that remained faithful to their traditional culture widened, as seen in the numerous uprisings and rebellions that occurred. An important factor exacerbating those differences was religious denomination. During the time of the Counter-Reformation, the area of today's Belarus was fraught with rivalry between Catholicism, supported first by the Crown and then by the Republic, and Orthodoxy, first supported by Moscow, and later Russia.

Progress in the polonisation of the nobility and the spread of Catholicism in Belarus was aided by two events, the first political, and the second religious but having political consequences. In 1569, the personal union that had been made between the Crown and the Grand Duchy of Lithuania was transformed at the Sejm in Lublin into a real union, and the confederation was replaced by a federation. The issue of the greater unification of the two states had long been on the agenda of the Polish aristocrats, who had been striving to strengthen their position by acquiring land and position in those areas belonging to the GDL. The Catholic Church also saw benefits in the conclusion of a real union, thanks to which it would obtain increased opportunities for expanding eastward and reinforcing its position in the struggle against not just Orthodoxy, but also Protestantism, which had found numerous supporters in the GDL. These expectations from the Polish side were met with those of the Lithuanian Rusian nobles, who demanded that the privileges of the "golden Polish freedom" be expanded throughout the GDL, and who sought military reinforcement. The Act of the Union of Lublin, concluded on 18 June 1569, proclaimed that the Crown of Poland and the Grand Duchy of Lithuania constituted from that moment on a single, inseparable state and a common Republic "which, from two states and nations raised up and bound together a single people" (Sahanowicz, 2001, p. 207). At the head of that state stood one monarch – the King and Grand Duke of Lithuania. There was to be one Sejm and one foreign policy. The nobility obtained equal rights within the territory of the entire state, and so the prohibition against Poles acquiring lands in the old territory of the GDL was lifted. The Union of Lublin led to a reduction in the political significance of the GDL and the loss of half of its territory.

The idea of the independence and power of the GDL remained strong among the nobility and the aristocracy, who used every opportunity that arose to see that it again became reality. In 1588, King Sigismund III Vasa signed the 3rd Statute of the GDL, which laid out its political system and at the same time provided civil and penal codes. The 3rd Statute undermined some of the provisions of the Union of Lublin, and defined the GDL as a separate state with a separate legal system. Poles were deprived of the property rights and political rights in Lithuania they had been granted as a result of the Union of Lublin[7]. The 3rd Statute also defined the official state language in the GDL as Old Belarusian, which was also deemed the national language.

3. The Union of Brest and its consequences

The Union of Lublin created political conditions amenable to the religious expansion of the Catholic Church, which in the mid-14th century had had almost no presence in the lands of today's Belarus. There were still no Catholic churches in Mogilev or Orsha at the end of the 16th century. The tendency to conclude a church agreement between the Catholic and Ortho-dox Churches in the Republic gathered strength after the appearance of the Society of Jesus, which was to serve in the fight against Protestantism and Orthodoxy. The idea of a union found support among the state authorities and with the monarchs Stefan Batory and Sigismund III. As in the case of the Union of Lublin, support also came from another direction. The upper echelons of the Orthodox hierarchy were dissatisfied with their socio-po-litical position, and saw a union as a way of gaining rights equal to those of the Catholic clergy. Moreover, the moral level of Orthodox bishops and the educational level of the lower clergy were very low, and a union was seen as a means of changing this. And so, in 1596, a church agreement was entered into between the Orthodox Church in the Republic and the Catholic Church. The union was concluded, though, by only some Ortho-dox bishops, and was not supported by the lower clergy or the faithful. Those Orthodox bishops who accepted the supremacy of the Catholic Church were promised a place in the Senate, as well as land and political status equal to that of Catholic bishops. The new denomination was to keep its ritual and liturgical traditions. Under the Union of Brest, King Sigismund III Vasa delegalised the Orthodox Church. Orthodox clergy were prohibited from conducting ceremonies or using churches or ceme-teries. The Orthodox Church went underground. Growing resistance against the union in the eastern regions of the Republic forced Sigis-

---

7 The 1st and 2nd Statues were issued in 1529 and 1566, at the behest of the Council of Lords of the GDL, in order to regulate all social, political and property relations in the state, as well as relations between the dukes and their subjects. The 3rd Statute was a response to the Union of Lublin.

mund's successor, King Władysław IV Vasa, to once again legalise the Orthodox Church within the state.

From that moment, rather than receding, the denominational divisions within the Republic only became ever stronger, contrary to what had been intended. It is a historical paradox of the Belarusian people that it was in Greek Catholic circles, and even among the Roman Catholic nobility, as Polish researchers argue, that the idea of the Belarusian nation arose in the 19th century (Radzik, 2012, p. 183; Pawluczuk, 2015, p. 35). This assertion is indisputable, but is conditioned as follows. Firstly, the Catholic nobles in the east, who did much to further the development of Belarusian national culture, had a Polish consciousness (Pawluczuk, 2012). Secondly, they were the descendants of polonised Rusian nobles. Thirdly, they were a minority, surrounded by rural Belarusians, often unaware even of their ethnic separateness, but bound to Orthodoxy, and there is no doubt that their goal was the religious conversion of the Belarusian people, deprived as it was of an Orthodox intelligentsia and a middle class. Fourthly, the cultural heritage created by those circles became the national heritage of Belarus, for whose people one of the fundamental components of their identity is Orthodoxy. An attempt at the beginning of the 1990s to establish Greek Orthodoxy as the national religion of Belarusia was not supported by either the Belarusians themselves or by the authorities, because, despite certain objective conditions, it was not a mass religion (Lazarevich and Leviash, 2014, pp. 43-44), and especially because the attempt was made in a post-atheistic society. The argument that Orthodoxy, which occupies a historic place in the Belarusian consciousness, was a factor that hindered the development of the Belarusian national movement, that preserved the pro-Russian or even Russian ethno-cultural orientation of Belarusians, that Belarusian nationalism "was created by Orthodox circles, and activists of that line of thought were often the sons of Orthodox clergy. Belarus saw itself as part of Russia, with Belarusians as a regional variety of Russians" (Radzik, 2012, p. 183) does not fully reflect the historical conditions of the Belarusian nation. Fifthly, Belarusian national culture is a synthesis of: 1) the Byzantine tradition as affected by Western culture (Catholicism, Greek Orthodoxy, latinisation), and 2) high culture (literature, the arts) and folk culture.

In the 17th century, foreign armies marched through Belarus, and the Republic took part in battles fought there. These were accompanied by internal conflicts between aristocratic families struggling for domination in the GDL. All these led to the destruction of economic potential, to a de-

cline in crafts and trade, to enormous human losses and – most importantly – to the decline of the Republic. An attempt was made to save the state
by adopting the Government Act, later known as the Constitution of 3
May 1791. Seeking to prolong the existence of an independent state, it
was decided to make a full political union and to abolish the GDL. No account was taken then of the differences, pride and customs of that part of
the Polish state. For 80% of the inhabitants of the GDL, their mother
tongue was Belarusian. This was used mainly by the people, but also by
some magnates and nobles when communicating with their subjects, who
knew no other language. The foundations and content of the Constitution
of 3 May grew out of the Enlightenment conception of a unified nation,
and invoked both the old Jagellonian tradition and the ideology of the
French bourgeoisie. It was assumed that the modern Polish nation should
be uniform, and that all regional differences – in language, culture and the
law, were harmful to the future of the state. The objective of this étatist
conception, then, was to transform a heterogenous population into a uniform nation by means of Polish language and culture.

In defence of the old order, and under Russian patronage, a confederation of aristocrats and nobles was formed, known as the Targowica Confederation. Yet, when, as a result of the Second Partition of Poland, a considerable part of the GDL was annexed by the Russian Empire, the mood
of the local nobles changed, and many supported the uprising led by
Tadeusz Kościuszko, who was himself born in Belarus. This, however,
was of little significance, and certainly did not save the Republic from
complete demise.

4. Polish-Russian rivalry over Belarusian "souls"

After the Partitions, the memory of the old, pre-Partition Poland remained
in the imaginations of the polonised Belarusian nobles. Patriotic circles in
the Kingdom of Poland made unsuccessful attempts to regain independence by force (in the November and January Uprisings), including within
the territory of the former GDL, that is, in much of today's Belarus. Yet,
due to the social and ethnic differences dividing the local, polonised nobility from the Belarusian people, these had no chance of success. During the
January Uprising, a newspaper was even published in Belarusian,
"Mużyckaja Prauda", on whose pages the pre-Partition Republic was ide-
alised and the Greek Orthodox Church promoted "as the only to respect

the language of the peasants"[8] (Mironowicz, 2001, p. 162); the Belarusian population was called on to support the uprising. One of the leaders in Belarus, Konstanty Kalinowski, stressed his ties to the Republic, without considering the distinctiveness of the Belarusian people. His use of the Belarusian language in his contacts with Belarusians was pragmatic – he wanted to be understood – and did not arise from any Belarusian consciousness on his part.

In Polish conceptions and imaginings concerning independence, an evolution occurred in relation to the territorial form of the future, reborn motherland, and thereby, in relation to the concept of the Polish nation, which changed from a political nation to a cultural one. This also affected relations with the Belarusian people. Initially, their ethnic distinctiveness from the Polish people was not recognised; they were treated as a regional group comprising an inseparable part of the Polish nation. For many representatives of Polish elites, the concept of a political nation was intellectually obvious given the pre-Partition borders of the Republic, and at that time the idea of giving up areas inhabited for the most part by non-Polish people was out of the question. Even if the Polish nobles were aware of ethno-cultural differences in those areas, they considered the people there to be Polish, or potentially Polish, regardless of the language they used: "In the far-flung territories from Podlasie to Mińsk, there were no clear language barriers, and it was common for people to communicate in a mixture of Polish and Belarusian" (Kosman, 1979, p. 257). Characteristic of how the Polish nation was understood in the 19th century is a study on Belarus by Aleksander Rypiński, in which he writes explicitly about the Polishness of those lands: "Rus, to the extent that it is and will remain Polish, constitutes an inseparable part of our dear motherland. Here lives a simple people of the Slavic tribe, long since crossed with the Lachy family, honest, but poor and little known in their motherland, Poland, though they love her beyond all else" (Pypin, 2005, p. 63). For a long time that nation had been a bone of contention among its neighbours, yet, despite their intrusions, it had endured to prove that it was capable of independently choosing its own leader and would not recognise foreign invaders. That is why Rypiński writes (1840): "...they chose Poland as their mother, throwing themselves into her embrace along with the Lithuanians, clinging to her with a son's love" (After: Pypin, 2005, p. 64). According to

---

8 Belarusian was introduced as the language of the Greek Orthodox liturgy.

Aleksander Rypiński, Belarusians are "far" from everything Muscovite. He also emphasised the significance of religion and language, asserting that "schism[9] is a synonym for paganism", and that the Belarusian language is closer to Polish than it is to Russian: "That language is not as "strong" as among "our" Ukrainians, less tatarised than among the inhabitants of Moscow or Kazan, not as Orthodox as in Galicia, yet despite it all it has its own national writing system that significantly distinguishes it from all of those languages and makes it, it seems to me, closest to Polish" (After: Pypin, 2005, p. 64). Polish intellectuals perceived the separateness of the Belarusian people, but it didn't occur to any of them that Belarusians could set out to develop their civilization other than in connection with Poland. Up to the 1860s, among the various conceptions of the Polish nation and the future, reborn Poland, the dominant idea was that of recreating Jagellonian Poland. Only the federalist concept did not treat all of the people in pre-Partition Poland as Poles, and allowed for national distinctions – Lithuanian-Belarusian and Ukrainian. As emphasised by Andrzej Walicki, this was a concession to the ethno-cultural concept of a nation whose purpose was to strengthen the foundations of Polish national identity by making a distinction between Poles and the non-Polish peoples of Belarus and Ukraine, while at the same time bolstering the historical ties of those lands with Poland and creating conditions under which Belarusians could engage in the process of nation-building independently of Russia (Walicki, 2009, p. 461). This was all the more important from the Polish perspective in that, after the January Uprising, the area saw the implementation of a stricter policy on unification with central Russia and the russification of the western fringes of the empire, known in Moscow as the Western Country. Despite Russian political dominion, Polish cultural influences continued to dominate in the area, and this was seen as a threat to the territorial integrity of the empire. The preponderantly Polish landowners waged a war against the minority of Russian landowners, who were supported by the state administration and Orthodox clergy, for the "souls" of the Belarusian population. The role of Poles and Russians in forming culture particularly involved religion and the organisation of the Church. A minority of Belarusians were Roman Catholic or Greek Catholic, which for the Russian authorities meant that they remained within the Polish cultural sphere, and in the broader context within Latin civilization, deemed

---

9 Orthodoxy was thus described.

the greatest threat to Russia as the centre of the Slavic world, both in nationalist circles and among the power elites. The depolonisation of the Western Country was to include its final decatholicisation as well (Jaśkiewicz, 2001, pp. 121, 128-129).

This intensification of russification in the Western Country resulted from the Russian authorities implementing the concept of the All-Russian nation, which was to include Great Russian (Russia), Little Russia (Ukraine) and Belarus. Further, the Russian imperial authorities assumed that these were "eternal Russian lands" – not because they were inhabited by peoples considered to be branches of the Russian nation, but because they were lands once ruled over by the Rurik dynasty, whose descendants the Romanovs were considered to be (Dolbilov and Miller, eds., 2007, p. 77). To restore the "Russian" character of those lands, however, ethno-cultural criteria were employed, such as religion (Russian Orthodoxy) and language, as well as colonisation through granting lands to Russian officials in return for serving the empire in the Western Country. Official Russian propaganda claimed that there had never been "real" Poles in the area, and that the forebears of the Polish nobles were polonised and catholicised Russian nobles. A Pole here was a Catholic, a noble, or, in the broader meaning, a person from another stratum, but not a peasant, born in the western provinces of the empire or in the Kingdom of Poland. For this reason, the study of Russian was disseminated, and officials who came from deep within Russia tried to impose their traditions, and customs typical of the Russian (Great Russian) people, on the local populace; this satisfied neither those people nor the Russian authorities: "We can be no one other than Russians, but not Muscovite Russians. No force can separate us from our common Russian Motherland, but no force can make us take on the Muscovite way of life or world view, for we are closer to Europe!... Let Moscow be envious of no one, let it humble itself and cease its destruction of the remote regions, with its condemnation of everything reminiscent of European civilization; let it learn from Europe" (Dolbilov and Miller, eds., 2007, p. 217). In support of the idea of an All-Russian nation, in Belarus the concept of *zapadnorusizm* (West Russia) arose; the belief was propagated that Belarusians were a branch of the Russian nation that had yielded to Polish and Catholic influence, which is why they differed somewhat ethnically. Belarusian-ness was identified with Orthodoxy, as a regionalism within *russkosti*, which was "something broader": "By supporting *zapadnorusizm*, Russians to some extent – and against their own wishes – expanded Belarusian-ness (always, however, measured in terms of Polishness). They ascribed it – and this affected the future of Belarus – to a specific historical dimension, and described it in cultural and linguistic categories" (Radzik, 2009, p. 41). Supporters of *zapadnorusizm* believed that, for Belarusians, the language of high culture and civilization should be Russian. Belarusian language and culture were thus to become an ethnographic dimension within the Russian nation (Belarusian ethnicity, Russian nationality), though the creation of a Belarusian literature was not opposed (Tokt', 2011, pp. 141-143). Belarusian regionalism posed no threat to the concept of a unified Russian nation, in contrast to the Ukrainian national movement, which was gathering force at that time. An important role in disseminating *zapadnorusizm* was played by the Orthodox clergy.

The appearance of a federalist conception marked the beginning of the evolution of the idea of the Polish nation from a political nation, which had begun to be seen as ineffective and unsuccessful, to an ethno-cultural (ethno-linguistic) nation. This second concept was for a long time unacceptable in Polish circles striving for political independence, for it meant giving up on the pre-Partition borders of the Republic. In an era of positivism, the ideal of "external autonomy" gave way to the ideal of "internal autonomy", understood as toiling for the civilizational development of the Polish nation. Positivists believed that promoting the "internal development" and democratic local government of the Polish nation would be easier in a society that was homogenous, and the rule of the Polish nobility over the Belarusian people began to be seen as a foreign yoke[10].

The positivist ethnic concept of the nation led to a break from the legacy of Jagellonian Poland and created fertile ground for the Piast concept of the nation acknowledged by National Democratic circles. Polish expansion to the east was seen as an unnecessary effort that weakened the Polish state (Dmowski, 1926, p. 506). According to the ND, the core of the reborn Polish state should be those lands that were ethnically Polish (Dmowski, 1926, p. 20)[11]. The more numerous the Polish population, the smaller the problem posed by the non-Polish population the state contains. Of key importance, then, was the "internal cohesion (independence)" of the state – impossible to achieve when expanding to the east and absorb-

---

10 A belief held by, among other people, Bolesław Wysłouch – a peasant movement activist born in Belarus.
11 Dmowski included in this area: Congress Poland, with part of the "Stolen Lands", Western Galicia, Greater Poland, West Prussia, Warmia, Silesia including Cieszyn Silesia, and the linguistically Polish Mazuria.

ing areas that were linguistically (ethnically) not Polish, for this would threaten the very existence of that state. In National Democratic circles, Belarusians were not considered a nation at all. Roman Dmowski empha-sised that, while Belarusians constituted more than 40% of the population of the former GDL, he considered them to be a tribal community: "As for the Belarusians – no one denies that one can speak of them as a race or a tribe, but not as a nation. To deserve that term, there must be at least some kind of elementary internal organisation, at least some kind of collective soul, at least some kind of political aspiration" (Dmowski, 1901, p. 618). Ironically, the Piast conception was implemented at the behest of Stalin in post-war Poland; the authorities, guided by internationalism, built a "so-cialist nation" on the basis of an ethnically homogeneous people (after the period of war-time exterminations and ethnic cleansing).

In opposition to the concept of National Democracy stood the federal-ism of the socialist camp and the traditionalists, who recognised the ethno-cultural distinctiveness of the Belarusians and Ukrainians, viewing them as part of a federal state, as a buffer between Russia and the ethnically Polish lands, even at the cost of Piast lands (Nowak, 1999)[12]. In its pro-gramme, the Polish Socialist Party (PPS) foresaw expanding its activities "to the provinces formerly connected with the Republic". This assertion was only made, though, in order to gain as much support as possible among society, and not to support the Belarusian national movement. The activities of the PPS for the benefit of Belarus at the beginning of the 20th century were limited to individual activists distributing texts written in Be-larusian and published abroad. Such activity, however, did contribute to the development of Belarusian national consciousness.

5. The beginnings of Belarusian nationalism

In 1902, at the initiative of a student of noble descent, Wacław Iwanowski, the first Belarusian political party was formed in St Petersburg – The Be-larusian Revolutionary Party (BPR). Most of its members were young members of the intelligentsia raised in Catholic circles. Despite its name,

---

12 The various approaches to the territorial form of a reborn Poland, and thereby the concept of the Polish nation itself, were undoubtedly affected by the personal lives of their creators. Roman Dmowski was born in Congress Poland, Józef Piłsudski in Lithuania.

the party was not out for revolution, but focused on working among the Belarusian peasantry to provide education in the mother tongue and to disseminate knowledge of the history of the Belarusian nation. The PPS worked together with the BPR, though the two parties differed in their approach to the question of Belarus. The PPS was in favour of restoring the First Republic, with its federal structure, while the BPR planned to create a sovereign Belarus. Political agitation on the part of the PPS led to a split within the BPR and the formation of the Belarusian Revolutionary Group (BSH), headed by the brothers Iwan and Antoni Łuckiewicz. At the first assembly of the new party in 1903, a programme was adopted in which the party demanded the freedom to pursue an independent path of political growth. One year later, the BRH changed its name to the Belarusian Socialist Group (BSH). It ran an active propaganda campaign, issuing proclamations in Belarusian thanks to its printing house in Minsk, and publishing *The Group (Hromada)* in St Petersburg. The PPS began working more closely with the BSH, viewing it as an ally in the struggle against tsarist authority. In 1904, the PPS even tried to create its own Belarusian party – the Socialist Party of Belarus[13]. This, however, was yet another example of a group treating the Belarusian movement instrumentally in order to further its own political aims. For Belarusian activists, the most important goal was to empower their own nation through national awareness and education and cultural activities. The more instrumental approach of Polish activists could result from the low level of national consciousness among Belarusians, which was characterised by the dichotomy of Catholic-Pole vs. Orthodox-Belarusian. Denomination, then, was to be replaced by national consciousness (Głogowska, 2012, pp. 36, 39). The problem of the inadequate development of Belarusian national consciousness included the facts that almost 90% of Belarusians were peasants, the intelligentsia was small in number, and the middle class had little such awareness. The area of Belarus within the Russian Empire was economically backward, whereas Poles and Jews dominated in the cities. Given, then, the low level of national consciousness and the social structure, Belarusians were treated paternalistically. It would seem that it was this paternalism and the instrumental treatment on the part of Poles that in 1905

---

13 The founding members of the new structure came from the areas of Minsk or Grodno; they spoke Belarusian and had experience in illegal party activities.

prompted the BSH to accept the BRH's demand for Belarusian autonomy within the borders of Russia.

The liberalisation of the Russian system of power as a result of the 1905 Revolution led to a rally in the Belarusian nationalist movement. A key role in this was played by the newspaper *Our Field* (*Nasza Niwa*), which ran from 1906-1915. The paper engaged in a wide range of publishing, cultural and educational activities. In one issue from 1913, the paper stated: "If we want to live as and be a nation, we should create our own literature, science and art. This is the main condition for our existence, for Belarusians, as a nation" (Glybinny, 2012, p. 14). A breakthrough in the formation of Belarusian national consciousness and for the Belarusian intelligentsia came in 1910 with the publication of a book by Wacław Łastowski, *A Short History of Belarus*. The author, who himself was Belarusian, took a negative view of the heritage of the Republic in the national history of Belarus. He highlighted Belarusians's loss of their political and cultural identity. At the same time the Belarusian historian and ethnographer Mitrofan Downar-Zapolski was beginning his academic work. Both these researchers interpreted the past from the perspective of their own national interests, striving to empower Belarusians. The Polish-Russian rivalry for cultural and political domination in Belarus began to be presented as a fight between two foreign imperialist agendas.

6. *The First World War and the October Revolution in Russia*

As a result of events during the First World War, in September 1915 Belarus was divided into two zones – German and Russian. The German authorities supported separatism among the nations of Russia in order to weaken their adversary. In the areas the Germans occupied, Polish and Lithuanian social, political, cultural and educational organisations arose. Despite these favourable conditions, however, the Belarusian movement suffered due to mass evacuations among the Orthodox population, who were withdrawn eastward along with the retreating Russian army. The Russians spread information concerning imminent repressions and cruelty against Orthodox civilians. It is estimated that, in this way, from 1.3 – 2.9 million people from the Belarusian provinces (Grodno, Vilnius and Minsk) moved deeper into Russia. The Roman Catholic and Jewish population remained (Mironowicz, 2001, p. 176; Głogowska, 2012, p. 87).

In December 1915, in the area captured by the Germans, a Temporary Council of the Confederation of the Grand Duchy of Lithuania was formed to unite Polish, Belarusian, Lithuanian and Jewish activists. Its goal was to maintain the territorial integrity of the Lithuania and Belarusian lands "on the principle of the independence of Belarus and Lithuania within a separate state" (Głogowska, 2012, p. 88). In the spring of 1916, the idea of the Confederation was completed with a project for a Belarus-Black Sea Union – developed by Iwan and Antoni Łuckiewicz. Apart from Belarus and Lithuania, the Union included Latvia and Ukraine, and was created in order for all of those nations to separate from Poland and Russia. Polish political circles also became more active in this area; in May 1917 they sent the German Chancellor a memorandum emphasising the "ethnographically mixed population of Belarus, with no nationality dominating" and the special role played by Polish society in the development of those areas (Głogowska, 2012, p. 90). Belarusian activists feared the polonisation of Belarusians, especially since, among those people who had not moved deeper into Russia, most were Catholics, identified with Poles.

There was also increased activity by Polish political circles in those areas still under Russian control. This was made possible by the democratisation of social and political life, particularly after the February Revolution. Minsk became a real centre of Polish political thought, with all streams present. The most significant Polish organisation was the Polish Council of Minsk Land, founded in May 1917; it declared that Belarus, as the motherland of Poles living there, had ties with the Polish state. Belarusians were also active in the area. Among the Belarusian elite, three orientations functioned at the time. The first favoured an independent state, if an imperfect one, that would raise the status of Belarusians to that of a nation-state in relations with the Russian Soviet Federative Socialist Republic and other states of the former Russian Empire. The second orientation, represented by Belarusian Bolsheviks, sought a union with Russia, while the third sought some form of integration with Poland.

In December 1917, the First Minsk All-Belarusian Assembly was announced, with the consent and financial support of the People's Commissariat for Nationalities of Soviet Russia. Delegates attended from various parts of Belarus, as well as from Russia and Ukraine. Soldiers, teachers and officials dominated the talks, and two orientations were evident. Representatives of the Vilnius, Grodno, Vitebsk and Minsk provinces argued for a Belarus having national and territorial autonomy. Representatives of the Mogilev and Smolensk provinces, as well as members of Belarusian socialist parties from St Petersburg, supported the unity of the Russian state and demanded national and cultural autonomy for Belarusians. The gathering attempted to establish a Soviet government, bypassing the Bolshevik structures of the Executive Committee of the Western District and Western Front in Minsk. It even appointed an Executive Committee of the First Council of the All-Belarusian Assembly, but its members were unable to develop its activities because they were arrested by the Bolshevik authorities. This occurred after Bolshevik units withdrew from the area and German forces returned. A fight for control of Belarus then arose between the Executive Committee of the First Council of the All-Belarusian Assembly and the Polish Council of Minsk Land. The Executive Committee declared on 19 February 1918 that it had taken power in Minsk, and two days later announced "to the nations of Belarus" that authority in Belarus should be formed in accordance with the will of the Belarusian people through democratic elections. Belarus's striving for independence was increasingly visible. The Polish Council of Minsk Land demanded a part in forming the national government, as well as various guarantees for Poles and Polish culture. Taking advantage of the support of the German occupying authorities, the Executive Committee of the First Council of the All-Belarusian Assembly announced the establishment of the Belarusian People's Republic. The council of the BPR was pro-Polish. One of its leading activists, Józef Lesik, stated: "Poland itself has experienced pressure as a nation, and so it is easier to reach an understanding with it. Polonisation is not so terrible, because the majority of the Belarusian population are against the Polish language... For Belarus, russification poses a bigger threat because both the rural and urban populations willingly accept the Russian language" (After: Malinovskiĭ, 2003, p. 153). This did not mean, however, that the BPR strove for some kind of formal association with the Polish state. On 25 March 1918, the Council of the BPR proclaimed the independence of Belarus. The BPR, however, was not recognised or supported, either internally or under international law.

In November 1918, the German army began retreating from Belarus, with its place taken by the Red Army. The Council of the BPR was forced to evacuate to Vilnius. Its pro-Polish orientation and the threat posed by the Bolsheviks, who soon formed the Belarusian Soviet Socialist Republic (transformed for a short period into the Lithuanian-Belarusian Soviet Socialist Republic) in the areas of Belarus they occupied, had an adverse effect on relations between the BPR Council and the reborn Polish state.

These relations were informal, because the Second Republic did not recognise the BPR in international relations. Nevertheless, when on 28 November 1918 the Polish head of state Józef Piłsudski signed a decree on elections to a Legislative Parliament, whose reach was to extend to the areas of Białystok and Bielsk Podlaski, the Council of Ministers of the BPR sent a note of protest to the Polish Foreign Minister, in which it stated that "the BPR opposes this attempt to annex part of purely Belarusian territory with the main industrial centre of Belarus – Białystok", and that if the decree was upheld in force, this would be treated as a position hostile to the Belarusian People's Republic (Głogowska, 2012, p. 104). The Polish government ignored the note.

7. *The reborn Republic and the lands of Belarus*

The independence of Belarus, or its state affiliation (with Poland or Russia) had not yet been determined. On 4 April 1919, the Polish Parliament adopted a resolution on the eastern borders of the Republic of Poland, in which it called upon the government and the supreme command to liberate the north-eastern areas of Poland, with the capital in Vilnius, from Bolshevik control with all speed, and to permanently unite them with the Republic. The Parliament also passed a resolution on the Eastern Borderlands in which it recognised neither the Lithuanian-Belarusian Soviet Socialist Republic nor the BPR as sovereign powers. Based on the position taken by the Legislative Parliament, Poland sought to make it understood that it would not give up on Belarus – the area was included in plans to implement a federalist conception whose aim was to create a powerful state standing in opposition to Russia (and Germany as well), irrespective of whether the Russian government was Soviet or "white".

After the outbreak of the Polish-Bolshevik War, the Polish army began taking control over Belarusian lands. In April 1919, the representative of the government of the BPR in Warsaw requested that the Polish government recognise Belarusian statehood. After Polish forces took Vilnius, Józef Piłsudski made an appeal to the inhabitants of the former Grand Duchy of Lithuania in which he spoke of their political empowerment and the creation of a civil government in the occupied territory. Yet Poland treated Belarus as its own pre-Partition province and, in principle, did not consent to any recognition of full independence, as attested to by its not acknowledging the BPR as the Belarusian state. After Minsk was taken by

Polish forces in August 1919, it was announced in the city that "with its sabres, the victorious Polish army brings the right to self-determination to the Belarusian people", yet shortly thereafter most Belarusian lands found themselves under Polish control. The majority of Belarusian politicians favoured an independent state. Among the Belarusian elites, those who had been pro-Polish were increasingly disappointed with Poland's policy towards Belarus, and this change was also hastened directly by actions of the Polish army and the Civil Administration of the Eastern Lands, such as filling positions with Polish Catholic landowners, plundering, committing acts of terror and executing those suspected of communist activities; these made the Polish presence reminiscent of that of an occupying power (Mironowicz, 2001, pp. 193-194). Repressions affected the Orthodox population because it was suspected of supporting the Bolsheviks. Orthodox churches were handed over to Catholics, who changed their denomination, even in places where the proportion of Roman Catholics was small. The Belarusian press was harassed, and even theatres – in Minsk, plays by Belarusian authors were prohibited. Despite all of this, some Belarusian politicians and soldiers fought on the Polish side in the Polish-Bolshevik War. In Lodz, a Belarusian War Committee was formed, and independently, troops under Gen. Stanisław Bułak-Bałachowicz also fought on the Polish side.

Despite its successful defence against Soviet Russia, Poland did not manage to implement the federalist conception. Under the Treaty of Riga signed on 18 March 1921, Belarus was divided between Poland and Soviet Russia. In exchange for concessions in Ukraine, the Soviet authorities offered Poland almost all of Belarus, including Minsk. Poland was wary of having too large an Orthodox population within its borders, though, and decided to establish the border along the Daugava, from the Latvian-Soviet border towards the central course of the Pripyat.

As a result of the Treaty of Riga, a significant number of Belarusians found themselves within the territory of the Second Republic. Exact figures are difficult to provide because a considerable number of Belarusians were unable to define their nationality, simply calling themselves "locals". Using criteria of religious denomination or language failed to resolve the issue, because part of the population considered Belarusian declared themselves to be Roman Catholics, while the people of the Eastern Borderlands were not clearly identified linguistically. This is why the number of Belarusians in the Second Republic was estimated as from 4-6% of the total population (Żarnowski, 1973, pp. 374-376).

8. Belarusians in the Second Republic and the Belarusian Soviet Socialist Republic

Many studies have been written on the subject of the policy of the Second Republic of Poland towards minorities, including towards Belarusians, as well as on the policy of the USSR towards the Belarusian Soviet Socialist Republic. We will not repeat the best-known facts and events, but it is necessary to mention that the Polish authorities implemented a policy of assimilation towards Belarusians, considering them to be unconsciously Polish by nationality, and thus ripe for polonisation. The social and occupational structure of Belarusian society also favoured this. More than 90% of Belarusians worked in agriculture, with the intelligentsia comprising only a tiny fraction. That is why it was thought that Belarusians were a group that could easily be assimilated. As it later turned out, the matter was not so simple, due to Belarusians's low level of awareness of their nationality or of what a nation is.

The policy of the Second Republic regarding nationality was, in a certain sense, a continuation of what had been started by the Civil Administration of the Eastern Lands. The Catholic Church and local administration played an important part in the policy of polonisation in the north-eastern provinces inhabited by Belarusians, and were given plenty of scope. The Belarusian language was discriminated against, the activities of Belarusian organisations were hindered, the number of Belarusian schools limited – it was claimed those schools offered a low level of teaching and spread pro-Communist ideas among children and adolescents. The education system was one of the instruments of polonisation most actively used throughout the interwar period.

The Orthodox population was especially exposed to hardship. They were treated as unreliable, and sympathetic towards the USSR (viewed as being the same as Russia); this was a paradox, since Orthodoxy was persecuted there in a manner comparable to the first Christians in Rome. And so, Orthodox property was seized, Orthodox churches turned into Catholic churches. This sometimes took place spontaneously, at the initiative of the local people themselves. The construction of new Orthodox churches was not permitted, except for the church in Baranowicze – the only one built between the wars. These measures were accompanied by the resettlement of people from central Poland who were to form a "zone of ethnographic influence" favouring the assimilation of Belarusians. There was an intensification of forced polonisation in the second half of the 1930s, and especially in the years just before the outbreak of the Second World War, when it was claimed that, to date, the assimilation carried out had been insufficient, because it had been confined mainly to building up loyalty towards the Polish state. After a period of not having recognised Belarusians as a nation, it was asserted that "the eastern lands are not sufficiently Polish, and they must be made Polish". There was a shift in emphasis, then, to assimilating the nation; the goal was to finally transform Belarusians into Poles. Consideration was given to abolishing all schools and outlets in which there was any form of teaching whatsoever in Belarusian, to dismissing non-ethnically Polish teachers, to filling school administrations posts with Poles only (preferably from the military), and abolishing other Belarusian organisations (Głogowska, 2012, pp. 224-225). It was also believed that a hallmark of Polishness in the borderlands was Catholicism, and so the policy against Orthodoxy was tightened up, with the engagement of the local state apparatus and the police. An attempt was even made to polonise the Orthodox Church by introducing the Polish language in sermons and Polish patriotic songs at the end of services, and by preparing a translation of the Orthodox liturgy from the Orthodox-Slavic language into Polish. The idea of an "Orthodox Polish" identity was propagated. And so, it is no wonder that some Belarusians looked with hope at the Belarusian Soviet Socialist Republic, where, in the 1920s, there was a policy of *korenizatsii* (indigenisation, from the Russian *korennoĭ* – root), that is, of belarusisation (in Belarusian *belarusizatsyiia,* in Polish *białorutenizacja*). People began to believe that within Soviet Belarus there were more opportunities for Belarusian culture to develop, and that the very existence of the BSRR was the first step towards an independent Belarus in the future. The goal of indigenisation was to give the construction of socialism a national form in accordance with the provision of the 12th Congress of the Communist Party (Bolsheviks) of Russia in 1923 (Rudzutak, 1924, pp. 169-171). This took place by supporting Belarusian language and culture and recruiting party and state officials from among Belarusians. An important role in this belarusisation was played by the Belarusian Institute of Culture of the Scientific and Terminological Commission. The statute of that institution, approved in 1924 by the Council of People's Commissars, obligated the Republic to undertake research work on language, ethnography, history, natural history, the economy, social movements and other problems. The Belarusian intelligentsia understood perfectly well that the development of Belarusian culture would enhance the formation of the Belarusian nation, and therefore of their aspirations for independence. Belarusisation, therefore, included introducing the history, geography, language, literature and economy of the Republic as compulsory subjects, as well as the creation of universities[14]. This policy in the USSR bolstered the activities of the communist underground among Belarusians in independent Poland, including the Communist Party of Western Belarus, and of those who sympathised with the communist movement, such as the Belarusian Peasants' and Workers' Assembly (BWRH)[15] in the years 1925-1927, thereby heightening repressions by the authorities of the Republic of Poland. In the 1930s, there was a shift in USSR policy away from indigenisation and towards sovietisation on the basis of russo-centrism, directed towards the Russian language and Russian culture, and towards Russians themselves as the element binding the multi-ethnic Soviet nation together. Sovietisation was accompanied by intensified atheisation, collectivisation, and the extermination of Belarusian national elites, who were accused of "bourgeois nationalism". If we compare, then, the overall policy of the Polish Republic towards Belarusians in the inter-war period with sovietisation on the basis of russo-centrism, then the former, despite its hostility towards the Belarusian minority, comes out well ahead of the policy of the USSR towards the Belarusian SSR in the 1930s. This is confirmed by the recollections of citizens of Belarus from the Brest region gathered by the author during interviews conducted from 2013-2016. They recall the period of affiliation with inter-war Poland more fondly than the period of affiliation with the USSR, particularly at the end of the 1930s and the beginning of the 1940s. In the Second Republic, despite everything, there were no exterminations of national elites or collectivisations depriving the Belarusian peasants of the basis of their existence.

After the failure of the federalist conception, interest grew among the Polish elites in the idea of Prometheanism. This had arisen during the time of the Partitions, and its goal was to weaken and divide the Russian Empire. After the fall of the Empire and the rise of Soviet government, Prometheanism was directed against the USSR. The idea was to support

---

14 The Belarusian State University and the Belarusian State Agricultural Academy in Minsk, and the Veterinary Institute in Vitebsk.

15 The BRWH existed from 1925-1927, when it was delegalised and its leading activists, including Polish MPs, were convicted of crimes and sentenced. It was a mass organisation counting about 100,000 members. Its programme combined socialist and nationalistic demands, such as schooling in the mother tongue.

non-Russian nationalities within that state in their quest for independence. After the end of the Polish-Bolshevik War, initiatives surfaced in Polish thought that were directed towards utilising the problem of the nationalities in the USSR in the interests of Polish foreign policy. The essence was for Poland to assist national movements seeking to cast off the yoke of Soviet power. Thus, at the beginning of the 1920s, with Polish inspiration, a "Promethean movement" began within the elite émigré circles of those nations conquered by the USSR, since, as stated above, the USSR was equated with Russia. Initially, the movement was defensive in nature, but over time it became an offensive conception that has remained a real force up to the present, e.g., in the form of "exporting democracy". Belarus and Belarusian émigrés do not belong to the strongest 'hotbeds' of Prometheanism, but they are within the area of interest of the movement (Kornat, 2008).

9. The Second World War and the post-war period

During the Second World War, as a result of the implementation of the provisions of the Ribbentrop-Molotov Pact and the invasion of eastern Poland on 17 September 1939 by the Red Army, the north-eastern provinces of Poland, referred to in Soviet propaganda and literature as Western Belarus, were annexed into the USSR. Most Belarusians perceived this as a unification of Belarus within the Soviet Union, and this tended to have a positive impact that outweighed the recent repressions of Belarusian elites. The Soviet authorities gave privileges to the poorest Jews and Belarusians, while treating Poles restrictively as "lords". The situation altered dramatically, of course, after the conquest of the area by the Germans in 1941, though some Belarusians believed that the Germans intended to erect an independent Belarusian state. Polish political circles, concentrated around the government-in-exile in London, favoured a restoration of Poland's pre-war borders, though this of course was not met with great enthusiasm among Belarusians. The end of the global war brought changes in the borders, and paradoxically, as stated above, this made it possible for Roman Dmowski's programme on the borders of Poland to be implemented. Belarus as the Belarusian SSR remained within the Soviet Union. The new borders, resettlements of people and the repatriation of Poles from the BSSR meant that socialist Poland became a state that was ethnically homogeneous, with only a small Belarusian minority.

When establishing the western borders of the BSSR after taking over the Białystok region in July 1944, a Soviet administration was established in Bielsk County. Yet, in August, it was replaced by an administration of Poles run by the Polish Committee for National Liberation. In August 1944, the Supreme Council of the BSSR adopted a resolution on handing over the lands of the Białystok region to Poland. This problem was taken up again by the Belarusian side during the initial phase of Polish-Belarusian relations after the collapse of the USSR, as discussed further in Chapter 3.

The Polish People's Republic that appeared on the map of Europe at the end of the Second World War was not a fully sovereign state, but it was recognised internationally. The Belarusian Soviet Socialist Republic, which had the attributes of statehood, had no international status at all, though it did have its own representation at the United Nations. Political relations between the PPR and the BSSR, then, were possible only within PRL-USSR relations. Economic and cultural cooperation provided somewhat more scope for development. Poland was a country that guaranteed more creative freedom than that found in the USSR, where cultural connections had to be subordinated to reinforcing the ideological and political influence of the USSR on the external world. Polish-Belarusian cultural relations, therefore, were formed as part of Polish-Soviet relations, which were restricted ideologically and politically (Waszkiewicz, 2005, p. 49). The complete sovereignty of Poland, and the international status of Belarus, became possible only after the demise of the USSR and the Soviet bloc.

References

Akademiia upravleniia pri Prezidente Respubliki Belarus', 2004. *Osnovy ideologii belarusskogo gosudarstva, 2004*. Minsk: Redaktsionno-izdatel'skiĭ tsentr Akademii upravleniia pri Prezidente Respubliki Belarus'.

Bukhovets, O., 2010. Istoriopisanie sovetskoĭ Belarusi. In: F. Bomsdorf and G. Bordiugov, eds., 2010. *Natsional'nye istorii na postsovetskom prostranstve – II. Desiat' let spustia*. Moskva: Fond Friedrikha Naumanna, AIRO-XXI, pp. 15-44.

Dmowski, R., 1901. Narodowiec. W naszym obozie. Listy do przyjaciół politycznych. *Przegląd Wielkopolski*, 10(7), pp. 609-625.

Dmowski, R.,1926. Na przełomie stuleci. Odrodzenie myśli politycznej w Polsce. In: R. Dmowski, 1926. *Polityka Polska i odbudowanie państwa z dodaniem memorjału „Zagadnienia Środkowo- i Wschodnioeuropejskie" i innych dokumentów polityki polskiej z lat 1914-1918*. Second edition, Warsaw. Nakładem Księgarni Perzyński, Niklewicz i Ska, pp. 3-35.

Dmowski, R.,1926. Memorjał o terytorium Państwa Polskiego złożony przez R. Dmowskiego Prezydentowi Wilsonowi w Waszyngtonie dn. 8 października 1918 r. In: R. Dmowski, 1926. *Polityka Polska i odbudowanie państwa z dodaniem memorjału „Zagadnienia Środkowo- i Wschodnioeuropejskie" i innych dokumentów polityki polskiej z lat 1914-1918*. Second edition, Warsaw: Nakładem Księgarni Perzyński, Niklewicz i Ska, pp. 506-520.

Dolbilov, M., Miller, A., eds. 2008. *Zapadnye okrainy Rossiĭskoĭ Imperii*. Moskva: Novoe literaturnoe obozrenie.

Evstigneev, Iu., 2005. *Ischeznyvshie ètnosy (Kratkiĭ ètno-istoricheskiĭ spravochnik)*. St. Petersburg: Asterion.

Głogowska, H., 2012. *Stosunki polsko-białoruskie w XX wieku: Od Imperium Rosyjskiego do Unii Europejskiej*. Białystok: Wydawnictwo Uniwersytetu w Białymstoku.

Glybinny, U., 2012. Dolia belaruskae kul'tury pad Savetami 1920-1957. In: A.Taras, 2012. *Dolia belaruskae kul'tury pad savetami 1920-1991 gg*. Minsk: Kharvest, pp. 3-17.

Hroch, M., 2008. *Małe narody Europy. Perspektywa historyczna*. Wrocław, Warszawa, Kraków: Zakład Narodowy imienia Ossolińskich.

Jaśkiewicz, L., 2001. *Carat i sprawy polskie na przełomie XIX i XX wieku*. Pułtusk: Wyższa Szkoła Humanistyczna w Pułtusku.

Kappeler, A., 2014. *Russische Geschichte*. München: Verlag C.H. Beck.

Konstitutsiia Respubliki Belarus' 1994 goda (s izmeneniiami i dopolneniiami, priniatymi na respublikanskikh referendumakh 24 noiabria 1996 g. i 17 oktiabria 2004 g.), 2006. Minsk: Amalfeia.

Kornat, M., 2008. Ruch prometejski – ważne doświadczenie polityki zagranicznej II Rzeczypospolitej, *Nowa Europa Wschodnia*, 2, pp. 76-86.

Kosman, M., 1979. *Historia Białorusi*. Wrocław, Warszawa, Kraków, Gdańsk: Zakład Narodowy imienia Ossolińskich.

Kosmarskaya, N., 2011. Russia and Post-Soviet 'Russian Diaspora': Contrasting Visions, Conflicting Projects, *Nationalism and Ethnic Politics*, 17(1), pp. 54-74.

Kravtsevich, A., 2011. Pogranich'e kak sud'ba (VI-XVIII vv.). Mezhdu Vostokom i Zapadom Evropy. In: A. Kravtsevich, and A. Smolenchuk, and S. Tokt',. *Belorusy: natsiia pogranich'ia*. Vilnius: Evropeĭskiĭ gummanitarnyĭ universitet, pp. 7-84.

Kuzio, T., 2001. Nationalising states" or nation-building? A critical review of the theoretical and empirical evidence. *Nations and Nationalism*, 7(2), pp. 135-154.

Lazarevich, A. and Leviash, I., 2014. *Belarus': kul'turno-tsivilizatsionnyĭ vybor*. Minsk: Belarusskaia navuka.

Leshchenko, N., 2004. A fine instrument: two nation-building strategies in post-Soviet Belarus. *Nations and Nationalism*, 10(3), pp. 333–352.

Łatyszonek, O., 2010. Białorusini. In: M. Kopczyński, and W. Tygielski, eds. 2010. *Pod wspólnym niebem. Narody dawnej Rzeczypospolitej*. Warszawa: Muzeum Historii Polski, Bellona, pp. 39-54.

Malinovskiĭ, V., 2003. *Istoriia belorusskoĭ gosudarstvennosti*. Minsk: Belarus'.

Mironowicz, A., 2001. *Kościół prawosławny w dziejach dawnej Rzeczypospolitej.* Białystok: Wydawnictwo Uniwersytetu w Białymstoku.

Mironowicz, E., 2001. *Historia Białorusi.* Białystok: Orthdruk.

Nowak, A., 1999. *Jak rozbić Rosyjskie Imperium? Idee polskiej polityki wschodniej (1733–1921).* Kraków: Wydawnictwo ARCANA.

Pawluczuk, W., 2012. W poszukiwaniu tożsamości. Kształtowanie się idei narodowej Białorusinów. In: M. Głowacka-Grajper, R. Wyszyński, eds. 2012. *20 lat rzeczywistości poradzieckiej. Spojrzenie socjologiczne.* Warszawa: Wydawnictwa Uniwersytetu Warszawskiego, pp. 155-167.

Pawluczuk, W., 2015. U źródeł idei narodu białoruskiego. In: M. Bieńkowska, W. Żelazny, eds. 2015. *Pogranicza. Księga Jubileuszowa Profesora Andrzeja Sadowskiego.* Białystok: Wydawnictwo Uniwersytetu w Białymstoku, pp. 33-44.

Picheta, V., 2003. *Istoriia beloruskogo naroda.* Minsk: Izdatel'skiĭ centr BGU.

Pypin, A., 2005. *Istoriia russkoĭ ètnografii.* Minsk: Belarusskaia Èntsyklopedyia.

Radzik, R., 2009. Kulturowo-cywilizacyjna tożsamość społeczeństwa Białorusi. In: I. Topolski, eds. 2009. *Białoruś w stosunkach międzynarodowych.* Lublin: Wydawnictwo Uniwersytetu Marii Curie-Skłodowskiej, pp. 39-75.

Radzik, R., 2012. *Białoruś. Między Wschodem a Zachodem.* Lublin: Wydawnictwo Uniwersytetu Marii Curie-Skłodowskiej.

Rudzutak, Ia., 1924. Tsyrkuliarnoe pis'mo TsK RKP(b) o meropiiatiakh po realizatsii postanovleniĭ po natsional'nomu voprosu, priniatykh XII s"ezdom RKP(b) i IV soveshchaniem TsK RKP(b) s otvestvennymi rabotnikami natsional'nykh republik i oblasteĭ, 2005. In: L. Gatagova, L. Kosheleva and L. Rogovaia, eds. *TsK RKP(b) i natsional'nyĭ vopros. Kniga I. 1918-1933.* Moskva: Rossiĭkaia politicheskaia èntsiklopedia, pp. 169-175.

Rypiński, A., 1840. *Białoruś. Kilka słów o poezji prostego ludu téj naszéj polskiej prowincji; o jego muzyce, śpiéwie, tańcach, etc. przez Alexandra Rypińskiego, członka akademii przemysłu, rolnictwa, rękodzieł i handlu francuzkiego.* Paris: W księgotłoczni J. Marylskiego.

Sahanowicz, H., 2001. *Historia Białorusi. Od czasów najdawniejszych do końca XVIII wieku.* Lublin: Instytut Europy Środkowo-Wschodniej.

Szybieka, Z., 2002. *Historia Białorusi 1795-2000.* Lublin: Instytut Europy Środkowo-Wschodniej.

Tokt', S., 2011. Belorusy v epokhu formirovaniia modernykh evropeĭskikh natsiĭ. In: A. Kravtsevich,. and A. Smolenchuk and S. Tokt', eds. 2011.*Belorusy: natsiia pogranich'ia.* Vilnius: Evropeĭskiĭ gummanitarnyĭ universitet, pp. 85-158.

Vonsovich, L., 2005. *Belorusovedenie.* Minsk: TetraSistems.

Walicki, A., 2009. *Naród. Nacjonalizm. Polska.* Prace wybrane. Kraków: UNIVERSITAS. Vol. 1.

Waszkiewicz, J., 2005. Białorusko-polskie kontakty kulturalne w latach 1945-1989. In: H. Chałupczak and E. Michalik, eds. 2005. *Polska Białoruś. Problemy sąsiedztwa.* Lublin: Wydawnictwo Uniwersytetu Marii Curie-Skłodowskiej, pp. 45-52.

Wierzbicki, A., 2012. Nacjonalizm i geopolityka w Europie Wschodniej. In: S. Bieleń, and A. Skrzypek, eds. 2012. *Geopolityka w stosunkach polsko-rosyjskich.* Warsaw: Oficyna Wydawnicza ASPRA-JR, pp. 87-121.

Wyszyński, R., 2010. *Narodziny czy śmierć narodu. Narodotwórcze działania elit białoruskich i buriackich po upadku ZSRR.* Warsaw: Wydawnictwo Naukowe Scholar.

Żarnowski, J., 1973. *Społeczeństwo Drugiej Rzeczypospolitej 1918-1939.* Warsaw: Państwowy Instytut Wydawniczy.

Chapter 2 Polish-Belarusian relations from the perspective of Polish policy towards the east

1. Transformation of the foreign policy of Poland and Belarus

The late 1980s and early 1990s ushered in a new era in the history of Poland and Belarus. Both countries set out on a path of political, social and economic transformation, and set new priorities for their foreign policy. The goal of the political reforms in Poland was a return to full sovereignty, the construction of a liberal democracy with a parliamentary republic, and the gradual creation of a three-level system of local self-government. Social and economic reforms included building the foundations of a market economy through radical change, and amending the pension, healthcare and educational systems. Fundamental changes were also made in the foreign policy of the Republic of Poland. According to an axiom of Stalin, Poland had been a satellite state of the USSR, which obviously affected both the internal and foreign policies of the Polish socialist state. At the beginning of the transformation, the Soviet Union still existed, yet the change in Poland's foreign policy was evident in its seeking membership in NATO and the European Union, that is, its seeking to join the Western community of nations. Although different issues have been accented, these main thrusts of Poland's foreign policy were, and continue to be, agreed on by all of the country's main political forces. The "occidentalisation" and "Europeanisation" of Polish foreign policy began directly after the election of 4 June 1989, which, while not completely free, did permit a gradual confirmation of values previously accepted, or the adoption of new values underlying Western Europe's and Poland's identity, such as the rule of law, human rights, minority rights, a market economy, free competition, and property rights (Parzymies, 2011, p. 37).

The internal transformations and choice of foreign policy priorities of Belarus ran a different, more complicated course. Up to the mid-1990s, in the political sphere Belarus headed in the direction of a parliamentary republic, implementing the national democratic model of systemic change. Supporters of this appealed to liberal democratic values, stressing that the history of Belarus is part of the history of Europe, while the European political idea is an element of what it means to be Belarusian. The country, then, had only one choice – to turn towards the West and build up a Belarusian nation-state. On the other hand, the construction of democratic institutions was accompanied by a drive to make Belarus more Belarusian and to transform it into a mono-ethnic state – a contradiction of those democratic ideals. This policy, in combination with an appeal to the European roots of Belarusian culture, was based on a negation of Belarus's ties with Russia, and so the Russian language, used throughout Belarusian society, was presented as the language of a foreign power. Supporters of this orientation denied Belarusian status to those inhabitants of the country who favoured the existence of an independent state but did not speak Belarusian. This led to a situation in which, paradoxically, Belarusian became synonymous with the opposition, and now public appearances by people using that language spark interest and surprise. Historians have attempted to demonstrate the oldest possible origin of the Belarusian ethnos, idealising its past. Yet a European consciousness and the sense of being distinct from Russia were not widespread ideas; confined to a very small elite, they were little understood by most people. During this period of change, the governments of Belarus were of a hybrid nature, described as anocracy (Wojtaszczyk, 1996, p. 15). When, after winning the presidential election in 1994, Alexander Lukaszenka came to power, by taking advantage of public feeling he changed the country's course, moving towards authoritarianism and tradition. The Belarusian version of tradition meant: the preservation of the Soviet tradition, a turning away from the belarusisation of the state, anti-occidentalism, and an evolutionary form of economic reform. The result of Lukashenko's internal policy was the creation of a Belarus consolidated by authoritarianism (Antoszewski, 2010, p. 107).

Supporters of the democratisation of Belarus were not unanimous as to which direction was best for the country's foreign policy. In the first half of the 1990s, there was a desire for complete independence, cooperation with other republics of the former USSR in order to create a common economic area and develop the Commonwealth of Independent States, and the inclusion of Belarus in pan-European processes, and so, from the moment Belarus's independence was proclaimed, there was a consensus on a foreign policy aimed at achieving neutrality. This was, at the same time, as Rafał Czachor has emphasised, the most paradoxical conception of contemporary Belarus. As it later turned out, it was an "instrumental neutrality" that remained a mere political declaration – including in the provision of the Constitution stating that "the Republic of Belarus aims at making the state neutral" (*Konstitutsiia Respubliki Belarus*, 2005). In practice, the requirement to maintain neutrality did not suit the particular political and economic interests of those in power (Czachor, 2011, p. 37). After the creation of the Collective Security Treaty initiated by Russia in 1992 (the Tashkent Treaty), some people at the highest levels of power in Belarus favoured Belarus's accession to the treaty; these were the Prime Minister, Wiaczesław Kiebicz, a supporter of greater cooperation with Russia, and the Foreign Minister, Piotr Kozłowski. They argued that, without Russia, Belarus would not be able to maintain its armed forces or protect itself against a collapse in its arms industry, which had up till then been based on serving the needs of the Soviet army. The chairman of the Supreme Council of Belarus, Stanisław Szuszkiewicz, remained a supporter of neutrality. Lest the country be caught in a "grey area of security", and in order to form a military alliance with Russia, in April 1993 the Belarusian parliament decided by a clear majority of votes to joined the Tashkent Treaty. Contrary, then, to what is commonly believed, the pro-Russian turnabout in the foreign policy of Belarus occurred before Lukashenko came to power – after which he continued the process at an accelerated pace. This fact should give food for thought to those Polish politicians who assume that the only barrier to the "europeanisation" of Belarus is Lukashenko. After Lukashenko came into office, there was increased cooperation, and even integration, with Russia, within the structures of the Commonwealth of Independent States. This caused a deterioration in Polish-Belarusian bilateral relations, even though a relevant agreement was signed in 1992 (Sulowski, 2007, p. 286). As we shall attempt to show further on, this resulted from the contrary interests of the two states, and from their divergent paths of political and economic development. Poland consistently built up the foundations of democracy and a market economy, seeking integration with the structures of the West, while since 1994 Belarus has reinforced authoritarianism, has transformed its economic system only gradually, and has been interested in integrating not with the West, but with the countries of the former USSR – above all with Russia. Ideologically, Lukashenko rejected integration with the West, on the assumption that "full political sovereignty can be enjoyed only by a block of states that share a common denominator – religion, ethnic values, cultural models, religious centres, a similar understanding of history. Such a foundation for the stable existence and dynamic development of Belarus in the system of contemporary international relations is provided by an affiliation with Russia" (*Akademiia upravleniia pri Prezidente Respubliki Belarus'*, 2004). Yet the paradox pointed out by Rafał Czachor remains – that the binding Constitution of the Republic of Belarus contains a provision on neutrality (Article 17).

These divergent paths of development also affected the legal and political situation of decision-making bodies in respect of foreign policy. In Poland, which built up a parliamentary and executive system with a strong president chosen in a general election (which certainly enhanced the legitimacy of the system), a conflict of competence arose between the President of the Republic and the Council of Ministers. The principles for demarcating the competences of the President vis-à-vis those of the government were not clear-cut, there was no well-established practice, and most importantly, the political culture was not at a high enough level for power struggles to be avoided (Nowak-Far, 2011, p. 191). Pursuant to Article 126 of the Constitution of the Republic of Poland, "The President of the Republic of Poland shall be the supreme representative of the Republic of Poland and the guarantor of the continuity of State authority" (par. 1), and "shall safeguard the sovereignty and security of the State as well as the inviolability and integrity of its territory" (par. 2) (*Konstytucja Rzeczypospolitej Polskiej*, 1997). In respect of foreign policy, the competences of the president are also based on Article 133 of the Constitution, under which the president is authorised to represent the State in external relations, including by ratifying and renouncing international agreements, appointing and recalling plenipotentiary representatives of the Republic of Poland to other states and to international organisations, receiving letters of credence and recalling diplomatic representatives of other states and international organizations accredited to him. Yet Article 146 (1)(2)(4) of the Constitution states that the Council of Ministers is in charge of foreign policy, exercising "general control in the field of relations with other States and international organizations".

The Constitution of the Republic of Belarus sets out less ambiguous competences between the highest bodies of state power within the scope of foreign policy; in 1996, an Eastern presidential (super-presidential) system was introduced characteristic of the post-soviet states. It places the president above other state authorities, although formally there is a tripartite division of power. The overriding idea of this system is that the president is, formally and factually, the centre of power (Bodio, Wojnicki and Załęski, 2007, p. 479). This is reflected in both specific provisions and political practice. Pursuant to Article 79 of the Belarusian Constitution, the president shall "guarantee the implementation of the main guidelines of domestic and foreign policy, represent the Republic of Belarus in relations with other states and international organizations... take measures to protect the sovereignty of the Republic of Belarus, its national security and territorial integrity" (*Konstitutsiia Respubliki Belarus'*, 2005). Whereas under Article 84, the president shall "conduct negotiations and sign treaties, appoint and recall diplomatic representatives... to/from foreign states and international organisations" (par. 20), shall "receive letters of credence and of recall from diplomatic representatives of foreign states accredited to him" (par. 21), and shall "address the people... with messages on the state of the nation and on the guidelines of domestic and foreign policy" (par. 13). Certain competences pertaining to foreign policy are also granted to the executive branch – the Council of Ministers. In accordance with the Constitution, the government shall "elaborate the basic guidelines of domestic and foreign policy and take measures for their implementation" (Article 107). There is no doubt, however, that, as one Polish author has rightly concluded, "the deciding voice in foreign policy rests with the President" (Dziemidok-Olszewska, 2009, p. 34).

Having become acquainted with the systemic conditions of Polish-Belarusian relations, we can now examine the geopolitical situations and the social and economic potential of the two states.

2. Geopolitical situation and social and economic potential

The geopolitical situations of Poland and Belarus have certain features in common. In terms of area, both states are considered "middle-sized". The international status of middle-sized states is determined by the politics of the great powers, and Poland and Belarus are no exception. Ryszard Zięba has pointed out that, as a rule, "states from this group prefer the method of multilaterialism, adopting a middle-of-the-road, mediatory and moderate posture. This makes them stand out as states stabilising the international system" (Zięba, 2011, p. 64). This conclusion, however, is not necessarily borne out in Polish-Belarusian relations. Both states are "front states", where the front means the border between the North Atlantic Treaty Organization, of which Poland is a member, and the "near abroad" of the Russian Federation, which includes Belarus; Belarus therefore is part of a joint security system together with Russia. The Polish-Belarusian border is also a border between the European Union and the Eurasian Union. Finally, the borderlands on either side of the Polish-Belarusian border mark the dividing line between Western civilization (Euro-Atlantic) founded on Western Christianity, and Byzantine-Orthodox civilization.

A common feature of both states, geopolitically and geo-economically, is that they lie along trade routes from Russia to Western Europe, which is important primarily with regard to the transport of commodities. Where the two countries differ is in their access to the sea, of which Belarus has none, being a landlocked state.

These common features of the geopolitical situation of Poland and Belarus ensure that the great powers are interested in each for their own purposes (Iwańczuk, 2009, p. 135). The geopolitical orientation of Poland has been clearly, expressly defined, which cannot be said of Belarus, according to the European Union and the United States. A paradox of this situation is that, in this rivalry over "middle-sized states", Poland – itself such a state – is a participant.

The social and economic potential of the two states differs significantly. Not only in area and population, but in every criterion used to define social and economic potential, Poland ranks higher than Belarus. There is no doubt, however, that each country's potential is considerable, and each is an attractive political and economic partner for the other (Table 1).

Table.1. Social and economic potential of Poland and Belarus

Criterion	Poland	Belarus
Area in thousands of square kilometers	312,679	207,595
Population in millions	38.4	9.5 (2017)
Growth in GDP	2.7	- 2.6
Income per capita[16] (USD)	24,117	15,629
Average earnings (EUR)	752 (EUR)	328 (EUR)
Life expectancy (inc. women and men)	77.6	71.5

---

16 Aggregate income of an economy generated by its production and its ownership of factors of production, less the income paid for the use of factors of production owned by the rest of the world, converted to international dollars using PPP rates, divided by mid-year population.

Criterion	Poland	Belarus
Position in UNDP classification According to Human Development Index[17] (2016)	36	52

Source: Human Development Report 2016. Human Development for Everyone, 2016; Average Salary in European Union, 2017, Quarterly statements of gross domestic product for the years 2012-2016, 2017.

Undoubtedly, Polish-Belarusian relations are determined by the geopolitical situations of the two countries and their affiliations with various military-political and economic-political formations. On the Polish side, these must be considered in the broader context of the Poland's eastern policy since 1989.

3. Poland's policy towards the east

In 1991, the USSR ceased to exist, and a new international situation opened up on Poland's eastern border. Instead of having a single neighbour, Poland now had four new neighbours, including the Republic of Belarus. The international situation forced the Polish government to elaborate a policy towards the east, that is, concerning its relations with the new post-Soviet states. That eastern policy is to be understood as undertakings (conceptualisation, activities, results) aimed at establishing contacts with those new neighbours, including on the basis of bilateral agreements. Initially, the implementation of the basic tenets of this policy enjoyed societal consent (Bieleń, 2012).

Poland's eastern policy was formed in part by the ULB[18] conception, which consisted in maintaining good relations with Ukraine, Lithuania and Belarus. This, in the opinion of Juliusz Mieroszewski, would permit both Russia and Poland to give up any imperialistic tendencies in the area. It should be emphasised that Mieroszewski was one of the first to admit that the inhabitants of Eastern Europe, including Belarusians, were entitled to

---

17 Human Development Index (HDI): A composite index measuring average achievement in three basic dimensions of human development — a long and healthy life, knowledge, and a decent standard of living.

18 An acronym of the first letters of the states Ukraine, Lithuania and Belarus.

consider Poland an empire in which polonisation posed a greater danger for them than russification: "Only for us does the Jagellonian idea have nothing to do with imperialism. For Lithuanians, Ukrainians and Belarusians, it constitutes the purest form of traditional Polish imperialism. The Polish-Lithuanian Commonwealth ended with the total polonisation of the Lithuanian nobility, while the most heartfelt declaration of love for Lithuania ("Lithuania, my motherland, you are health itself") was written in Polish (Mieroszewski, 1974, p. 7). After the collapse of the USSR, that conception was transformed into a kind of *ULB first* doctrine, under which relations with Ukraine, Lithuania and Belarus were given top priority. The aim was intra-political and geopolitical Westernisation, that is, a "geopolitical turnabout" to the West conducted by the authorities of those states. With regard to Belarus, it was acknowledged that, for this to happen, the country must be democratised, and in this sense the ULB concept became an expression of "exporting democracy". Lately, opinions have been put forward suggesting it's time to "say goodbye to Giedroyć[19]" and forego such activities, focusing rather on supporting Polish culture and language in Belarus (Pełczyńska-Nałęcz, 2017), which attests to an evolution in this conception.

In the context of the ULB conception, two factors forming Poland's Eastern policy predominate (Vezhbitski, 2015). The ideological component of Polish eastern policy comprises "exporting democracy" and "human rights". Since the beginning of the transformation, many Polish politicians have been convinced of the superiority of democracy over the non-democratic states of the former USSR. This was something of a "neophyte syndrome", since Poland itself had only just set out on the democratic path; democracy had not yet firmly established itself. But this did not stop Polish political elites from spreading democracy among other nations. The priorities of Poland's foreign policy in the years 2012-2016 included "supporting activities serving to disseminate human rights, the rule of law and democracy, in order to foster a friendly international environment and avoid conflicts" (*Priorytety polskiej polityki zagranicznej 2012-2016*, p. 6). This was undoubtedly a manifestation of "missionism", according to which Poland, being on the fringes of Western civilization, took on the role of "missionary" of that civilization's values, directed eastward

---

19 Jerzy Giedroyć – editor in chief of the émigré periodical *Kultura*, published in Paris, in which Mieroszewski put forward his conception.

(Jedlicki, 1988, p. 31). This certainly applies to Polish-Belarusian relations. After Alexander Lukashenko came to power, Poland repeatedly raised this issue in bilateral contacts, pointing out violations of human rights and attempting to convince the Belarusian government and citizens that democracy is a better form of exercising power. One cannot deny the disinterested and noble intentions of many Polish politicians, including those in government. Nevertheless, "exporting democracy" had a broader, deeper context. The political elites in Poland counted on liberal democracy being a factor uniting the nations of Eastern Europe in opposition to Muscovite despotism. With the help of democratisation and the fight for human rights, Poland tried to create a "sanitary cordon" in Eastern Europe that would separate Poland from Russia. It was not, then, a matter of whether democracy was an effective or ineffective form of government; besides, there is more than one type of democracy, and every nation has the right to choose its own course of development. The policy of promoting democracy was implemented as a part of an anti-Russian policy (Zięba, 2011, p. 70)[20]; it was not an aim in itself, of which Russia was perfectly well aware. Yet it caused more harm than good. Poland did not gain supporters in the countries concerned, and at the same time worsened its relations with Russia. Poland tried to exert influence on the Lukashenko regime by means of non-governmental organisations, including that of the Polish minority in Belarus, as presented in more detail in a later chapter. In providing support to the Polish minority, the aim was not so much to protect the rights of Belarusian citizens of Polish nationality as to use the Polish minority organisation instrumentally in order to bring about a regime change or force the Lukashenko government to make political reforms. There was a hope that the removal of Lukashenko from power would result in a "European" and "Euro-Atlantic" choice by Belarus (Wierzbicki, 2012, p. 117). The conviction that the geopolitical orientation of a given state depends on a single person is irrational. The President of Belarus criticises Russia from time to time, but one must face that fact that there is more potential in the country for russo-centrism than there is for euro-centrism, and Lukashenko is well aware of this. Belarus's pro-Russian orientation is not likely to change if another person, or another regime, comes to power. It would even be safe to assume that future governments may be

---

20 Poland's best-known programmes of cooperation with its Eastern neighbors providing for the export of democracy were *Partnership for transformation* from 1994 and *Principles of Polish foreign policy towards Russia* from 2000.

even more pro-Russian than the current one (*Lukashenka budet ubezhdat' èlektorat, chto v krizise vinovata Rossia*, 2015).

As an "exporter of democracy" to the east, Poland fulfilled its role inconsistently and without conceptual cohesion. Azerbaijan was no more democratic than Belarus, but was not subjected to such severe criticism as was Belarus. This was probably because Azerbaijan was not conducting an unambiguously pro-Russian foreign policy, and was included in plans to build an oil and gas pipeline that would circumvent Russian pipelines.

The efforts of the Polish government and opposition politicians met with little success, however. Their arguments fell on deaf ears with the Belarusian authorities, and also within Belarusian society, for three reasons. Firstly, such practices did not take account of the political and socio-cultural reality of Belarus, and led only to a type of "canonisation" and "idealisation" of democracy as an "exceptional", "unique", "positive" model of a political system. At the same time, there was a "deification" of the democratic, pro-European opposition. Thus, the "export of democracy" took on a confrontational character. Striving for democracy at any cost, without considering local traditions and the local political culture, had an effect opposite to that intended, since it was seen as something imposed from the outside, something "foreign". Democracy and democratisation became an attempt to impose "higher" values upon "backward" countries and societies. Secondly, the citizens of Belarus, who observed the democratisation that took place in Russia in the 1990s, feared similar adverse consequences on their own standard of living and sense of social security. Thirdly, for many Belarusians, the Polish political and cultural presence in the country was perceived as a remnant of the colonial era.

Another factor related to how Poland's eastern policy shaped Polish-Belarusian relations is Poland's location between Germany (involved in the process of European integration and NATO, and therefore not as threatening as it once was) and Russia, with the latter seen as a "perpetual threat". Polish-Belarusian relations are subordinate, therefore, to Polish-Russian relations. For Poland, Belarus is not as significant as Ukraine, although it is true that the interests of Poland and Russia intersect in Belarus. For both states, historically, Belarus constitutes part of their national territory: "Both the Polish and Russian identities, formed as they exist today during different epochs and looking back nostalgically on different centuries, intersect in space: the whole of Western Rus (comprising today's Belarus and Ukraine) is an area that both ordinary Poles and ordinary Russians believe is part of their national territory. This is the basis of the fundamental differences in how historical events are interpreted and of the differences in their policies towards each other" (Nemenskiĭ, 2010); "Both neighbouring nations strove for domination in the area between the ethnically Polish lands and those inhabited by ethnically Russian peoples. From the start, Russia developed as an imperial state. Jagellonian Poland was a Republic of many nations" (Rotfeld, 2012, p. 42). That is why today's Belarus remains a bone of contention in the rivalry between the West, represented by Poland, and Russia. In the Polish consciousness, Belarus is part of the Eastern Borderlands, an inseparable component of a common political and cultural past, a memory of a single state, nation and culture, the era of the apex of Poland's power. From this perspective, for Belarus to choose "Russia" instead of "Europe" is perceived as a threat to the geopolitical interests of Poland, and the Union State of Belarus as an attempt to at least partially restore the USSR and to absorb Belarus within an imperial Russia reaching out ever closer to the borders of the Polish Republic. This is why Poland tries to take on the role of a kind of "European advocate" of Belarus, as in the Eastern Partnership programme it initiated. This "missionary" aspect of Poland's Eastern policy is summed up by the Polish researcher Stanisław Bieleń: "...Poland, which has a weak position in the West, can make up for this lack of recognition and prestige in the East. It can show that it is active in promoting Western values, even when it does not itself fully implement those values. The worst of this feature, however, is its missionary conviction that Western values are the only right values in the modern world. It can be forgotten that this world, in all of its complexity, is pluralistic; there is room for different systems and values. In the context of Russia, Ukraine, Belarus and Georgia, people forget that these states have inherited their own cultural and civilizational traditions, and that no Western model will ever be grafted onto them entirely successfully. They will always remain hybrids. Accepting models from the outside would mean their abdicating their own identity, whereas identity is more valuable than sovereignty" (Bieleń, 2017, p. 323).

European integration is treated as a "guarantee of democracy, human rights and liberation from the Russian threat". The Belarusian authorities were in favour of the Eastern Partnership, but called it a pragmatic step of the EU that should have been taken much earlier. Belarus does not aspire to EU membership. Above all, it expects measurable material benefits, developmental aid, an opening to European markets for Belarusian production, and funds for modernising the economy and infrastructure. It also expected a liberalisation of visa traffic. It did not look at the Partnership as a step towards integration with the EU. According to the Belarusian authorities, the Eastern Partnership cannot be directed against Russia, which remains Belarus's most important ally. Democratisation and the development of civil society do not hold much interest for those in power; for them, Belarus being invited to join the Partnership legitimises the regime. Some of those in the pro-democratic and pro-European Belarusian opposition called the Partnership a betrayal of EU values, and demanded that the Belarusian authorities be excluded from cooperation until the system was changed.

The European Union's policy towards Belarus must be guided by an understanding of the specific conditions of the state- and nation-building process in that country. Otherwise, the actions the EU takes will be viewed as a "civilizing mission" of the West borne out of a "feeling of superiority" aimed at political and cultural westernisation and at an expansion of Western capital into the Belarusian market. This is important to the extent that Belarus, unlike Orthodox Romania and Bulgaria, which are EU members, has no need to be "appreciated" by the West.

This discussion of Poland's eastern policy provides a basis for a better understanding the development of relations between today's Poland and Belarus since their inception, particularly within the sphere most important for political science – the political sphere.

References

Akademiia upravleniia pri prezidente Respubliki Belarus', 2004. *Osnovy ideologii belarusskogo gosudarstva.* Minsk: Redaktsionno-izdatel'skiĭ tsentr Akademii upravleniia pri Prezidente Respubliki Belarus'.

Antoszewski, A., 2010. Instytucjonalne uwarunkowania rywalizacji politycznej w państwach poradzieckich. In: T. Bodio, ed. 2010. *Przywództwo, elity i transformacje w krajach WNP. Problemy metodologii badań*, Warszawa: Oficyna Wydawnicza ASPRA-JR, Vol.1, pp. 91-110.

Bieleń, S., 2012. O polskiej polityce wschodniej. *Polityka Wschodnia*, 1(10), pp. 11-33.

Bieleń, S., 2017. *Czas próby w stosunkach międzynarodowych.* Miscellanea. Warszawa: Oficyna Wydawnicza ASPRA-JR.

Bodio, T., Wojnicki, J. and Załęski, P., 2007. Transformacja ustrojowa państw postsocjalistycznych. In: K.A.Wojtaszczyk, W. Jakubowski, eds. 2007. *Społeczeństwo i polityka. Podstawy nauk politycznych.* Warszawa: Oficyna Wydawnicza ASPRA-JR, pp. 468-485.

Czachor, R., 2011. *Polityka zagraniczna Republiki Białoruś w latach 1991-2011. Studium politologiczne.* Polkowice: Wydawnictwo Dolnośląskiej Wyższej Szkoły Przedsiębiorczości i Techniki w Polkowicach.

Dziemidok-Olszewska, B., 2009. Konstytucyjne ośrodki decyzyjne Republiki Białoruś. In: I. Topolski, ed. 2009. *Białoruś w stosunkach międzynarodowych*. Lublin: Wydawnictwo Uniwersytetu Marii Curie-Skłodowskiej, pp. 17-38.

Iwańczuk K., 2009. Pozycja geopolityczna Białorusi. In: I. Topolski, ed. 2009. *Białoruś w stosunkach międzynarodowych*. Lublin: Wydawnictwo Uniwersytetu Marii Curie-Skłodowskiej, pp. 129-135.

Konstitutsiia Respuliki Belarus' 1994 goda (s izmeneniiami i dopolneniiami, priniatymi na respublikanskikh referendumakh 24 noiabria 1996 g., i 17 oktiabria 2004 g.), 2005. Minsk: Amalfeia.

Konstytucja Rzeczypospolitej Polskiej z dnia 2 kwietnia 1997 r.,1997, 2001, 2006. Dziennik Ustaw Rzeczypospolitej Polskiej [Journal of Laws], 78, item, 483; 28, item, 319; 200, item 1471,114, item, 946.

Lukashenko budet ubezhdat' èlektorat, chto v krizise vinovata Rossia. [online] Available at: <naviny.by/rubrics/politic/2015/01/17/ic_articles_112_188014/> [Accessed 22 February 2015].

Mieroszewski, J., 1974. Rosyjski „kompleks polski" i obszar ULB. *Kultura*, 9(324), pp. 3-14.

Nemenskiĭ, O., 2010. *Poliaki i russkie: narody raznykh vremen i raznykh sudeb*. [online] Available at: <http://www.apn.ru/publications/article22387.htm> [Accessed 2 September 2017].

Nowak-Far A., 2011. Conflicts powers in the realm of Poland's foreign Policy decisions. In: S. Bieleń, ed. 2011. *Poland's Foreign Policy in the 21st Century*. Warsaw: Difin SA, pp. 185-196.

Parzymies S., 2011. Successes and failures in building Poland's Western identity. In: S. Bieleń, ed. 2011. *Poland's Foreign Policy in the 21st Century*. Warsaw: Difin SA, pp. 21-38.

Pełczyńska-Nałęcz K., 2017. *Pożegnanie z Giedroyciem*. Warsaw: Fundacja im. Stefana Batorego, styczeń 2017. [online] Available at: <http://www.batory.org.pl/upload/files/pdf/rap_otw_eu/Pozegnanie%20z%20Giedroyciem.pdf> [Accessed 26 June 2017].

Priorytety polskiej polityki zagranicznej 2012-2016, 2012. Warszawa: Ministerstwo Spraw Zagranicznych.

Rotfeld A., 2012. *Myśli o Rosji ...i nie tylko*. Warsaw: Świat Książki.

Sulowski S., 2007. Transformacja polskiej polityki zagranicznej. In: J. Błuszkowski, ed., 2007. *Dylematy polskiej transformacji*. Warszawa: Dom Wydawniczy ELIPSA, pp. 282-293.

Vezhbitski A., 2015. Paradigmy pol'skoĭ vostochnoĭ politiki po otnosheniiu k stranam byvshego SSSR. *Memlekettik Zhoene Qyzmet. Gosudarstvennoe upravlenie i gosudarstvennaia sluzhba. Public administration and civil service*. Available at: <http://www.pa-academy.kz/index.php?lang=ru> [Accessed 15 November 2015].

Wierzbicki A., 2012. Nacjonalizm i geopolityka w Europie Wschodniej. In: S. Bieleń, A. Skrzypek, eds. 2012. *Geopolityka w stosunkach polsko-rosyjskich*. Warszawa: Oficyna Wydawnicza ASPRA-JR, pp 87-121.

Wojtaszczyk K.A.,1996. Transformacja ustrojowa w krajach Europy Wschodniej, Środkowej i Południowej. In: E. Zieliński, ed. 1996. *Transformacja ustrojowa państw Europy Środkowej i Wschodniej.* Warszawa: Dom Wydawniczy ELIPSA, pp. 9-20.

Zięba R., 2011. The search for an international role for Poland: conceptualizing the role of a „middle-ranking" state. In: S. Bieleń, ed. 2011. *Poland's Foreign Policy in the 21st Century.* Warsaw: Difin SA, pp. 61-79.

Chapter 3 Political relations

1. A good beginning and a lost opportunity

In the consciousness of Poles, Belarus remains part of the former Eastern
Borderlands of the Republic, and therefore part of the old Polish state and
within the Polish cultural sphere. Up to 1991, Belarus was part of the Soviet Union. After Belarus declared independence, and after the change in
the political and economic system in Poland, the two countries began to
look for areas in which they could cooperate. Poland needed to guarantee
security and stability on its eastern boundaries, while for Belarus, Poland
could act as a bridge in Belarus's relations with the West. In the period
preceding the demise of the USSR (1989-1991), Poland had a dual policy
towards its eastern neighbours. That policy was conceived by the Polish
Foreign Ministry (Czachor, 2011, p. 70) presented in the spring of 1990
during a parliamentary *exposé* by Krzysztof Skubiszewski, the Foreign
Minister in the government of Tadeusz Mazowiecki (*Sejmowe exposé ministra spraw zagranicznych RP Krzysztofa Skubiszewskiego 1991*, pp.
11,17). The policy involved, on the one hand, Poland's first non-commu-
nist government since the end of the Second World War maintaining official relations with the central authorities of the USSR, while on the other
hand, seeking to establish diplomatic relations with those republics on the
western edge of the Soviet empire, including with Belarus (since it was
evident that the USSR was about to collapse) (Snapkoŭski, 2003, p. 18).

Despite these favourable prospects and the absence of serious conflicts
in the past, the beginnings of Polish-Belarusian relations proved difficult.
Bilateral cooperation began later with Belarus than with Poland's other
eastern neighbours. The first visit to Minsk by Polish Foreign Minister
Krzysztof Skubiszewski ended in failure. At that time, the policy of the
Belarusian government was heavily influenced by the Belarusian National
Front (Habowski, 2009, p. 236). Under pressure from it, Belarus refused
to sign a declaration on the principles and foundation for the development
of mutual relations, when similar declarations were signed by Poland with
the Ukrainian SSR and the Russian Soviet Federative Socialist Republic.
The reason for Belarus's refusal was the fact that Belarus had not taken
part in the signing of the Polish-Soviet agreement of 16 August 1945 con-

cerning the borders of the state, and therefore did not deem the existing border binding. This issue concerned the area of Białystok, which had been annexed as part of the Belarusian SSR after the Soviet aggression of 17 September 1939. The Belarusian side rejected the formula on the inviolability of the Polish-Belarusian border; it demanded a provision in the declaration stating that Białystok is an ethnically Belarusian land, though it did not put forward any territorial claims against Poland. Poland did not consent to that provision. Minister Skubiszewski argued that the permanence of the borders was to be a fundamental assumption of any agreement Poland signed with its neighbours.

At the same time, the Polish parliament took an active part in building relations with Belarus. After the Supreme Council of the BSSR approved the Declaration on the state sovereignty of the BSSR on 27 July 1990, the Polish Senate adopted a resolution addressed to the people of Belarus, greeting the Belarusian declaration with joy and writing that "the Poles, for whom independence and a free state are fundamental values, totally understand this critical moment in the history of Belarus – a neighbour with whom we wish to live as nations that are equal and close to one another. On either side of our common border live citizens belonging to the Belarusian and Polish nations. We hope that our relations will develop in accordance with the best traditions of the former Republic, its tolerance and the co-existence of many cultures. We wish to develop cooperation with Belarus in all areas of life. Our wish for the Belarusian nation, which for many centuries was deprived of its own statehood, is that it will be able to freely form its own countenance and conditions of life, and will have a successful future" (*Uchwała Senatu Rzeczypospolitej Polskiej z dnia 3 sierpnia 1990 r. do narodu Białoruskiego z okazji proklamowania suwerenności państwowej Białorusi*, 1990). The Polish Parliament adopted a relevant resolution on 31 August 1991, in which it recognised the right of all nations to self-determination, and welcomed the announcement of Belarusian independence on 25 August 1991. "Poland, which has made the independence and liberty of its own state an overriding value, completely understands and appreciates the significance of this historic decision by the Belarusian Parliament. It is the fulfilment of the yearnings of the Belarusian nation, an expression of the right of Belarus to freely determine its external and internal position. The Parliament of the Republic of Poland expresses its conviction that an independent Belarus will proceed along the path to democratic transformation, creating conditions for mutual, neighbourly international cooperation between Poland and Belarus"

(*Uchwała Sejmu Rzeczypospolitej Polskiej z dnia 31 sierpnia 1991 r. w sprawie ogłoszenia niepodległości Białorusi*, 1990).

There was a revival in Polish-Belarusian relations after the coup in August 1991 in Moscow. On 25 August, the Supreme Council of the BSSR passed a law granting constitutional status to the Act on the Declaration of the Supreme Council of the BSSR on the state sovereignty[21] of the Belarusian Soviet Socialist Republic, and to a resolution on the political and economic independence of the BSSR (Malinovskiĭ, 2003, p. 190). Essentially, this was a proclamation of independence.

The problem of the border was preliminarily resolved in October 1991. The Prime Ministers of both countries (Jan Krzysztof Bielecki for Poland and Wiaczesław Kiebicz for Belarus) signed a Declaration on neighbourly relations, mutual understanding and cooperation between the two states. The Declaration contained a provision that: "Mutual relations between the Republic of Poland and the Republic of Belarus are based on the principles of equality, respect for the sovereignty and territorial integrity of both states, non-intervention in internal matters, freedom of choice concerning the social and political system, good neighbourly relations, mutual understanding and mutually beneficial cooperation. The existing border between the Republic of Poland and the Republic of Belarus established on the basis of the Agreement between the Republic of Poland and the Union of Soviet Socialist Republics on Polish-Soviet state border of 16 August 1945 cannot be changed now or in the future. The border between the Republic of Poland and the Republic of Belarus is an important element of peaceful regulation in Europe (*Deklaracja o dobrym sąsiedztwie, wzajemnym zrozumieniu i współpracy między Rzeczypospolitą Polską i Republiką Białoruś*, 1991, pp. 18-22).This was the first Polish-Belarusian document to regulate bilateral relations between Poland and Belarus. On 27 December 1991, by a resolution of the Council of Ministers, Poland recognised the independence of Belarus, which accelerated the development of Pol-

---

21 The process of acquiring sovereignty among the Soviet republics had three dimensions. The first concerned relations between the centre of the Soviet empire and the republics, and involved making them equal and horizontal, rather than vertical. The second dimension concerned greater autonomy in implementing economic and social policy within the territory of those republics, while the third involved real empowerment in international relations, with the right to conclude international agreements. It did not mean, however, a complete break with the centre in Moscow.

ish-Belarusian relations. At that time there was a intensive exchange of contacts and visits, including at the ministerial level, with an important event in political relations being an official visit to Poland by the Belarusian Foreign Minister, Piotr Krauczanka, on 23 March 1992. Krauczanka met with President Lech Wałęsa, the Polish Foreign Minister Krzysztof Skubiszewski, the Prime Minister Jan Olszewski, and Polish MPs. A result of the visit was the signing of an understanding on the establishment of diplomatic relations and a consular convention. The issue of cross-border traffic was discussed. Poland wanted those belonging to the ethnic minorities of the two countries to have the right to cross the border freely. In March 1992, Prime Ministers Kiebicz and Olszewski held a working meeting in Puszcza Białowieska, while from 23-24 April 1992, a Belarusian government delegation headed by Prime Minister Kiebicz appeared in Warsaw. They met with President Wałęsa and the speakers and Deputy Speakers of the Polish Parliament and Senate. During the visit, they initialled the text of a treaty on neighbourly relations and friendly cooperation, and signed many bilateral agreements and understandings (Czachor, 2011, p. 74). As a result of these two meetings, a packet of agreements was concluded at the government level: on opening up three new border crossings, on additional supplies of Polish coal to Belarus, on the rules of cross-border cooperation, on the movement of people, on supporting and protecting investments, on the creation of Polish-Belarusian commercial bank, and on combating crime.

The most important event of the first period of Polish-Belarusian relations was the between the Republic of Poland and the Republic of Belarus on Neighbourly Relations and Friendly Cooperation signed on 23 June 1992 during a visit to Poland by the chairman of the Supreme Council of the Republic of Belarus, Stanisław Szuszkiewicz. This was the first ever visit to Poland by the head of an independent Belarus. Also of symbolic importance at that time was the opening of the opening of the Belarusian embassy in Warsaw – Belarus's first embassy in the world.

International treaties are of a political nature, yet also contain legal obligations that are binding on both parties. They are the highest and most general form of agreement summarising discussions and procedures concerning the relations between the parties to the treaty (Kukułka, 1998, pp. 9-10). The Polish-Belarusian treaty is similar. In the preamble, emphasis is placed on both parties's attachment to the idea of a just peace and order in Europe, and to respect for human rights and fundamental freedoms. Mention is also made of "the significance of friendly Polish-Belarusian relations in strengthening trust and cooperation on the European continent" and that "to a large extent, Poland and Belarus share a common history, of which the best tradition is co-existence and a mutual enrichment of culture". The treaty refers to the "ethnic and cultural closeness of the Polish and Belarusian nations" and to the fact that "Poles and Belarusians inhabiting the territories of the Parties, make an important contribution to the development of both countries and the cultures of both nations" – a reference to ethnic minorities (*Traktat między Rzecząpospolitą Polską a Republiką Białoruś o dobrym sąsiedztwie i przyjaznej współpracy*, 1992). Both parties to the treaty undertook to form their relations "as friendly states, in a spirit of mutual respect, neighbourliness and partnership" (Art. 1). They finally confirmed the inviolability of their common border (Art. 2) and their will to strengthen "European mechanisms of security, stability and cooperation" (Art. 3). The treaty obligated both side to legally and institutionally guarantee the development of cooperation between regions, near the border, and at border crossings (Art. 11), as well as contacts between citizens, organisations and institutions (Art. 12). A significant number of the treaty's provisions concerned the mutual protection of ethnic minorities (Art. 13-17)[22].

In the economic sphere, both states undertook to create suitable conditions for economic, financial, fiscal and legal cooperation. They undertook to support and protect investment, to comply with copyright and patent standards, and to facilitate the movement of goods, services, labour and capital (Art. 18-20). The treaty also contained obligations concerning cooperation in the fields of science, culture, education and information (Art. 22), and legal guarantees for developing consular relations and legal circulation, for combating organised crime, and providing legal protection to cemeteries, graves and burial places (Art. 24-25). The treaty was concluded for a period of 15 years, that is, to 2007. After that period, it was to be subject to automatic extension if neither side gave notice of termination at least one year before the end of a given period (Art. 28).

The Polish-Belarusian Treaty provided a foundation for regulating bilateral relations, namely cooperation in various areas of social and economic life. Apart from the treaty itself, in the years 1992-1995 a number of agreements and understandings were signed to regulate specific areas of those mutual relations, including on cooperation in the areas of culture,

---

22 More on this subject in Chapter 4.

science and education (1992), on avoiding double taxation within the scope of income and property tax (1992), on cooperation in the field of science and technology (1992), on civil air transport (1993), on bilateral military contacts, a report on consultations between the foreign ministries of Poland and Belarus (1994), and others (Kukułka, 1998, p. 98). Some of these were signed during a visit by Prime Minister Hanna Suchocka to Belarus on 18-19 November 1992. The purpose of the visit was to develop further Polish-Belarusian political, economic and trade cooperation. The programme also included talks with Prime Minister Wiaczesław Kiebicz and a meeting with representatives of Polonia, including activists of the Association of Poles in Belarus. Poland signed more agreements and understandings with Belarus than with any other post-Soviet country. After her return home, Prime Minister Suchocka expressed concern over the rapprochement taking place between Belarus and Russia, as attested to by the signing in July of that year of about twenty economic and military understandings. In response, Prime Minister Kiebicz stated that the government of Belarus was maintaining a balanced policy towards its neighbours, and gave his assurance that similar understandings would be signed with Poland. There was also a tightening of cooperation on defence between Poland and Belarus. In December 1992, the Polish Defence Minister, Janusz Onyszkiewicz, hosted his Belarusian counterpart, Paweł Kozłouski, in Warsaw. During the visit, a joint declaration of the ministers was signed that contained provisions on the establishment of permanent working contacts, reciprocal training, and exchanges of experience and viewpoints on defense concepts. In April 1993, during a return visit to Minsk by the Polish Defence Minister, an agreement on defence cooperation was signed. The activities of the Polish authorities with regard to Belarus in the political, economic and military spheres clearly show that Poland placed great emphasis not only on the development of bilateral relations, but also on strengthening the European identity of Belarusians. Poland's Eastern policy, as discussed previously, included maintaining the sovereignty and independence of its eastern neighbours. Belarus was seen by the Polish government as a prospective buffer state separating Poland from Russia – which was traditionally viewed as a danger and a threat. According to Krzysztof Skubiszewski, Poland was interested in the success of democratic and market reforms in Belarus, and in strengthening Belarus's independence as a guarantee of Poland's own security. It was in Poland's interest to support pro-independence, democratic forces in Belarus, while at the same time avoiding any steps that could be perceived as interference in its neighbour's internal affairs (yet this was to occur eventually). Things got off to a good start, and there was a mutual rapprochement, not only in the political sphere.

Certain changes in those relations – not yet acute – began in 1993. At the beginning of the year, speaking at a New Year's meeting with the diplomatic corps, President Lech Wałęsa emphasised the importance of the East, including relations with Belarus, to Polish foreign policy. He stated that Poland's relations with its eastern neighbours (Belarus, Russia and Ukraine) had undergone a qualitative change based on the pillars of democracy, sovereignty, partnership and truth, as well as similarity to Poland in terms of experience, interests and problems. Poland was to take on the role of a bridge between the West and the East (*Przemówienie prezydenta RP Lecha Wałęsy wygłoszone na spotkaniu noworocznym z korpusem dyplomatycznym*, 1993). Although the process of reform in Belarus in 1993 ran a course similar to that in Ukraine, Poland's political cooperation with Belarus was not as close as Poland's cooperation with Ukraine. Polish-Belarusian relations became dominated by economic issues. Finding itself in a difficult economic situation, Belarus was looking for help that Poland, itself overcoming its own economic hardships, was unable to give. Belarus became increasingly interested in integration with the post-Soviet states and cooperation with Russia, whereas Poland was taking increasingly decisive steps to accede to the European Union and NATO. And so, as noted by Rafał Czachor, the interests of the two countries became increasingly polarised, and their paths diverged (Czachor, 2011, p. 77). The hope of a Polish-Belarusian rapprochement that would balance Russian influence in Belarus diminished. At the beginning of 1993, a Belarusian economic delegation came to Poland. During the visit, a cooperation agreement was signed on transport, post and telecommunications.

On 28-29 June 1993, the Polish President Lech Wałęsa made an official visit to Belarus. In Minsk, he met with the Chairman of the Supreme Council of the Republic of Belarus, Stanisław Szuszkiewicz, as well as Wiaczesław Kiebicz and Foreign Minister Piotr Krauczanka. Wałęsa spoke very positively about Belarus, but was unable to reverse an adverse tendency. Changes had taken place in both countries that had clearly led to a weakening and deterioration in Polish-Belarusian relations. In Poland, the new SLD-PSL government coalition had no good ideas for Poland's eastern policy, while in Belarus, after the introduction of the institution of President, the President chosen was Aleksander Lukashenko, a politician who had not been the favourite in the election and did not have Russian support. Yet he chose to deepen cooperation with Russia in the political, economic and military spheres.

The effects of Polish-Belarusian relations from 1991-1994 were not very satisfying; though they provided a solid foundation for further development, this was not fully capitalised on. One would even be justified in calling this a period of lost opportunities. On the other hand, as will be shown further on, this was in fact the best period in the history of relations between the two countries. This is confirmed by our assumption that those relations were determined by ideology and geopolitics, not as much by the state of Polish-Russian relations as by the sense of a threat from that direction. It seemed that the end of the Cold War would favour the development of Poland's cooperation with its eastern neighbours, including Belarus, and that new divisions would not arise. For Poland, Belarus's rapprochement with Russia – a country viewed in Poland as a "perpetual threat" – constituted a barrier. For Belarus, whose political elites had been formed within Soviet political culture, the greatest threat was NATO, which could extend to Belarus's border with Poland if Poland was successful in joining the alliance. Polish fears that Belarus could become dependent on Russia and lose its independence were met with counterarguments from the Belarusian side that Poland was dependent on the West, and its sovereignty limited. Mirosław Habowski aptly commented on this situation: "Pity over Belarus's "regressive sovereignty" sounded quite odd in Poland, since at the same time Polish society was slowly being convinced to give up its sovereignty in favour of the European Union, or being told that after EU accession Poland would continue to be sovereign – it would only be necessary to change the definition of sovereignty" (Habowski, 2009, p. 241). Habowski goes on to point out that, paradoxically, Belarus has a greater scope of freedom and independence within the Commonwealth of Independent States or the Union State of Russia and Belarus than Poland has in the EU.

Distrust and divergent geopolitical orientations outweighed the real opportunities for cooperation. Both countries, then, suffered from a lack of pragmatism and realism, which would have allowed them to develop neighbourly relations and mutually beneficial cooperation, regardless of their geopolitical orientation. On this issue, I let the Polish philosopher and historian of ideas, Bronisław Łagowski, have the floor: "The problem of Poland's eastern "policy" is not its missionary character, its exhumed Promethenaism, its ignorant, irrational drive or its servility towards America, anticipating the USA's wishes...The worst is that that "policy" is devoid of any analysis of reality in relation to the real national interest... Incompetence and unwillingness to face facts as they are, an excess of evaluations, the dominance of assertions over descriptions, a total disregard for the point of view of the other side, the immediate dismissal of the idea that the other side could be right; add to this the self-conceit that releases one from the obligation to prove one's supposed certainties, and the moral and intellectual vices that make up the Polish collective mentality and turn the eastern "policy" into a mere caricature" (Łagowski, 2016, p. 75). In such conditions, all that remained possible was a "critical dialogue".

2. *"Critical dialogue"*

Changes in the internal policy of Belarus also led to the consequences for its foreign policy mentioned above. As a result of the two countries's different geopolitical orientations, Polish-Belarusian relations began to worsen progressively. The election of Aleksander Lukashenko as President of Belarus was greeted in Poland with concern. Lukashenko was seen as a provincial populist and demagogue who did not even speak Belarusian. Nevertheless, when the new President was sworn in, a Polish delegation with Prime Minister Jan Oleksy was in attendance. This shows that the Polish government was trying to keep the dialogue going. Apart from Oleksy's visit, 1994 also saw Belarus visited by the Polish Foreign Minister, Andrzej Olechowski; Olechowski met with President Lukashenko, Prime Minister Michaił Czyhir and Foreign Minister Uładzimir Sieńko. The Polish government made an effort to have Belarus accepted into European regional organisations, which could have a beneficial effect on cooperation between Belarus and countries to the west. This coincided with Belarus's attempt to balance Russian influence by engaging in multilateral regional cooperation with the countries of Central Europe. The idea of Belarus acceding to the Visegrad Group was even contemplated, but despite the support of Poland, the other members of the group rejected the idea. Yet Belarus was successfully accepted into the Central European Initiative in 1996 thanks to the efforts of Poland, which held the chairmanship at that time.

In 1995, bilateral political contacts continued. In January, the Prime Ministers of the two countries, Waldemar Pawlak and Michail Czyhir, met in Brest, and as a result, four documents were signed: a declaration on economic cooperation, an agreement regulating Polish-Belarusian border issues, a scientific, technical and industrial cooperation programme for 1995, and an agreement on the protection of graves and historic sites. On 26 January, during the 50th anniversary of the liberation of the Auschwitz concentration camp, the Belarusian President Aleksander Lukashenko met with the Polish President Lech Wałęsa. This was followed by several meetings, and by the conclusion of an understanding and an agreement on economic and cultural cooperation. An important event of 1995 was the opening of a Consulate General of the Republic of Poland in Grodno on 15 June; the consulate was opened by the Polish Foreign Minister Władysław Bartoszewski, and coincided with the fifth anniversary of the founding of the Union of Poles in Belarus. In turn, a Consulate General of the Republic of Belarus was opened in Białystok (Głogowska, 2012, pp. 407-408). In November, at the invitation of Prime Minister Józef Oleksy, the Belarusian Prime Minister Michaił Czyhir made a two-day visit to Poland. The result was the signing of a series of inter-state agreements, including an Agreement on cooperation in the fields of culture, science and education that expanded on the provisions of the treaty of 1992. During that visit, both sides reached the conclusion that "in principle, there are no contested issues between us", while Prime Minister Czyhir stated that "for Belarus, Poland can be a bridgehead to the West, and for Poland, Belarus can be a bridgehead to the East" (Czachor, 2011, p. 136). Contacts were maintained at the parliamentary level. In April 1995, the Polish Senate sent a delegation to Belarus, headed by the speaker of the Senate, Adam Struzik. Yet, despite all these contacts, the tendencies indicated earlier-Poland's cooperation with NATO and Belarus's rapprochement with Russia – continued unabated, and intensified mutual distrust and negative perceptions.

A new Polish President, Aleksander Kwaśniewski, tried to enter into a dialogue with the President of Belarus. On 30 March 1996, in the Belarusian part of the Bialowieża Forest, the two met. The presidents exchanged views on bilateral relations, European security, and projects for integrating Belarus and Russia. Lukashenko explained that Belarus was not directly engaged in the issue, given much attention in early 1996, of building a "Kaliningrad corridor" from Grodno to Kaliningrad. He also declared his support for trans-border cooperation with the Bug and Niemen Euroregions, and for expanding the number of border crossings. The visit of the Polish President to Belarus was very controversial in Poland, because it took place at rather an unfortunate time, namely, just several days before the creation of the Union State of Belarus and Russia, which took place on

2 April, and just before an upcoming meeting between the Polish President and the President of Russia, Borys Yeltsin. Despite opposition protests, Aleksander Kwaśniewski did not call off the visits, stating that "a sovereign Belarus is necessary for Poland and Europe, but Poland cannot intervene in the choice of options of Belarusian foreign policy. Belarus can integrate with Russia, just as Poland can with the European Union or NATO". Kwaśniewski's visit, however, brought no measurable results.

In May 1996, a much-talked-about incident in Polish-Belarusian relations took place that confirmed the authoritarian tendencies of the Belarusian President. On 14 May, Marian Krzaklewski, the chairman of the Solidarity Trade Union in Minsk, was arrested, along with several activists of the union. The Belarusian authorities charged them with organising an illegal rally and making inappropriate attempts to intervene in the internal affairs of Belarus. The delegation was taken into custody and transported by convoy to the Polish-Belarusian border. Poland criticised the conduct of the Belarusian authorities as a drastic violation of the freedom of trade union activities.

The last meeting at a high level between Poland and Belarus took place on 21 September 1996 between the Polish Prime Minister Władysław Cimoszewicz and the Belarusian Prime Minister Michaił Czyhir, in connection with the opening of a Belarusian-language school in Kleszczele in Podlasie and the simultaneous opening of a Polish-language school in Grodno.

A milestone in Polish-Belarusian relations was the referendum on the Belarusian constitution conducted on 24 November 1996. As a result, President Lukashenko severely restricted the role of parliament and the constitutional court, removing opposition members from the parliament. After the referendum, a new constitution was adopted, on whose basis full power came into the hands of the President, and the presidential term of office was extended by a year and a half. The heightening of internal tensions in Belarus raised serious concern in Poland, and led to the Presidents of Poland, Ukraine and Lithuania issuing a joint declaration in November 1996 in which they called for a solution to the conflict by constitutional means and for civil rights and democratic freedoms to be respect in accordance with international standards. Belarus rejected that declaration as an intervention in its internal affairs; the event had an adverse effect on Polish-Belarusian relations and deepened Belarus's isolation internationally. Increasing autocracy, a withdrawal from pro-market transformation, combating the opposition by administrative and repressive means, violations of human rights and the suspension of democratic principles led to a gradual reduction in the level of diplomatic contacts between Poland and Belarus. Another factor that had an adverse effect on bilateral relations was that Polish Catholic priests were running a campaign of evangelisation within Belarus. Yet Poland recognised that the total isolation of Belarus could strengthen its integration with Russia, and this could in turn harm Polish interests and worsen the position of the Polish minority in Belarus, and so it began to implement a policy that became known as "critical dialogue". Poland condemned violations of human rights and democratic principles, but did not withdraw completely from dialogue with the Belarusian authorities. The intensity of contacts certainly declined at the political level, but an attempt was made to develop contacts at the lower and working levels; these were mainly economic contacts and regional, transborder cooperation (Fedorowicz, 2009, p. 98). At the same time, it became a priority of Poland's Belarusian policy to support democratisation and the construction of a civil society through dialogue and financial and organisational assistance to the opposition, non-governmental organisations, and the Polish minority in Belarus. One of the most spectacular manifestations of Poland's support for the democratisation of Belarus was the founding of Radio Racja[23] (Barwiński, 2013, p. 15; Sulowski, 2007, p. 286). In January 1999, the Polish Parliament adopted a Message of the Parliament of the Republic of Poland to the Belarusian Nation, in which in expressed its moral support for those delegated to the Supreme Council of the Republic of Belarus, 13th term of office, which had been dissolved by Lukashenko. The message also called for talks between the government and the opposition, and emphasised that "Poland is vitally interested in the restoration of democratic institutions, and in the strengthening of the national identity and state sovereignty of Belarus" (*Posłanie Sejmu Rzeczypospolitej Polskiej do Narodu Białoruskiego*, 1999). Such measures were greeted with criticism and disapproval on the part of the Belarusian authorities as an intervention in Belarus's internal affairs.

---

23 A non-public radio station broadcasting from Białystok and Biała Podlaska in the Belarusian language (also available online), intended for the Belarusian minority in Poland and the citizens of Belarus, funded by the Polish Ministry of Foreign Affairs, operating in 1999–2002 and again since 2006. The main objective of the station is to provide Belarusian citizens with access to information about events and the situation in Belarus, Poland and the world that is independent from that provided by the Belarusian authorities.

Hope for a renewal of Polish-Belarusian political dialogue appeared in 1998 when Poland took over the chairmanship of the OSCE (Organization for Security and Cooperation in Europe). In February, the Polish Foreign Minister Bronisław Geremek officially opened an OSCE observation mission in Minsk – the Consultation and Observation Group. During his visit, Geremek held talks with the Belarusian Foreign Minister Iwan Antonowicz. Belarus declared its openness to a dialogue with Poland, though this was not accompanied by any relevant changes in foreign or internal policy. In the same year, as a result of a diplomatic scandal around the residence of ambassadors in the "Drozdy" estate in Minsk caused by the Belarusian authorities, the dialogue begun in the forum of the OSCE quickly fell apart. In June, the Polish ambassador was recalled for consultations in Warsaw, and returned to Minsk only in January 1999. The conflict around Drozdy had an adverse effect on Polish-Belarusian relations. For the next several years, political contacts were confined to a very low level, and brought nothing new in bilateral relations. Both minor incidents and spectacular actions by the two states over the next several years solidified the positions of both sides that contacts between them were in a bad way. The main causes of this stagnation were that the policy of Belarus was contrary to European principles, and that the two countries differed on key issues of international security. It must be said that Poland's policy towards Belarus was less rigorous than that of most European Union member states, where the prevailing approach was to isolate Belarus totally. Poland, which was not yet a member of the EU, was not obliged to subordinate its decisions to those of the EU, and could allow itself a more flexible policy. When, after the crisis around the ambassadors' residence near Minsk, EU countries introduced a ban on the Belarusian President and 130 state officials entering their territories (rescinded in February 1999), Poland did not join the sanction, arguing that it would hinder contacts vital to neighbouring countries and the activities of the OSCE in Belarus, and would not lead to the desired changes in Belarus. The Polish position was accepted with understanding by the EU Council for External Relations (Krzysztofowicz, 2003, p. 30). Yet, as a country that was seeking to become a member of the EU, Poland took part in a series of diplomatic conflicts between the EU and Belarus that began in July 1998.

Without justifying the actions of the Lukashenko regime in curtailing human rights and political freedom, it is still necessary to consider why Belarus chose the path of becoming closer with Russia and why it consistently implemented that policy. We find the answer in the ideological

Foundations of the Belarusian State, where we read that "in a globalising world, full political sovereignty can be enjoyed only by a block of states that share a common denominator – religion, ethnic values, cultural models, religious centres, a similar understanding of history. Such a foundation for the stable existence and dynamic development of Belarus in the system of contemporary international relations in provided by an affiliation with Russia" (*Akademiia upravleniia pri Prezidente Respubliki Belarus'*, 2004, p. 34). From this it results, firstly, that Russia is culturally closer, and therefore more important, for Belarus than is the West – while the latter remains very attractive economically and technologically, culturally it is more "alien". Secondly, as Aleksander Lukashenko has stated, Belarus is disappointed by Western policy: "Russia was, is and will be a great power. Sooner or later, having overcome the economic crisis, it will once again be a powerful, thriving country. As for the economically developed countries of the West, our state is ready to cooperate with them on the basis of mutual benefit and equality. But the West, which declares that its economy is open, has in fact put up fences against the countries of the former USSR in the form of quotas and tariffs that do not permit equitable commercial and economic cooperation to develop" (*Akademiia upravleniia pri Prezidente Respubliki Belarus'*, 2004, p. 57). Polish politicians, touting their efforts to promote EU integration and NATO membership, offered explanations concerning civilization, yet failed to perceive that, for this very reason, "Minsk is closer to Moscow", when geographically it is farther from Moscow (700 km) than it is from Warsaw (500 km). At the same time, as observed by Mirosław Habowski, the Belarusian President was accused of being authoritarian, though it was admitted that he had the support of the majority of society (Habowski, 2009, p. 241). Belarus's "Russian choice" need not mean the marginalisation of the Western vector of the country's foreign policy. True economic integration with the more advanced market economy of Russia could stimulate cooperation with neighbouring countries, including those belonging to the European Union. Openness to the West need not be an alternative for Belarus, but could be a supplement to its economic cooperation with Russia: "We have not and will not be led down the path of those who obstinately try to convince us of the inevitability of the dilemma –Belarus either with the East (Russia) or with the West (Europe). Our task is to be a bridge connecting the East with the West (*Poslanie Prezidenta Respubliki Belarus' A.G. Lukashenko belorusskomu narodu i Natsional'nomu sobraniiu Respubliki Belarus' „Blagopoluchie rodnoĭ zemli – delo vsekh i kazhdogo"*, 2009). As noted by Adam

Eberhardt, Western states did not question Belarus's sovereign right to integrate with Russia politically and economically, but only pointed out that decisions in this regard should be taken in accordance with the will of Belarusian society (Eberhardt, 2003, p. 46). In principle, this should be no cause for concern. In the referendum held on 14 May 1995, 83.3% of Belarusians voted for integration with Russia.

In 2001, Poland attempted to end the crisis in Polish-Belarusian relations under conditions of international solidarity in the wake of the terrorist attacks in the United States on 11 September. In November, President Lukashenkos's chief of administration was invited to a regional conference in Warsaw on combating terrorism. Poland continued to maintain a political dialogue with Belarus, as attested to in November 2002 when Poland opted out of further sanctions against Belarus in the form of a ban on the highest representatives of Belarus travelling to 14 EU countries (apart from Portugal) and the USA. Belarus expressed its appreciation of Poland's gesture, but this did not lead to any real revival of Polish-Belarusian relations. Certain symptoms of this, however, did appear in the years 2002-2003. In 2002, a new initiative was addressed to Belarus, with the participation of Polish diplomats; the idea was to help Belarus get out of its international isolation through a "last-chance visit" by representatives of the European Parliament to Belarus in order to create a new forum for discussion. Moreover, during a visit to Poland in 2002 by the President of the Russian Federation, Vladimir Putin, a proposal was put forward to create a Polish-Russian group for Belarusian issues. Yet neither of these initiatives came to fruition. The Polish authorities renewed contacts with Belarus at higher levels in the form of informal meetings between the heads of national security offices, vice premiers and foreign ministers. In May 2002, the first joint Polish-Belarusian border guard exercises were conducted in order to fight cross-border crime. Poland convinced Belarus to open itself up to the West. In this regard, it is also worth noting a visit by Polish high-level politicians to Belarus in the autumn of 2003. The Speaker of the Senate, Longin Patusiak, took part in the unveiling of a monument to Adam Mickiewicz in Minsk, and Prime Minister Leszek Miller took part in the commemoration of the 60th anniversary of the Battle of Lenino (Czachor, 2011, p. 228). It was at this time that Poland's accession to the European Union was approaching, which raised the issue of border crossings by citizens of both states. As from 1 October 2003, in accordance with the accession treaty, Poland introduced a visa obligation for Belarusian citizens, which created new barriers in Polish-Belarusian relations. In 2004, the Polish-Belarusian dialogue resumed at a high level; in February a meeting of the Foreign Ministers of both countries was held. In the same year, Poland acceded to the European Union, while in Belarus another referendum was held, as a result of which the limit of two terms of office for one person as President was abolished, opening the door to a third term for Aleksander Lukashenko. In response, the European Union imposed sanctions on representatives of the regime in Belarus. Initially, these concerned Lukashenko and five of his collaborators, but two years later, in March 2006, after the next presidential election which, according to the EU, did not fulfil democratic standards, further sanctions were imposed on 35 more representatives of the regime. They also included a ban on entering EU territory and a freezing of Belarusian financial assets in EU countries. Moreover, for violations of employee rights, the EU excluded Belarus from the group of countries having privileged customs tariffs in trade with the EU (Zięba, 2010, p. 237).

Poland's accession to the European Union caused certain changes in Poland's foreign policy towards Belarus. The need arose to accept the *acquis communautaire* also in those areas concerning relations with third countries (trade and visa policy), and the possibility appeared of Poland using its own and EU economic potential to shape bilateral relations. Being a neighbour, and with a large Polish minority in Belarus, Poland had its own interest in its relations with Belarus, which is why it employed an "individualised" policy towards that state. The development of bilateral relations could have broader significance for both countries. As one Polish author wrote, "for Poland, good relations with Belarus can result in a greater role within the EU, while for Belarus they can mean a strengthening of its relations with Russia" (Krzysztofowicz, 2003, p. 32).

3. New challenges and problems after the expansion of the European Union

In the years 2005-2007, Polish-Belarusian relations worsened still; this was caused by a conflict around the Union of Poles in Belarus and the Polish Card accepted in Poland. The consequences of that conflict have continued to affect relations between the two countries up to the present. The source of the conflict can be found, again, in ideology and geopolitics. The active part taken by Polish politicians, non-governmental organisations and civil society in the events of the "Orange Revolution" in Ukraine in

2004 made Poland appear to Belarus as a "crusader" bearing the "banner" of democracy. Fearing that some other coloured revolution might be brought into its territory by Polish activists, Belarus used the conflict over the Union of Poles in Belarus to make certain changes that were not accepted by Poland. Belarus objected to the adoption of the Polish Card, stating that it could destabilise inter-ethnic relations in Belarus[24]. And so, when Poland was governed by the Law and Justice Party, and then by a coalition formed by Law and Justice, the League of Polish Families and the Self-Defence Party in 2005-2007, Polish-Belarusian relations remained tense.

The governments of Kazimierz Marcinkiewicz, and especially of Jarosław Kaczyński, criticised the internal policies of Aleksander Lukashenko. In 2006, the Polish Foreign Minister Stefan Meller sent a letter to the High Representative of the Union for Foreign Affairs and Security, Javier Solana, and to the heads of EU diplomacy, proposing an expansion of visa sanctions and the freezing of assets of members of the Belarusian regime. This time Poland was also demanding the introduction of repressive measures against the Belarusian political elite. In response to growing repressions against opposition activists and non-governmental media, in 2006-2007 the Polish government was often invited by representatives of the Belarusian opposition, which aroused the ire of the pro-Belarusian media. For Belarusian students expelled from university for taking part in opposition demonstrations, a Kalinowski Scholarship Fund was created to support their continuing studies in Poland[25]. Also in Poland, a satellite television channel, *Belsat TV*, was established that broadcast in Belarusian in order to provide an alternative to state television within Belarus. This noble intention of supporting the Belarusian language and propagating liberal democratic values turned out to be of little use, however, because the content of the programmes broadcast never reached the Russian-speaking population of the country.

---

24 This is discussed further in Chapter 5.
25 The author had the opportunity to conduct classes in which Belarusian students covered by this programme took part. They were well-informed "Belarus-centrically", which supposedly distinguished them from supporters of the regime. While advocating the dissemination of the Belarusian language, among themselves they conversed in Russian. When an attempt was made to speak with them in that language, they replied that they "weren't going to speak in an imperialistic language".

At the end of 2007, an opportunity arose for improving bilateral relations, thanks to the appointment of a new Polish Ambassador in Minsk in December of that year – Henryk Litwin. This came about at the initiative of the new Civic Platform and Polish People's Party coalition government. From the spring of 2008, the new ambassador began rebuilding official contacts with Belarus at various levels: customs and border services, and frequent consultation on consular and economic affairs. In February 2008, the President of Belarus spoke mildly on the topic of the Polish Card, placing the blame for the criticism on his government and the Foreign Minister.

In a parliamentary address in May 2008, the new Polish Foreign Minister, Radosław Sikorski, stated that Belarus could count on Poland's support wherever human rights, dialogue and compromise were respected, and where there was openness to Europe. In mid-2008, the Belarusian regime partially renounced its repressive policy against the political opposition and its restrictions of freedom of the press; it released political prisoners and declared its willingness to improve relations with the European Union and with Poland. Representatives of the OSCE were invited to observe the parliamentary election planned for September 2008, and the opposition was allowed to take part. In connection with this reduction in repressions in Belarus, Poland became interested in including Belarus in the Eastern Partnership that had been initiated by Poland and Sweden in the EU in 2008. The task of the Eastern Partnership was to achieve one of the key goals of Polish foreign policy – a rapprochement and integration of the states of Eastern Europe with the EU. After the parliamentary election in Belarus in September 2008, there was a certain warming of relations between those countries and Belarus; the OSCE took a critical view of the election, but found it had been more democratic than the previous one. On 5 September 2008, in the EU Council, EU foreign ministers discussed opportunities and conditions for a renewal of the political dialogue between the Union and Belarus. The EU lifted its sanctions against representatives of the Belarusian government. On 12 September, the first meeting in more than four years between the foreign ministers of Poland and Belarus was held, and was deemed a harbinger of improved bilateral relations. During the meeting, the issues of the Union of Poles in Belarus, border security, energy cooperation, security of commodities transport, and the Belarusian privatisation programme were discussed. A warming in Polish-Belarusian relations occurred after 1 November 2008, when Poland reduced the price of visas for Belarusian citizens, and talks were held on liberalising the rules for granting such visas. In 2009, the Vice Premier and Minister of Economy Waldemar Pawlak paid a visit to Belarus. The whole period from 2008-2010 can be described as a rapprochement in mutual relations, at the cost of a certain compromise in Poland's stance towards the Union of Poles in Belarus. Yet, in 2010, this "thawing" in Polish-Belarusian relations practically ended before it had really developed, because of two events.

The first was a renewed sharpening of the conflict over the Union of Poles in Belarus[26], to which the Polish government reacted in a statement by Prime Minister Donald Tusk concerning "repression against the Polish minority", in a protest sent by President Lech Kaczyński to Aleksander Lukashenko, and in a parliamentary resolution of February 2010 condemning the Belarusian authorities. Consequently, the Polish ambassador in Minsk was recalled, and there was again a tightening of sanctions against persons holding the highest offices in Belarus. The opposition party in Poland at that time, the Law and Justice Party, began a mass campaign criticising the policy of the Polish government towards Belarus, in which President Kaczyński took part.

The second event was the Smolensk air crash of 10 April 2010 in which the Polish president Lech Kaczyński was killed. After this, relations between Poland and Belarus became increasingly unfriendly. Belarus was the only eastern neighbour of Poland that did not declare mourning and that, at the funeral ceremony on 18 April, was represented "only" by the Chairman of the Council of the Republic of Belarus, Boris Batura. In this way, as Oleg Nemenski wrote, "Aleksander Lukashenko passed up a chance to meet with the leaders of European countries. At the level of symbolic gestures, to which Warsaw was at that time very sensitive, Minsk behaved very brusquely, and this cooled off relations between the two countries even more" (Nemenskiĭ, 2010).

Towards the end of 2010, because of the presidential election in Belarus, the regime began a 'diplomatic game' with Poland and the EU, suggesting that it would run democratic elections if it obtained specific political and economic benefits. In November, the Polish and German Foreign Ministers met with Lukashenko in order to convince him to hold a democratic election campaign and voting, as this would help improve relations with the EU. The election was held in December, and Aleksander

---

26 This is discussed further in Chapter 5.

Lukashenko won again, with 80% of the vote. In the opinion of the OSCE, the election fell far short of fulfilling democratic requirements (Robiński, 2010).

The Belarusian government dealt decisively with opposition protests after the presidential election, and Polish-Belarusian relations fell to an all-time low (Yeliseyeu, 2017, p. 160). Radosław Sikorski spoke with his Belarusian counterpart, and demanded the release of all those members of the opposition arrested or detained. He also gave notice that Poland would demand the imposition of "intelligent" sanctions against Belarus. Poland announced that, as from 1 January 2011, it would increase its visa fees for citizens of Belarus and simultaneously close the border to everyone who took part in repressions against the opposition. A 'black list' was prepared of those persons who would not be permitted to enter Poland. The sanctions included Aleksander Lukashenko himself, two of his sons, and his closest political circle.

In September 2011, Warsaw hosted the second Eastern Partnership, to which Aleksander was not invited due to the sanctions. Lukashenko called Poland "the leader of EU anti-Belarusian policy". Further, he accused Warsaw of wanting to restore the pre-1939 Polish borders, that is, by annexing the western part of Belarus. Relations between the two countries gradually moved towards a new confrontation (Nemenskiĭ, 2015). At the same time, at the initiative of several non-governmental organisations, Belarus House was established in Warsaw as a place to unite the Belarusian diaspora, coordinate the activities of Belarusian émigré opposition organizations, support repressed activists of the Belarusian opposition, and hold discussions among all the organisations fighting for political change in Belarus. Belarus House also serves to inform the Polish public about events in Belarus (Barwiński, 2013, p. 15).

In response to the extension of EU sanctions, in February 2012 Belarus recalled its Ambassador in Warsaw for "consultations", while the Polish Ambassador in Minsk was expelled, along with the EU Ambassador, Maira Mora. Belarusian media attacked the Polish government and its eastern policy, accusing it of financing armed units whose goal was to destabilise Belarus and lead to an overthrow of the Lukashenko regime. Poland was seen by the Belarusian authorities not as an independent entity in international relations, but as a mouthpiece for American interests. Under these conditions, it was surprising that the Polish authorities decided to provide Belarus with financial information on the Belarusian defender of human rights, Aleś Białacki – as Andrei Yeliseyeu claims, this undermined Poland's credibility in the eyes of the Belarusian opposition (Yeliseyeu, 2017, p. 161).

In the document referred to earlier, *Priorities of Polish Foreign Policy 2012-1016*, it is written that the further development of relations with Belarus will be totally dependent on the process of democratisation and europeanisation: "In terms of civilization, it is worth having partners that recognise the same values on both sides of the Polish border. That is why Belarusian society must be supported in activities benefiting freedom and political pluralism while opposing all types of repressions, whose victims include Poles in Belarus" (*Priorytety polskiej polityki zagranicznej 2012*-2016, p. 17).

A change in Polish-Belarusian relations was favoured by the events in Ukraine in the years 2013-2015, namely, the demonstrations in favour of a European-oriented foreign policy for Ukraine, the annexation of Crimea to Russia, and the war in Donbass.

4. The "Ukrainian factor" and the honeymoon

In the face of the Russian-Ukrainian conflict, Belarus came to view closer relations with the EU as a means of decreasing its political and economic dependence on Russia. In addition, Western sanctions contributed to economic stagnation in Russia, provoking a deeper downturn in the Belarusian economy as well (Yeliseyeu 2017, p.169). Other factors favouring a renewal in Polish-Belarusian relations were that neither country recognized Russia's annexation of Crimea, and that Belarus tried to act as a mediator in the civil war in Ukraine. In 2014, then, the diplomatic scandals between Poland and Belarus disappeared, and dialogue between Belarus and the EU was revived. Polish-Belarusian relations slowly began to improve.

The renewal in mutual relations began on 17 April 2014 with a meeting between President Lukashenko and the Polish Prime Minister, Donald Tusk. This was the first such discussion since the Belarusian presidential election on 19 December 2010. On 9 June 2014, in an interview with Serbian media, Lukashenko said that the policy and position of the European Union towards Belarus was gradually changing for the better: "At least, now they greet me and talk with me. Even that is big progress" (quote after Nemenskiĭ, 2010).

The Belarusian President managed to convince the leaders of those states involved in the armed conflict in Ukraine to come to Minsk for peace negotiations. In this way, the most important politicians in the EU visited Minsk, as later did the President of France and the Chancellor of Germany. For Poland, Belarus's partial emergence from diplomatic isolation was neither a success nor a defeat. Even though Donald Tusk became the President of the European Council in December 2014, Poland's influence on that process was minimal. On 28-29 August 2014, the Belarusian Foreign Minister Uladzimir Makej paid a visit to Warsaw. He and his counterpart Radosław Sikorski discussed events in Ukraine and the problems of Polish-Belarusian bilateral relations[27]. This opened the way towards, above all, economic contacts. In December, the Vice Premiers of the two countries – Janusz Piechociński and Mikhail Rusy – chaired meetings of the Belarus-Poland Commission on economic cooperation. Throughout 2014, there were numerous meetings of working groups concerning transport, tourism and agriculture, and the following year brought continued economic and technical contacts between the two countries.

The victory of the Law and Justice Party candidate Andrzej Duda in the Polish presidential election in May 2015, and that party's return to power in October of the same year, did not suggest any fundamental change in the "cool co-existence" of the two states, as described by Mieczysław Czasnouski (Czasnouski, 2015, p. 77). In the previous period when that party had been in power, alone or in coalition with the League of Polish Families and Self-Defence, policy had differed little from that of the Civic Platform[28]. Yet, in 2015 there was an unexpected, consistent attempt at a rapprochement between the two states that was greater than that made in 2014. Grigory Ioffe has called this most recent period in Polish-Belarusian

---

27 Even before the visit of the Belarusian foreign minister, two symbolic events took place that showed a real improvement in the atmosphere. The first was a meeting in April 2014 of the Polish-Belarusian Working Group for Trade and Investment together with the Economic Cooperation Committee and a business forum of Polish and Belarusian entrepreneurs. The second was a forum of Polish and Belarusian partner cities in May 2014, after a 12-year break.

28 The conflict over the Union of Poles in Belarus began during the presidency of Lech Kaczyński. At that time, Radio Racja was also started up, as well the television station Belsat, and the Polish government harshly criticised the Belarusian presidential election in 2006. In 2010, Law and Justice signed an agreement with the Belarusian opposition, against the leaders of the Belarusian National Front (BNF).

relations a "honeymoon" (Ioffe, 2016). The heads of the foreign ministries have spoken on the subject with enthusiasm (*Ministerstwo Spraw Zagranicznych RP*, 2016; *Makeĭ v Polshe: My khotim uĭti ot sil'noĭ zavisimosti ot Rossii*, 2016)[29].

The current policy of the Law and Justice Party government is, in fact, opposite to the policy implemented from 2005-2007 (Petrovskaya, 2017 p. 96). The improvement in relations is evident most of all in the number of state visits that have taken place. After a hiatus of several years, Foreign Minister Waszczykowski became the first politician at such a high level to visit Belarus (in March 2016) after the European Union lifted its sanctions against Belarus, and he was met by Lukashenko himself[30]. He thereby "recreated", as he put it, contacts in a new format (*Ministerstwo Spraw Zagranicznych RP*, 2016). In August, a Polish parliamentary delegation headed by the Deputy Speaker of the Parliament Ryszard Terlecki went to Belarus. This visit was of particular significance because is expressed a desire to cooperate with the Belarusian parliament, which was not recognised by other European countries[31]. To the end of 2016, there was an observable increase in the frequency of similar visits at the highest level of state. On 10 October, in response to an official invitation, the Belarusian Foreign Minister Uladzimir Makiej visited Poland, where he met with President Andrzej Duda and Foreign Minister Witold Waszczykowski. Makiej and Waszczykowski discussed prospects for developing bilateral economic cooperation, as well as the regional situation. They also discussed NATO and problems within the European Union, and the issue of movement near the Belarusian-Polish border.In the same month, the Polish Vice Premier and Minister of Finance and development Mateusz Morawiecki went to Minsk, and in December the speaker of the Polish Senate, Stanisław Karczewski, followed suit. In its policy towards Belarus, Poland

---

29 Witold Waszczykowski, the Polish foreign minister, has deemed the new character of Polish-Belarusian relations as one of the greatest foreign policy successes of the new government. In turn, the Belrusian foreing minister Uladzimir Makej has stated that "currently, Belarus and Poland are going through a historic moment, entering a new phase of bilateral relations in which there will be no room for mistrust, confrontation, intrigue, outdated stereotypes or any ideological prejudice whatsoever".

30 During the trip, Waszczykowski visited Vawkowysk, his mother's home town.

31 Interestingly, Poland acted against the position of the European Parliament, which differs from the positions of other EU structures in respect of Belarus, because it was approved under the influence of the Belarusian opposition.

is looking for positive opportunities and is changing the mentality of its citizens towards Belarus, which had been cast in a bad light and had been called "the last dictatorship in Europe". There is no doubt that, in the well-known triad of Juliusz Mieroszewski of Ukraine-Lithuania-Belarus, it was the last of these three that became the "jewel in the crown" of Poland's eastern policy[32].

The essence of the change in the policy of the Polish government towards Belarus is a decline in interest in democratising Belarusians or imposing on them the values of Western civilization. This approach by the Law and Justice Party government corresponds in a way to that of the EU, which, by lifting its sanctions, has shown that it accepts Belarus's internal policy[33]. In turn, Aleksander Lukashenko is demonstrating the formal implementation of EU recommendations. Political prisoners have been freed, and the presidential election in 2015 and the parliamentary election in 2016 were run without excesses and with certain concessions made. The methods employed in fighting the opposition have definitely become more restrained. Belarus's readiness to improve its respect for human rights has been demonstrated in a relevant inter-ministerial action plan for the years 2016-2019, approved by the government. Furthermore, the Belarusian President has altered his rhetoric on democratisation, indicating a willingness to introduce certain changes similar to those previously implemented in Poland. Lukashenko's position on democracy echoes the criticism heard from the EU and the USA of the changes the Law and Justice Party has introduced in Poland in the areas of the judiciary and the media.

The Law and Justice Party's policy towards Belarus does not completely preclude support for civil society, meaning essentially the Belarusian opposition, with which Polish politicians continue to meet. Minister Waszczykowski emphasised in Minsk that his party grew out of Solidarity, and problems of human rights and democracy "are problems about which we never forget". At the same time, he added that "peace did not prevail at once, for some processes require time" (*Èto nenormal'no, kogda bliskie sosedi ne obshchaiutsia i ne vstrechaiutsia"*, 2016). From this statement

---

32 Minister Waszczykowski paid a visit to Belarus in March 2016, but went to Kiev only in September, and to Vilnius not at all at the time of writing.

33 The EU's political expectations of Belarus are at present minimal, confined to the introduction of amendments in electoral law, a simplification of the activities of political parties and non-governmental organisations, and the introduction of a moratorium on capital punishment.

we can conclude that democratic issues have been put on the back burner until some unspecified time in the future, as attested to by the fact that assistance is now granted to Belarusian non-governmental organisations that act mainly in the social, and not the political, sphere (*Anna Dyner: „Iz Varshavy Minsku podadut ruku"*, 2016)[34]. The future of Belsat TV is also unclear, because in December 2016 the Polish Ministry of Foreign Affairs reduced the station's subsidy by 2/3 (*Dotacje dla TV Biełsat obcięte o 2/3? Romaszewska: to oznacza likwidację stacji*, 2016). Instead, there was a plan to prepare retransmission in Belarusian of TV Polonia, which broadcasts in Polish for Poles around the world. Also, support would go to the Belarusian Polish minority rather than to opposition groups. Finally, however, under Prime Minister Beata Szydło the subsidy was maintained, yet Belsat's future remains uncertain.

The "recreation" of Polish-Belarusian relations in the years 2014-2016 was also reflected in Polish geopolitical concepts – essentially, that cooperation between Poland and Belarus should be based on their shared history, since Belarus is practically the only neighbour with which Poland has not had conflicts. From this perspective, one priority of Polish foreign policy should be to establish friendly contacts, or even an alliance, with Belarus. One of the best-known advocates of such an alliance, Andrzej Zapałowski, a lecturer at the University of Rzeszow, emphasises that the West, and especially the USA, do not take account of the interests of the countries of Central and Eastern Europe; their overriding goal is to "liberate" the region from Russian influence. According to Zapałowski, Belarus has recently been engaged in a balancing act between Moscow and Washington. Talks on regulating the conflict in Donbass in February 2015 confirm the genuine sovereignty of the Belarusian state and an elevation of its status in international relations. Zapałowski draws attention to violations of human rights in Belarus, but stresses that, from the Polish perspective, what is most important is the existence of its neighbour to the east as a sovereign state: "If we're not bothered by a dictatorship in Saudi Arabia,

---

34 „There are many NGOs operating that deal with apolitical issues, and have results. Such organisations should be helped, so that Belarusians can work in such organisations and see that there is support, everything is run properly, and there are results from those activities. It is also necessary to support youth exchanges – for example, to create opportunities for large numbers of Belarusian students to attend EU universities for a half-year or year, so they can see how things function there." – Dyner, 2016.

or the dictatorship now forming in Turkey, then why should we treat Belarus – which is more important for us – any differently?" (*Dr Zapałowski: nie warto odwracać się od Białorusi*, 2017).

In Zapałowski's view, Poland's intervention in Belarusian internal affairs, connected with the split in the Union of Poles in Belarus into one part recognised by the Polish government and another by the Belarusian government, is irresponsible, and could have serious, adverse consequences in the future: "We are part of the West and are connected with it by alliances we must adhere to, but putting Poland into conflict does not eradicate the dangers, but gives third states a license to play with us in this respect... Unfortunately, in recent years we have allowed various irresponsible politicians to try to exploit our compatriots to support the Belarusian opposition. This was seriously irresponsible, and will come back to haunt us" (*Dr Zapałowski: nie warto odwracać się od Białorusi*, 2017).

Another supporter of strengthening cooperation with Belarus, and even of Polish neutrality towards the West and Russia, was also a candidate for president in the 2015 election, Grzegorz Braun. He does not enjoy mass support as a politician, but his views are worth examining. Braun also points to the absence of historical conflicts between the two states: "Belarus, a beautiful country laid waste in the past century by German national socialists and Soviet international socialists, should be treated with particular affection by Poles – but not with the protectionist disregard propagated in the last quarter-century. That propaganda – spread, unfortunately, with considerable involvement on the part of Polish agents and useful idiots – is completely divorced from the real and important priorities of our national interest" (*Białoruski klucz do geopolityki polskiej*, 2016). According to Braun, Belarus has the potential to change the consequences of the Second World War as dictated by the victors. Belarus is able to act on its own in international relations, and its partner of choice should be Poland – but a Poland that implements a foreign policy that is independent, not alien. Clientelism has always been bad for Poland, whether in relation to the USA or Russia. Poland needs a new eastern policy, but, as Braun underlines, "in Polish-Belarusian relations we have wasted the last quarter-century". In his opinion, Poland is more to blame for this than is the Belarusian regime, "which repeatedly sent out signals indicating a willingness for a rapprochement. One government after another... with little difference between them, unfortunately, whether left or right, implemented an insane policy of squandering chances with Minsk, a policy that was clearly contrary to our interest" (*Białoruski klucz do geopolityki polskiej*,

2016). A joint declaration by the Presidents of Poland and Belarus "on the absence of any mutual pretensions, on their joint determination to effectively combat any external claims whatsoever, combined with a decisive call to respect the inviolability of the borders and the sovereignty of the government of Eastern Europe" would be a guarantee to maintain the sovereignty of Poland and other Eastern European states.

The new policy of the Polish government towards Belarus has also drawn criticism from the opposition in Poland, on the one hand for not completely withdrawing support for democratisation, and on the other for making too many concessions in this regard. The first view is represented by the National Movement led by Robert Winnicki, an MP from the Kukiz 15 parliamentary club: "I believe that Poland's policy towards Belarus is just awful. Poland and Belarus are the most natural partners in this region of Europe, and they have the fewest potential problems between them. I don't understand at all why Poland finds itself in the front ranks of those criticising Belarus, while other countries manage to find agreement and common interests with it... Absolutely, we should stop supporting the opposition" (*Robert Winnitskiĭ: "Politika Pol'shi v otnoshenii Belarusi prosto uzhasna"*, 2016). The second point of view, which cannot be reconciled with the change in Poland's foreign policy towards Belarus, is represented by the Belarusian opposition and the Civic Platform in Poland. Belarusian oppositionists are concerned by the lifting of sanctions against Belarus, but even more so by the Belarusian government's efforts to monopolise contacts with the European Union, thereby becoming a more important partner for the West than the fragmented, quarrelsome opposition. On this question, the opposition itself is divided. Part of it, led by Nikolai Statkiewicz, believes that talks with the government make no sense, because they mean giving up on democratic principles. On the other hand, Aleksander Milinkiewicz, a presidential candidate in 2006 and leader of the "On Freedom" movement, takes a positive view of "dialogue" with the authorities – "the closer to Warsaw, Berlin and Brussels, the farther away from Moscow". In his opinion, dialogue with the West will favour a change away from the soviet mentality of Belarusians and towards a pro-Western view (*Glava MID Pol'shi planiruet 22 marta posetit' Belarus'*, 2016).

It is clear that in 2015-2016, there were no great differences in principle between the Civic Platform and the Law and Justice Party in terms of eastern policy, including within the scope of Polish-Belarusian relations. Yet two tactical lines were observable – romanticism and pragmatism (Bodio,

2001; Nemenskiĭ, 2012, p. 118). If Law and Justice was a bit closer to geopolitical romanticism in which ideological and historical determinants, messianism and a readiness for a radical confrontation with Russia prevailed, the Civil Platform leaned more in the direction of geopolitical pragmatism, taking account of the hard facts of the international environment. As a result of the "recreation" of Polish-Belarusian relations, the roles of the two parties reversed in some cases. Law and Justice became more pragmatic towards Belarus, and the Civic Platform moved to the side of romanticism.

The former Polish Ambassador to Russia, Katarzyna Pełczyńska-Nałęcz, and MP Maciej Święcicki have spoken out against the departure from the long-standing policy of protecting human rights and cooperating with Belarusian civil society organisations. In the newspaper *Gazeta Wyborcza*, Pełczyńska-Nałęcz argues that "pragmatic cooperation with Minsk may be beneficial for Poland, but you have to understand the complexities of the game". She emphasises Belarus's dependence on Russia, pointing out that decisions of Minsk are actually taken in Moscow. It is to Russia's advantage that Belarus become closer to the West, because this to some extent relieves it of the burden of propping up the regime there (Pełczyńska-Nałęcz, 2016).

Święcicki, a former Minister of Economic Cooperation and Foreign Minister, and the former Mayor of Warsaw, has stated that "international relations require contacts with the authorities of Belarus, but those talks don't have to be held at the cost of human rights. Here, the European Union should stand by the values that unite us" (*Okolo 70 chelovek proshli shestviem v Varshave po sluchaiu Dnia Voli*, 2016).

The "recreation" of political relations does not mean that "difficult issues" have been eliminated, though there are decidedly fewer of them and they are "milder" in character than in Poland's relations with its other neighbours. Nevertheless, the need to at least partially resolve them remains.

References

Akademiia upravleniia pri Prezidente Respubliki Belarus', 2004. *Osnovy ideologii belarusskogo gosudarstva.* Minsk: Redaktsionno-izdatel'skiĭ tsentr Akademii upravleniia pri Prezidente Respubliki Belarus'.

Anna Dyner: „Iz Varshavy Minsku podadut ruku", 2016. [online] Available at: <https://www.bsblog.info/anna-dyner-iz-varshavy-minsku-podadut-ruku/> [Accessed 17 September 2017].

Barwiński M., 2013. Polish interstate relations with Ukraine, Belarus and Lithuania after 1990 in the context of the situation of national minorities. *European Spatial Research and Policy*, 1(20), pp. 5-26.

Białoruski klucz do geopolityki polskiej, 2016. [online] Available at: <http://www.grze gorzbraun.pl/2016/05/01/bialoruski-klucz-do-geopolityki-polskiej/> [Accessed 28 June 2017].

Bodio, T., 2001. *Między romantyzmem i pragmatyzmem. Psychopolityczne aspekty transformacji w Polsce*. Warszawa: Dom Wydawniczy ELIPSA.

Chasnouski, M., 2015. Belarus' i regional'naia integraciia v Tsentralnoĭ i Vostochnoĭ Evrope: vyzovy XXI v. In: J. Tymanowski, A. Daniluk and J. Bryll., eds. 2015. *Polska i Białoruś we współczesnej Europie*. Warszawa: Wydział Dziennikarstwa i Nauk Politycznych, pp. 71-89.

Czachor, R., 2011. *Polityka zagraniczna Republiki Białoruś w latach 1991-2011. Studium politologiczne*. Polkowice: Wydawnictwo Dolnośląskiej Wyższej Szkoły Przedsiębiorczości i Techniki w Polkowicach.

Deklaracja o dobrym sąsiedztwie, wzajemnym zrozumieniu i współpracy między Rzeczypospolitą Polską i Republiką Białoruś, 10 października 1991, *Zbiór dokumentów*, 2(48).

Dotacje dla TV Biełsat obcięte o 2/3? Romaszewska: to oznacza likwidację stacji, 2016. [online] Available at: <http://kresy.pl/wydarzenia/dotacje-dla-tv-bielsat-obcie te-o-2-3-romaszewska-to-oznacza-likwidacje-stacji/> [Accessed 17 September 2017].

Dr Zapałowski: nie warto odwracać się od Białorusi, 2017. [online] Available at: <http://kresy.pl/wydarzenia/dr-zapalowski-nie-warto-odwracac-sie-od-bialorusi/> [Accessed 26 June 2017].

Eberhardt, A., 2003. Integracja białorusko-rosyjska a stosunki Białorusi z Unią Europejską. In: A. Eberhardt, U. Ułachowicz, eds. 2003. *Belarus' i Pol'shcha. Polska i Białoruś*. Warszawa: Polski Instytut Spraw Międzynarodowych, pp. 41-47.

„*Èto nenormal'no, kogda bliskie sosedi ne obshchaiutsia i ne vstrechaiutsia*", 2016. [online] Availableat: <https://gazetaby.com/cont/art.php?sn_nid=111151> [Accessed 17 September 2017].

Fedorowicz K., 2009. Białoruś w polskiej polityce wschodniej w latach 1990-1996. In: S. Jaczyński and R. Pęksa, eds. 2009. *Stosunki polsko-białoruskie. Tom I. Historia i polityka*. Siedlce: Wydawnictwo Akademii Podlaskiej, pp. 85-100.

Glava MID Pol'shi planiruet 22 marta posetit' Belarus', 2016. [online] Available at: <http://www.belaruspartisan.org/politic/336738/> [Accessed 17 September 2017].

Głogowska, H., 2012. *Stosunki polsko-białoruskie w XX wieku. Od Imperium Rosyjskiego do Unii Europejskiej*. Białystok: Wydawnictwo Uniwersytetu w Białymstoku.

Habowski, M., 2009. Stosunki Białorusi z Polską. In: I. Topolski, ed. 2009. *Białoruś w stosunkach międzynarodowych*. Lublin: Wydawnictwo Uniwersytetu Marii Curie-Skłodowskiej, pp. 233-253.

Ioffe, G., 2016. Belarus Charts Course Between Russia and Poland. *Eurasia Daily Monitor*, 13(166). Available at: <https://jamestown.org/program/belarus-charts-course-russia-poland/> [Accessed 16 September 2017].

Krzysztofowicz, M., 2003. Wpływ rozszerzenia Unii Europejskiej na stosunki polsko-białoruskie. In: A. Eberhardt and U. Ułachowicz, eds. 2003. *Belarus' i Pol'shcha. Polska i Białoruś.* Warszawa: Polski Instytut Spraw Międzynarodowych, pp. 27-32.

Kukułka, J., 1998. *Traktaty sąsiedzkie Polski odrodzonej.* Wrocław – Warszawa – Kraków: Zakład Narodowy Imienia Ossolińskich – Wydawnictwo.

Łagowski, B., 2016. Parcie na Wschód. In: B. Łagowski, 2016. *Polska chora na Rosję.* Warszawa: Fundacja Oratio Recta, pp. 73-76.

Makeĭ v Polshe: My khotim uĭti ot sil'noĭ zavisimosti ot Rossii, 17.10.2016. [online] Available at: <https://news.tut.by/politics/515492.html> [Accessed 16 September 2017].://news.tut.by/politics/515492.html

Malinovskiĭ, V., 2003. *Istoriia belorusskoĭ gosudarstvennosti.* Minsk: Belarus'.

Ministerstwo Spraw Zagranicznych RP, 2016. *#Dobry Rok w MSZ – minister Witold Waszczykowski podsumował rok w polskiej polityce zagranicznej,* 17.11.2016. [online] Available at: <http://www.msz.gov.pl/pl/aktualnosci/wiadomosci/0_dobryrok_w_msz___minister_witold_waszczykowski_podsumowal_rok_w_polskiej_polityce_zagranicznej [Accessed 16 September 2017].

Nemenskiĭ, O., 2012. Politika Pol'shi v otnoshenii Belarusi v kontse nulevykh – nachale desiatykh godov: glubokiĭ krizis i ego prichiny. In: Informatsionno-analiticheskiĭ tsentr pri Administratsii Prezidenta Respubliki Belarus', 2012. *Politika Evropeĭskogo soiuza v otnoshenii Sojuznogo gosudarstva Belarusi i Rossii.* Minsk: Biznesofset, pp. 117-127.

Nemenskiĭ, O., 2015. Politika Pol'shi v otnoshenii Belorusii v sisteme belorussko-evropeĭskikh otnosheniĭ. [online] Available at: <http://geo-politica.info/politika-pol shi-v-otnoshenii-belorussii-v-sisteme-belorussko-evropeyskikh-otnosheniy.html> [Accessed 16 September 2017].

Okolo 70 chelovek proshli shestviem v Varshave po sluchaiu Dnia Voli, 2016. [online] Available at: <http://www.belaruspartisan.org/m/politic/337245/> [Accessed 17 September 2017].

Pełczyńska-Nałęcz, K., 2016. Ostrożnie z graczem Łukaszenką. *Gazeta Wyborcza.* [online] Available at:<http://wyborcza.pl/1,75968,20896047,ostroznie-z-graczem-lukas zenka.html?disableRedirects=true> [Accessed 17 September 2017].

Petrovskaya, O., 2017. Povorot v pol'sko-belorusskikh otnosheniiakh: faktory sblizheniia, mekhanizmy vzaimodeĭstviia. *Problemy natsional'noĭ strategii,* 1(40), pp. 95-127.

Poslanie Prezidenta Respubliki Belarus' A.G. Lukashenko belorusskomu narodu i Natsional'nomu sobraniiu Respubliki Belarus' „Blagopoluchie rodnoĭ zemli – delo vsekh i kazhdogo", 23 aprelia 2009 g. [online] Available at: <http://pravo.by/docum ent/?guid=3871&p0=P009p0001> [Accessed 7 September 2017].

Poslanie Sejmu Rzeczypospolitej Polskiej do Narodu Białoruskiego, 1999. Available at: <http://orka.sejm.gov.pl/proc3.nsf/uchwaly/780_u.htm> [Accessed 7 September 2017].

Przemówienie prezydenta RP Lecha Wałęsy wygłoszone na spotkaniu noworocznym z korpusem dyplomatycznym, Warszawa, 14 stycznia 1993 r. *Rocznik Polskiej Polityki Zagranicznej 1993.*

Robert Winnitskiĭ: „Politika Pol'shi v otnoshenii Belarusi prosto uzhasna", 2016. Available at:<https://www.bsblog.info/robert-vinnickij-politika-polshi-v-otnoshenii -belarusi-prosto-uzhasna/> [Accessed 17 September 2017].

Robiński, A., 2010. OBWE: wybory na Białorusi nie były wolne. Rzeczpospolita. Available at: <http://www.rp.pl/artykul/581806-OBWE--wybory-na-Bialorusi-nie-b yly-wolne.html#ap-1>[Accessed 16 September 2017].

Sejmowe exposé ministra spraw zagranicznych RP Krzysztofa Skubiszewskiego, 26 kwietnia 1990 r., Available at: <http://www.msz.gov.pl/resource/432b9164-91e5-4e f7-8c7a-3e0656cc48d9:JCR> [Accessed 5 September 2017].

Snapkouski, U., 2003. Stosunki polsko-białoruskie (1990-2003). In: A. Eberhardt and U. Ułachowicz, eds. 2003. Belarus' i Pol'shcha. Polska i Białoruś. Warszawa: Polski Instytut Spraw Międzynarodowych, pp. 17-25.

Traktat między Rzecząpospolitą Polską a Republiką Białoruś o dobrym sąsiedztwie i przyjaznej współpracy, podpisany w Warszawie dnia 23 czerwca 1992 r., 1993. Dziennik Ustaw Rzeczypospolitej Polskiej, 118, item 527. Available at: <http://dziennik ustaw.gov.pl/du/1993/s/118/527> [Accessed 5 September 2017].

Uchwała Sejmu Rzeczypospolitej Polskiej z dnia 31 sierpnia 1991 r. w sprawie ogłoszenia niepodległości Białorusi. Available at: <isap.sejm.gov.pl/DetailsServlet? id=WMP19910290206> [Accessed 12 January 2017].

Uchwała Sejmu Rzeczypospolitej Polskiej z dnia 22 stycznia 1999 r. Posłanie Sejmu Rzeczypospolitej Polskiej do Narodu Białoruskiego, 1999. Monitor Polski, 4, item 15, 16 i 17. Available at: <http://dziennikustaw.gov.pl/mp/1999/s/4/16/1> [Accessed 7 September 2017].

Uchwała Senatu Rzeczypospolitej Polskiej z dnia 3 sierpnia 1990 r. Do narodu Białoruskiego z okazji proklamowania suwerenności państwowej Białorusi. Available at: <https://www.senat.gov.pl/prace/senat/uchwaly/> [Accessed 12 January 2017].

Yeliseyeu, A., 2017. The Poland–Belarus relationship: Geopolitics gave new impetus, but no breakthrough. In: A. Kudors, ed. 2017. Belarusian Foreign Policy: 360°. Rīga: University of Latvia Press, The Centre for East European Policy Studies. Available at: <http://appc.lv/wp-content/uploads/2017/05/book_Belarusian_360-w ww-2.pdf> [Accessed 7 September 2017].

Zięba, R., 2010. Główne kierunki polityki zagranicznej Polski po zimnej wojnie. Warszawa: Wydawnictwa Akademickie i Profesjonalne.

Chapter 4 "Difficult issues"

The fact that there are no very serious problems in Polish-Belarusian relations as there are in Poland's relations with its other neighbours does not mean that there are no problems at all in maintaining neighbourly contacts. These include issues arising out of 20th-century history, the status of ethnic minorities – especially the Polish minority in Belarus – and cross-border and visa traffic.

1. The historical dialogue

In Polish-Belarusian relations, history does not play as important a role as it does in Polish-Russian or Polish-Ukrainian relations; the difference is a positive one, though this does not mean that those relations are idyllic. In June 2017, a series of seminars began in Minsk on "difficult issues", and one hopes that this will lead to some progress in the historical dialogue (*Polscy i białoruscy historycy rozpoczęli dialog o „sprawach trudnych"*, 2017). There is no agreement between the sides as to how to interpret the events and processes relating to the beginnings, course and consequences of the Second World War. This is of considerable importance, since the current government of the Republic of Belarus continues a state-building process that has its roots in the Belarusian Soviet Socialist Republic.

The first dispute concerns that entry of the Red Army into the territory of the Republic of Poland on 17 September 1939 as a result of the Ribbentrop-Molotov Pact. From the Polish perspective, this was aggression by the USSR against the Second Republic that accelerated the fall of Poland and was a kind of "stab in the back". It resulted in the fourth partition of Poland, with the existing state being divided up between the Third Reich and the Soviet Union. Yet, that event is interpreted by Belarusia in a completely different way: on 17 September 1939 the Red Army began its march of liberation to the west. The USSR did not declare war on Poland, whose government recognised that no state of war with the USSR exists (*Natsional'naia akademiia nauk Belarusi. Institut istorii*, 2014, p. 15). According to Belarusian historians, on 17 September 1939, Western Belarus was united with the BSSR: "The predominantly Belarusian structure of the people of Western Belarus, the tradition of the historic struggle against Polish rule for national autonomy, and the spiritual bonds with blood relations in the east large determined the process of unification in the autumn of 1939. Most Belarusians saw the events of the time as an act of historical justice; they greeted the Red Army with bread and salt, as their saviour from oppression" (*Natsional'naia akademiia nauk Belarusi. Institut istorii*, 2014, p. 16).

A second historical problem in Polish-Belarusian relations is the actions of the Red Army in the Eastern Borderlands – in Belarusian terminology, Western Belarus. The Belarusian side accuses the Polish Home Army of being passive against the German army while fighting against the Soviet army. Even before the Germans entered the USSR, i.e. before 1941, the Home Army is said to have committed "a series of terrorist acts" in the western part of the BSSR. During the initial stage of the Great Patriotic War, Home Army troops conducted armed operations against small groups of retreating Soviet soldiers, Communist party structures being evacuated and the first Soviet partisan groups: "At the same time," we read in a study by Belarusian historians, "Polish military underground formations did not carry out armed actions against German forces" (*Natsional'naia akademiia nauk Belarusi. Institut istorii*, 2014, p. 18). At that time, for the Home Army command, the most important task was to withhold the Soviet offensive as much as possible and to provoke armed conflict between the USSR and the USA and Great Britain: "This policy gave rise to mercilessness between the Home Army and Soviet partisans in Belarus" (*Natsional'naia akademiia nauk Belarusi. Institut istorii*, 2014, p. 18). According to Belarusian historians, the Home Army also conducted a campaign of pacification against the Belarusian civilian population, which, they say, "did not want a rebirth of the Polish state in its 1939 borders and supported the Soviet partisans", which provoked an aggressive reaction. In the concept of history promoted in Belarus, there is no room for the cult of the "cursed soldiers" propagated by Poland's current government. In the Belarusian version of history, the Soviet armed forces are seen as heroes[35].

In evaluating and interpreting the post-war past, the two sides have a common position on one issue – the actions of the National Military Union Special Forces (NZW PAS) under the command of Romuald Rajs,

---

35 In 2016, in Belarus the film "Traces in the Water" was shot. It tells the story of the NKVD's fight against the post-war underground, portraying today's Polish heroes as criminals.

nom de guerre "Bury", which in 1946 pacified villages inhabited mainly by Orthodox Belarusians. Information on a march in memory of the armed underground, organised in Hajnowka in 2016, was shown on Belarusian television because participants were carrying posters bearing images of Rajs. The Institute of National Remembrance, however, did not share the enthusiasm of the organisers of the march, because in the activities of Rajs they detected the hallmarks of genocide, and issued the following statement: "Without questioning the idea of the fight for an independent Poland conducted by organisations opposed to the imposed government, among which was the National Military Union, it must be stated categorically that the murder of wagon-drivers and the pacification of villages in January and February 1946 cannot be identified with the fight for the existence of an independent state, for they bear the hallmarks of genocide. On no account can this be justified by the fight for an independent State of Poland. On the contrary, "Bury's" actions against the inhabitants of villages in Podlasie helped the communist authorities, primarily by lowering the prestige of the underground organisations, and by providing propaganda arguments about the lawlessness of partisan groups. Without doubt, they also helped the government agreement to move ethnic Belarusians out of Poland. It is true that the resettlement campaign was implemented under the national slogan "Poland for the Poles", but at that time it more furthered the purposes of the Polish and Soviet Communist state apparatus. The pacifications led by "Bury" in no way helped further proper Polish-Belarusian relations or understanding of the fight of the Polish underground for an independent Poland. On the contrary, they often created intransigent enemies, or supporters of separating Belarus from Poland. There is no circumstance that would permit anyone from holding that what happened was right" (*Informacja o ustaleniach końcowych śledztwa S 28/02/Zi w sprawie pozbawienia życia 79 osób – mieszkańców powiatu Bielsk Podlaski w tym 30 osób tzw. furmanów w lesie koło Puchał Starych, dokonanych w okresie od dnia 29 stycznia 1946 r. do dnia 2 lutego 1946*, 2016).

A third historical problem that divides the two countries is their relationship to the end of the Second World War. In Belarusian historiography, this is seen as a "victory over fascism" and the "liberation" from German occupation. This results from the fact that contemporary Belarus, in official interpretations, refers to the Soviet process of state-building as the most significant in the history of Belarusian statehood – and indeed, it is the process that exists most authentically among Belarusians themselves.

In accordance with the post-Soviet mentality of Belarusians – which we do not assess here, but only report – the Belarusian Soviet Socialist Republic was the first real (not counting the short-lived BPR), though not sovereign, political organism known as Belarus. In the 20th century, the BSSR shared the fate of the USSR. Passing through the territory of the Belarusian Republic, the fronts and the terror employed by the German occupiers against the Belarusian people brought enormous losses, both material and human. That is why the Independence Day of the Republic of Belarus (Republic Day) is held on 3 July. It was on that day in 1944 that the capital of Belarus – Minsk – was liberated. That date was not, though, imposed by the authorities, but was accepted by the people in a referendum held in 1996[36]. Another public holiday is 7 November – October Revolution Day (*Ukaz Prezidenta Respubliki Belarus' ot 26 marta 1998 goda Nr 157 o gosudarstvennykh prazdnikakh prazdnichnykh dniakh i pamiatnykh datakh v Resublike Belarus'*, 1998).

For Poland, the Belarusian view of the end of the Second World War is unacceptable. The date of the signing of the capitulation of the Third Reich, 8 May 1945, is celebrated as the day of the end of the War, but not as a day of victory. Poland could not be a victor in the struggle because the German occupation was replaced with Poland becoming a USSR satellite state and with a Soviet military presence. The most important decisions in the internal and foreign policy of Poland, especially up to 1956, were not sovereign decisions, but resulted from directives established by the CPSU, and later, the Polish United Workers' Party (PZPR). Those who refused to subjugate themselves to the new geopolitical situation existing after the defeat of the Third Reich, that is, to dependence upon the USSR, took up an armed struggle against the new government, and for this they were persecuted and repressed.

The above issues are to be dealt with by a Polish-Belarusian joint commission; we will have to wait for the results of their work. There is reason to hope that, in a climate of "recreation" and Polish-Belarusian rapprochement, those issues will be clarified bilaterally, and that this will lead to the further development of mutual contacts. What is important is that history should remain the domain not of politicians, but of professional historians. One "difficult" but not unsolvable problem is the situation of the Polish

---

36 It is interesting that, apart from religious holidays in both the Orthdox and Catholic traditions, public holidays also include others that are a part of the Soviet cultural legacy, such as 8 March and 9 May.

minority in Belarus, and in particular its organisational structure – the Union of Poles in Belarus.

2. National minorities – Poles in Belarus and Belarusians in Poland

Poland and Poles, together with Belarusians, have created joint state bodies since a long time ago. In the Polish-Lithuanian Commonwealth, Rusians, as both Belarusians and Ukrainians were described, constituted an ethnic root of the Grand Duchy of Lithuania. The eastern parts of the Commonwealth were an ethnocultural borderland, and this affected the Commonwealth's ethnic structure. As a result of this intersection of cultures, of migrations, and later, of changes in the borders, especially after the Second World War, today's Polish-Belarusian borderland is home to compact clusters of people some of whose historical motherland is on the other side of the border. This is true of both Poles in Belarus and Belarusians in Poland. These are populations that can be considered, over a span of several centuries, as indigenous – though this term is rather vague (Gumilow, 1997, p. 21)[37]. There is no doubt that both groups consider themselves to be a local population, not foreigners, and their ties with their territory is one component of their ethnicity (Smith, 2009, pp. 38-40). The "little motherland" constitutes part of the two-dimensional "greater motherland". There is the state of which these people are citizens, and there is also the second "mother" on the other side of the border. This has consequences, not only in terms of national identity, but also in the area of political, social, economic and cultural rights in the "civic motherland" and in a striving to maintain ties with the historical motherland. Poles in Belarus and Belarusians in Poland could form a bridge between the two nations and states. Unfortunately, however, this is not happening, and the presence of the two minorities seems to cause divisions between the countries.

---

37 The Russian historian and geographer Lew Gumilow wrote: "There is no country in which – beginning from the Paleolithic – there haven't been numerous exchanges of peoples". This shows that, in many areas, it is practically impossible to define which nationalities are indigenous, and which 'alien'. This hypothesis of Gumilow on the dynamically changing ethnic structure of that part of Eurasia known as the Great Steppe can, with considerable simplification, be applied as well to the Polish-Belarusian borderland.

The problems of ethnic minorities features prominently in the Polish-Belarusian Treaty of 1992, which deals with mutual relations between the states as well as their internal policies. Within this scope, the 1992 treaty concluded between the Republic of Poland and the Republic of Belarus was in accordance with international standards pertaining to the protection of the rights of ethnic minorities, and met the expectations of the minorities concerned. International documents and domestic regulations obligate ethnic minorities to be loyal towards the state in which they live and of which they are citizens. The introduction of protections for minorities cannot question territorial integrity or national unity – something feared by states in whose territories sizeable minorities live (Łodziński, 2004).

A precise determination of the number of Poles living in Belarus is not possible due to discrepancies between official figures derived from population censuses and estimates made by Polish organisations, including the Polish Community Association (Table 1). These discrepancies also result from belarusisation and, in the case of the Polish population, from the connection made between national identity and affilation with the Roman Catholic Church. Belarusisation, combined with sovietisation on the basis of the russification of the language, has meant that the Polish language may no longer be a strict criterion of Polishness. In the Belarusian census of 2009, only 16,000 persons declaring themselves as of Polish nationality indicated Polish as their mother tongue (*Naselenie po natsional'nosti i rodnomu iazyku. Respublika Belarus'*, 2009). Data from 1999 show that 57.6% of Poles spoke Belarusian at Home, and 37.7% Russian (*Raspredelenie naselenia Respubliki Belarus' po natsionalnostiam i iazykam v 1999 godu*, 1999).

Roman Catholic affiliation is often used as an indicator of Polish ethnicity. This was the case in the past (Gatagova, Kosheleva and Rogovaia, eds. 2005, p. 335), and while Catholicism remains an important component of national identity, in recent years the importance of the Catholic church in this respect has weakened somewhat (Kabzińska, 2012, p. 323). Unfortunately, Belarus does not compile any official statistics on religious denomination. The Catholic Church in Belarus provides a figure of 1.4 million faithful, i.e. 14.8% of the population, which exceeds by many times the official figures on the number of Poles in Belarus (*Eparkhi. Rimo-Katolicheskaya Cerkov' v Belarusi*, 2017).

Table1. Poles in Belarus

	Number of Poles	
	Official data	Estimated data*
Belarus	294,549**	900,000
Total	485,774	1,895,000

* Polish Community 2007

** Census 2009

Source: Natsional'nyĭ sostav naseleniia, grazhdanstvo, 2009; Number of Polish diaspora, 2017.

Polish Belarusians are concentrated in the Grodno Region, where they comprise 1/5 of the population and where almost 80% of all Poles in Belarus live. The headquarters of the Union of Poles in Belarus is in Grodno, where it has access to Grodno television and radio, and broadcasts in Polish every week; also in Grodno, the periodical *Głos znad Niemna* [*Voice from the Neman*] is published, which was started up in cooperation with *Kurier Wileński* [*Vilnius Courier*] and *Kurier Podlaski* [*Podlasie Courier*] from Białystok. Since 1992, the quarterly *Magazyn Polski* [*Polish Magazine*] has also been published, and other Polish-language publications exist, such as *Echa Polesia* [*Voice of Polesia*] and *Słowo Ojczyste* [*Patriotic Word*].

Table 2. Poles in the ethnic structure of Belarus, based on the 2009 census

Area	Total population	Poles	% of population	% of Poles
Belarus	9,503,807	294,549	3.1	100
City of Mińsk	1,836,808	13,420	0.7	4.6
Brest Region	1,401,177	17,539	1.2	5.9
Grodno Region	1,072,381	230,810	21.5	78.4
Homel Region	1,440,718	1,958	0.1	0.6
Minsk Region	1,422,528	17,908	1.2	6.1
Mogilev Region	1,099,374	1,773	0.1	0.6
Vitebsk Region	1,230,821	11,141	0.9	3.8

Source: Natsional'nyĭ sostav naseleniia, grazhdanstvo, 2009.

The Polish general census of 2002 was the first since 1946 in which there was a question on nationality[38]. In 2011, another census was taken, in which two answers were possible to the question concerning nationality. The results of both these censuses differ from estimates made by the Polish authorities based on information obtained from national/cultural minority organisations and scholarly studies (Chodubski, 2016, p. 405; Chałupczak, 2006, pp. 267-270)[39].

Table 3. Belarusians in the ethnic structure of Poland

Minority	General census of 2011	First identification	Second identification	Ministry of Interior Affairs date (report of 2002 for the European Council)	Region of concentration
Belarusians	47,000	37,000	10,000	200-300,000	Podlaskie province

Source: Report for the Secretary General of the European Council from the Republic of Poland's implementation of the provisions of the Framework Convention of the European Council on the Protection of National Minorities, 2002, p. 11; Results of the National General Census of Population and Inhabitants 2011, Basic information on the demographic and social situation of the population of Poland and on residential resources, 2011, p. 18.

---

38 Polish experience in assessing national and ethnic minorities in the post-war period differs from that of the states of the former Soviet republics. After the Second World War, as a result of changes in its borders and the displacement of peoples, Poland became a mono-ethnic country in which 95% of the population belong to a single titular nation. Despite this ethnic homogeneity, national and ethnic minorities do exist, but in Socialist Poland little weight was placed on this issue, on the assumptions that, firstly, a mono-ethnic state has no minorities, and secondly, if they do exist, it is natural that they will assimilate. A public consequence of this disregard for the existence of minorities was the absence of statistics on nationality.

39 According to various estimates, from 1 to 6.3 million people belong to non-Polish nationalities.

The reasons most often mentioned for such phenomena are assimilation, the fact that data are collected by activitists of national/cultural minorities, the unreliability of census-takers, and fear of admitting one's ethnic origin in the local community (Wierzbicki, 2008, p. 226). Measures aimed at mitigating these factors are taken not only in Poland and Belarus, but all over the world, in order to prepare better records in international documents and bilateral agreements.

Before analysing the Polish-Belarusian Treaty signed in 1992 in respect of minority rights, let us reflect on the three most important problems in this area. The first of these is that modern standards of international law concerning the protection of members of national minorities include both universal human rights and regulations that directly concerns rights associated with being a member of a national minority. Between such members and the dominant majority, a special type of relationship is formed, because the essence of belonging to a national minority is not only numerical (demographic), but also political and cultural, in the desire to preserve ethnocultural distinctiveness (Arutiunian, Drobizheva and Susokolov, 1998, pp. 38-39). The essence of protecting minority rights, then, as has been stated by Sławomir Łodiński, is to guarantee members the right to preserve their own identity and an equal opportunity to take part in public and cultural life along with the majority (Łodziński, 2002, pp. 5-6). The Russian researcher Valeriĭ Tishkov has pointed out, though, that in no country, not even the most democratic, do minorities enjoy full linguistic or cultural equality, because inequality results from the very nature of a minority. For this reason, the ethno-political duty of the state is to strive to balance the more difficult conditions faced by minorities in preserving and developing their identity ("affirmative action")[40] (Jackson-Preece, 2007, pp. 97-98; Martin, 2001, pp. 9-15) and to create appropriate mechanisms and institutions to prevent ethnocratic tendencies on the part of the majority

---

40 A typical example of affirmative action is the policy of the USA towards racial and ethnic minorities, which aims at compensating for harm caused by the policy of racism, and extends to the labour market and education, where access to employment and universities is facilitated, mainly for Afro-Americans. This is also a kind of attempt to atone for the institution of slavery. Critics of the policy argue that it serves to perpetuate racial categories and classification. The American researcher Terry Martin also considers the policy of the USSR towards nationalities as affirmative action.

and undue politicisation of the ethnicity of minorities (Tishkov and Shabaev, 2011, pp. 13-164).

The second most important problem is the recognition of collective minority rights. Many states are not very eagerly disposed towards recognising this type of right, out of fear of secession, separatism or autonomisation. That is why international documents and domestic legal systems use a compromise formula on rights guaranteed "individually or together with others". The lack of acceptance of "group rights" also results from the "group" nature of state authorities and differences among minority communities. Not everyone who is a nominal member of such a group wishes to be treated as a representative of the group (Łodziński, 2002, p. 8).

The third problem to be considered is how to define a national minority. To date, no single, universally accepted and binding such definition has been formulated. The most important international documents[41] having global reach do not define the term, though definitions are proposed in certain international documents of regional scope (Wierzbicki, 2008, p. 233)[42]. Another disputed issue is the difference between a national and an ethnic minority. Several tendencies arise here. In European documents, the term "national minority" is used, while in other documents, e.g. those of the United Nations and in anglophone countries, the term "ethnic minority" is most often used. According to another tendency, national minorities are defined as those groups having their historical motherland outside the borders of their country of residence, while ethnic minorities are defined as those groups that have no such state (Łodziński, 2002, p. 8; Wierzbicki, 2008, p. 235). These problems are reflected in that part of the Polish-Belarusian Treaty that deals with the protection of national minority rights in Poland and in Belarus.

There is also a fourth problem concerning the international protection of national minority rights that unfortunately is somewhat neglected – the

---

41 The International Covenant on Civil and Political Rights, the UN Declaration on the Rights of Persons Belonging to National or Ethnic, Religious and Linguistic Minorities, and the Council of Europe Framework Convention for the Protection of National Minorities.

42 In Article 1 of the Convention on Guarantees of the Rights of Persons Belonging to Minorities, signed by some members of the CIS on 21 October 1994, a national minority is defined as *"persons, permanently residing in the territory of participating states and holding citizenship thereof, who differ in their ethnic origin, language, culture, religion or traditions from the majority of the population of a given state"*.

loyalty of members of minorities to the state of which they are citizens. The Framework Convention for the Protection of National Minority Rights approved by the Council of Europe on 1 February 1995 addresses this issue in Article 20, which stipulates that: "Every person belonging to a national minority who enjoys the rights and freedoms resulting from the principles contained in this framework convention has a duty to respect the legal system of the country and the rights of other persons, in particular those belonging to the majority or another national minority". Article 21 states that: "None of the provisions of this framework convention shall be interpreted as acknowledging the right to participate in any activities whatsoever or conduct any activities whatsoever that are contrary to the fundamental principles of international law, in particular the sovereign equality, territorial integrity and political independence of states" (*Konwencja Ramowa o ochronie mniejszości narodowych*, 1995). These articles touch on extremely sensitive matters. When acting to protect their rights and when benefiting from aid from their homeland abroad, representatives of national minorities must maintain their loyalty towards the state of which they are citizens. This tripartite relationship is described by what is known as the Brubaker triangle, created – or made visible – when there is a discrepancy between ethnic and political borders; it primarily concerns Central and Eastern Europe, in particular those countries that were once part of Yugoslavia and the USSR.

Diagram1. The Brubaker triangle

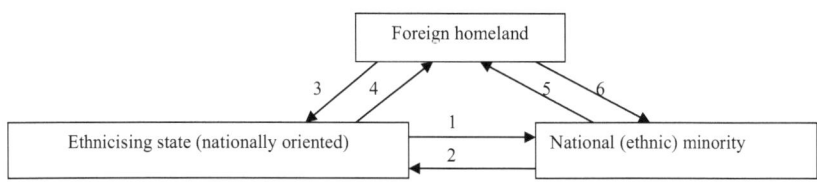

1 – effort (perceived effort) to assimilate national minorities

2 – political activism in defence of own distinctiveness and identity

3 – attempts to intervene and exert pressure in defence of national minorities

4 – reaction against intervention in internal affairs

5 – appeal for help by leaders of political minorities from the elites of the foreign (historical) homeland

6 – organisational and financial support to minorities

Source: own study on the basis of: Brubaker, 1998, pp. 70-98.

By nature, the Brubaker triangle involves conflict. The first entity in the configuration is an ethnically heterogenous state oriented nationally (nationalising itself, ethnicising itself) that is seeking to become a nation state. It is conceived of as a state defined by the titular nationality, where the elites believe the state was created by that nation and only for that nation. In order to implement this idea, the state is subjected to nationalisation (ethnicisation), that is, to "appropriation". This involves using demographic dominance, as well as the language and culture of the majority nation, to establish political, cultural (linguistic) and economic hegemony within the state. A state undergoing this process forces the second component of the triangle – national minorities – to assimilate, or is perceived by them as doing so, with the result that they become politically active in order to defend their own identity, publicly declaring their allegiance to an ethno-cultural nation other than the titular nation, demanding recognition of their ethno-cultural distinctiveness and of certain political or cultural rights in the form of national territorial or national cultural autonomy. The elites of the foreign homeland, that is, those states with whom the minorities identify, are the third component of the triangle. They keep a close watch on the situation of their compatriots in the state undergoing ethnicisation, with whom they feel connected by the conviction that they all belong to a national community that is above political borders or citizenship, and they feel responsible for them. That is why they protest against real or imagined violations of their rights, and seek to put pressure on the governments of the ethnicising state, and provide organisational and financial support for the minorities (Brubaker, 1998, pp. 73-87). The ethnicising state, however, is not passive in this regard, and objects to what it sees as attempts to intervene in its internal affairs. Thus, the problem of national minorities becomes politicised. The dependencies resulting from the 'Brubaker triangle' are unavoidable where political and ethnic borders do not follow the same lines, as is the case most everywhere in Central and Eastern Europe.

The role played in this triangle by the foreign homeland is especially worthy of attention. By exploiting the politicisation of the minority, it can cross the very fine line between demands focused on improving the situation of fellow nationals and attempts to exert influence on the internal situation of the ethnicising state – including up to changing the government. This is a politicisation of the problem of minorities that is not so much about protecting rights as it is about using minority issues to change the political regime in the state in which those minorities live, or forcing the government there to implement reforms or amend its geopolitical orientation. In such situations, the 'Brubaker triangle' must be modified such that what is crucial is not to protect the political and ethno-cultural rights of fellow nationals, but to change the rulers of the ethnicising state with whom the foreign homeland is "uncomfortable".

In its first version, the 'Brubaker triangle' applies, with certain reservations, to the situation between the Belarusian minority in Poland and the Belarusian government, whereas Polish-Belarusian relations can be described by a specific modification of the triangle. The Polish minority in Belarus is used by the foreign homeland (Poland) in an internal political struggle as one organisation that politically opposes Aleksander Lukashenko. This modification of the 'Brubaker triangle' is interesting in that Belarus is not a state that is nationally oriented, but a state that is de-ethnicised (de-nationalised), if we accept that ethnicisation (nationalisation) is a process in which the state is "appropriated" by the titular nation, and by its language and culture. In reality, Belarus is a state that has been ethnicised by Russian culture and language – which are close to Belarusians, but are not their own national culture and language. Official documents show that the basis of Belarusian statehood is the *belorusskaia ideia*, yet the authorities are guided ideologically by the traditions of East Slavic society. In the Polish-Belarusian 'minority conflict', the key issue is not the defence of Polishness as such, but the hope of Westernising Belarus internally and geopolitically.

Diagram 2. Modified Brubaker triangle

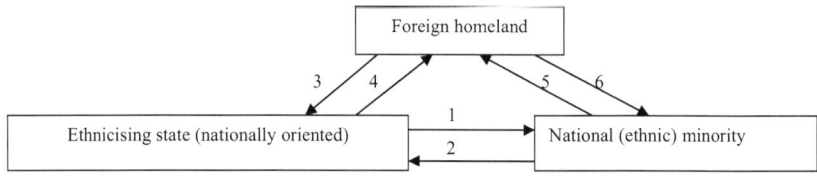

1 – effort (perceived effort) to marginalise national minorities politically while preserving basic cultural rights

2 – political activism addressed against the government, using demands to protect own distinctiveness and identity

3 – attempts to intervene and exert pressure in defence of national minorities as a pretext for far-reaching interference in the internal affairs of the ethnicising state involv-

ing the removal from power of the governing camp/a change in current geopolitical orientation

4 – reaction against intervention in internal affairs

5 – appeal for help by leaders of political minorities from the elites of the foreign (historical) homeland

6 – organisational and financial support to minorities, introduction of "national cards"

Source: own study on the basis of: Brubaker, 1998, pp. 70-98.

The Treaty between the Republic of Poland and Belarus contains a quite well-developed catalogue of national minority rights. The parties undertook to respect international principles and standards concerning the protection of national minority rights[43]. The treaty contains an important provision stipulating that adherence to a national minority is the individual matter of each citizen, and cannot entail any adverse consequences. Adherence to a national minority is related to the freedom to preserve, develop and express one's ethnic, cultural, linguistic and religious identity[44].

Article 15 of the treaty contains a detailed catalogue of the rights of members of national minorities that can be implemented individually or in consort with other members of the same group. These include:
– the freedom to use the mother tongue in private and public life, access to information in that language, the right to disseminate it and engage in interchange in it, and the right to use one's first and last name as pronounced in the mother tongue
– the right to establish and maintain one's own educational, cultural or other institutions, organisations or associations, which can seek voluntary financial or other aid, as well as state aid, in accordance with domestic law; the right to access mass media and to take part in the activities of international non-governmental organisations
– the right to belong to and practice one's religion, including by acquiring and using religious materials, and by conducting religious educational activities in the mother tongue

---

43 These include the international human rights covenants, the Final Act of the Conference on Security and Cooperation in Europe, the Document resulting from the Copenhagen meeting on the human dimension, and the Paris Charter for a New Europe.

44 Articles 13 and 14 of the Treaty between the Republic of Poland and the Republic of Belarus on Neighbourly Relations and Friendly Cooperation, signed in Warsaw on 23 June 1992.

- the right to establish and maintain undisrupted contacts between members of the group within the territory of their State, as well as contacts with citizens of other countries who share a common ethnic or national origin, cultural heritage or religious convictions
- the right to access legal means foreseen by the internal legislation of the country of residence in order to actualise and protect the above rights.

Poland and Belarus also undertook to develop constructive cooperation within the scope of protecting the rights of persons who belong to a national minority; this is to be treated as a means of strengthening mutual understanding and neighbourly relations between the Polish and Belarusian nations. Moreover, both states undertook to take account of the social and economic interests of minorities in their policies for region development (of particular importance given that, as described above, the Polish minority in Belarus and the Belarusian minority in Poland live in compact clusters), to strive to provide courses on the mother tongue, or schooling in that language in educational outlets, and, where possible and necessary, to provide public services in that language. In educational programmes in which persons belonging to national minorities take part, the two countries undertook to take broad account of their history and culture. Another important provision of the treaty is the right of representatives of national minorities to take part in public life, in particular when this concerns protecting and strengthening identity, and to take part in consultations with the authorities within this scope conducted by minority organisations and associations.

Provisions on national minorities are also found in other bilateral agreements concluded between Poland and Belarus at the governmental and ministerial levels. In the Agreement between the Government of the Republic of Poland and the Government of the Republic of Belarus on Cooperation in the Areas of Culture, Science and Education of 27 November 1995, persons belonging to the Polish minority in Belarus or the Belarusian minority in Poland are guaranteed conditions that favour the preservation, development and expression of their national, ethnic, cultural, linguistic and religious identity, without any discrimination whatsoever and under conditions of full equality before the law. The parties to the Agreement also undertook to create legal guarantees for the comprehensive support of the activities of social, educational and cultural organisations of persons belonging to the above minorities, and conditions under which they can obtain material aid from the territory of the other party to the Agreement.

In the same Agreement, the parties undertook as well to create conditions for the Polish minority in Belarus and the Belarusian minority in Poland in which they can learn their mother tongue; this constitutes an extension of the provision approved in the treaty of 1992. Those conditions foresee:

– ensuring interested persons voluntary access to knowledge about their mother tongue and schooling conducted in the mother tongue in preschools, elementary schools and middle schools, within the education systems of the Republic of Poland and the Republic of Belarus, and striving to create opportunities to learn the mother tongue at the university level

– supporting teaching and raising the level of teaching of the language, history and culture of the other party to the Agreement at all levels of education outside the state education system

– preparing and improving the qualifications of teachers for national minority schools

– providing, upon mutual consent, opportunities for teachers directed towards schools by the other Party to the Agreement.

For a dozen years or so, Belarusian legislation did not define the concept of a national minority, though the term did appear in legal acts[45]. Since 1996, Belarus has been outside the structures of the Council of Europe, and in 2010 the Parliament of that organisation voted to suspend contact with Belarus at the parliamentary-government level. This means that Belarus did not sign the Council of Europe Framework Convention for the Protection of National Minorities, nor did it accept the obligations resulting from the European Convention on Human Rights and Basic Freedoms (Janusz, 2005, p. 61). Belarus is a member of the Central European Initiative and of the Commonwealth of Independent States, and therefore has formally committed itself to the obligations resulting from understandings concluded within those organisations (Janusz, 2005, pp. 59-61).

Although Belarus is currently outside the structures of the Council of Europe, as early as 1992 it passed a law on national minorities – before the Council of Europe's adoption of the Framework Convention. In an amended version of 2004, that law included a definition of *national minority* that

---

45 In the Belarusian Constitution in force, the term *national community* is used.

refers to the definition contained in the Convention on the Legal Guarantees of Persons Belonging to a Minority, signed by some CIS countries in 1994. In the Belarusian law, national minorities are defined as persons permanently residing within the territory of Belarus who hold Belarusian citizenship and whose linguistic, cultural or traditional origins differ from those of the majority of the population of the country (Art. 1, Zakon Respubliki Belarus' ot 5 ianvaria 2004 g. Nr 261-3 „O vnesenii izmeneniĭ i dopolneniĭ v Zakon Respubliki Belarus'; „O natsional'nykh men'shinstvakh v Respublike Belarus,' 2004). Adherence to a minority is an individual matter of choice of every citizen. According to that law, the Belarusian State guarantees national minorities a series of rights and freedoms, such as:

- aid in the development of national culture and education
- the right to use the mother tongue, free choice of the language of communication, and the right to freely choose the language of upbringing and education
- the right to establish means of mass communication, to start up publishing activities, and the right to maintain, preserve and disseminate information in the mother tongue
- the right to establish cultural connections with fellow nationals abroad
- the right to profess any religious or none, to take part in ceremonies connection with a religious cult, rituals and services in the mother tongue
- the right to preserve historical, cultural and spiritual heritage, to freely develop culture, including through professional and amateur artistic activities
- the right to establish social organisations and join existing organisations
- the right to participate actively or passively in elections according to the principles of universality, equality, directness and confidentiality
- the right to equal access to public office (*Zakon Respubliki Belarus' ot 5 ianvaria 2004 g. Nr 261-3 „O vnesenii izmeneniĭ i dopolneniĭ v Zakon Respubliki Belarus' „O natsional'nykh men'shinstvakh v Respublike Belarus'*, 2004).

The Polish Parliament passed an Act on National and Ethnic Minorities and on Regional Language in 2005. The law makes a distinction between national and ethnic minorities. A national minority is defined as a group of Polish citizens that meets the following conditions: 1) it is less numerous than the rest of the population of Poland, 2) its members differ significantly from other citizens in terms of their language, culture or traditions, 3) they are conscious of their own history as a national community and wish to express and protect it, 4) their ancestors lived in the current territory of the Republic of Poland at least 100 years ago, 5) they identify with a nation that is organised within its own state (*Ustawa z dnia 6 stycznia 2005 r. o mniejszościach narodowych i etnicznych oraz o języku regionalnym*, 2005)[46].

The Polish "Minority Act" refers to the Framework Convention of the Council of Europe of 1995 and, obviously, to the Polish Constitution. It contains the compromise mentioned above of combining individualism and collectivism in the implementation of the rights and freedoms resulting from adherence to a national minority. Particular attention is paid to the issue of the languages of national and ethnic minorities. Persons belong to such minorities have, in particular, the right: 1) to freely use the minority language in private and public life, 2) to disseminate and exchange information in the minority language, 3) to communicate information of a private nature in the minority language, 4) to teach the minority language or teach in the minority language. What is most important to note is that, in districts in which the number of inhabitants belonging to a given minority is at least 20%, it is possible to use the minority language as a supplementary language before district authorities and as an additional writing system for traditional place names and buildings, as well as for streets, alongside the binding forms in the Polish language.

Pursuant to the Act, public authorities are obliged to take appropriate measures to support activities aimed at protecting, preserving and developing minority culture (*Ustawa z dnia 6 stycznia 2005 r. o mniejszościach narodowych i etnicznych oraz o języku regionalnym*, 2005)[47]. Further, representatives of national and ethnic minorities in Poland are present on the

---

46 In the meaning of this Act, an ethnic minority is a group of Polish citizens that meet all of the following conditions: 1) it is less numerous than the rest of the population of the Republic of Poland, 2) its members differ significantly from other citizens in terms of their language, culture or traditions, 3) they are conscious of their own history as a national community and wish to express and protect it, 4) their ancestors lived in the current territory of the Republic of Poland at least 100 years ago, 5) they do not identify with a nation that is organised within its own state.

47 Such measures can be in the form of subsidies for: 1) activities of cultural institutions, artistic movements and creativity of minorities and artistic events of importance for the minority culture; 2) investments serving to preserve minority cultural

Joint Commission of the Government and National and Ethnic Minorities, formed on the basis of the Act as a body for giving opinions to and consulting with the Council of Ministers[48]. In accordance with that Act, Belarusians in Poland have the status of a national minority. For them, the adoption of the Act was important because they mostly live in compact clusters in the southeastern part of Podlaskie province[49].

As researchers of the problem state, in contrast to Poland, the rights of national minorities in Belarus – both those resulting from the possession of citizenship and those resulting from adherence to a minority, are violated (Żołędowski, 2003, p. 285). These negative tendencies in the policy of the Belarusian state towards minorities became visible after 1994, and have both an ideological and a political basis[50]. The authorities began to

---

identity, 3) publications in minority languages or in Polish, in printed form or in other techniques of recording images and sounds, 4) supporting television and radio programmes created by minorities, 5) protecting sites associated with minority culture, 6) educational activities, 7) running libraries and documenting the cultural and artistic life of minorities, 8) various forms of education for children and youth, 9) propagating knowledge about minorities, 10) other programmes having the above goal and supporting the civic integration of minorities.

48 The tasks of the Joint Commission include: 1) issuing opinions on the implementation of minority rights and needs, including by assessing how those rights are implemented, and formulating proposals pertaining to activities aimed at ensuring the protection of minority rights and needs, 2) issuing opinions on programmes serving to create conditions that favour the preservation and development and minority cultural identity and that preserve and develop regional language, 3) issuing opinions on draft acts of law concerning minority issues, 4) issuing opinions on the amounts and rules for dividing funds from the state budget allocated to support activities aimed at protecting, preserving and developing minority cultural identity and to preserve and develop regional language; 5) taking measures to combat discrimination against persons belonging to a minority.

49 These are the counties: Hajnowski (39.1% of inhabitants of the county), Bielski (19.80%), Siemiatycki (3.46%), Białostocki (3.2%) and Białystok (2.53%). In 12 districts of Podlaski province, the Belarusian minority constitutes more than 20% of the inhabitants, including more than 50% in 4 districts.

50 Yet here as well, there are "difficult issues". At the end of 1992, Polish Catholic priests were accused of a lack of loyalty towards Belarus and of conducting political activity, while superiors in the Catholic Church in Belarus were accused of having taken many decisions without taking account of the position of the Orthodox Church hierarchy. The Polish side, in turn, accused the Belarusian authorities of numerous cases of hindering the development of Polish education in Belarus, of restricting the use of the Polish language, and of preventing manifestations of Polishness in the Catholic Church.

distance themselves from the ethno-cultural belarusisation of the country begun in the 1990s. The political component of the process, which affected the *politicisation of the problem of the Polish minority*, was anti-presidential and pro-opposition activities on the part of the Union of Poles in Belarus. The complex situation of the Polish minority, and especially of Polish organisations, had a serious impact on Polish-Belarusian relations. To a large extent, this was the result of the nature of the political regime that developed in Belarus in the second half of the 1990s. The Belarusian authorities assumed that national minority organisations, including that of the Polish minority, should concern themselves with preserving and developing the culture of their nations, but should not become politically engaged. The *politicisation of ethnicity* was forbidden. And yet, since the 1990s, while in Belarus there has not been a *politicisation of ethnicity* as has been observed throughout the post-Soviet states (Rotschild, 1981, p. 6)[51], there has been a *politicisation of the problem of the Polish minority*. Cezary Żołędowski rightly points out that the role of minorities in forming inter-ethnic relations in a given country increases along with their level of national identity, the amount of support provided by fellow nationals from foreign homelands, and the degree to which the ethnic majority accepts the preservation of ethno-cultural distinctiveness (Żołędowski, 2003, p. 10). Poles in Belarus became well aware of the possibility of using politics to preserve their own values and culture, but this became an instrument used in the struggle to democratise the Belarusian political regime (Głogowska, 2009, p. 205). This resulted, firstly, in a hostile reaction by the Belarusian authorities, who understood the political activities of the Polish minority as interference in internal affairs and a weakening of their loyalty towards Belarus, and secondly, in a deterioration of relations between the two countries. Thirdly, the politicization of the problem of the Polish minority in Belarus stands as an example of the conflicted, modified nature of the relations between the nationally oriented state, the national minority, and the foreign homeland.

---

51 According to Rotschild, to politicise ethnicity means: 1) to render people cognitively aware of the relevance of politics to the health of their ethnic cultural values, and vice versa, 2) to stimulate their concern about this nexus, 3) to mobilise them into self-conscious ethnic groups, 4) to direct their behaviour toward activity in the political arena on the basis of this awareness, concern, and group consciousness.

.

The first problem related to the Polish minority in Belarus is the conflict revolving around the Union of Poles in Belarus, which split up in 2005. The organisation was formed on 16 June 1990 in Grodno as an independent social organisation assembling all Poles in the Belarusian Soviet Socialist Republic and continuing the activities of the Adam Mickiewicz Polish Cultural and Educational Society. The first chairman of the UPB was Tadeusz Gawin. The statutory goals of the Union were: to protect the civil and national rights of the Polish population in the BSSR and to assist in meeting their needs; to support the teaching of the Polish language and education in Polish; to rebuild and develop Polish national culture in Belarus; to promote Poles living in Belarus in all areas of society (Giebień, 2014, p. 75). The UPB sought to achieve these goals by popularising the active role taken by the Union and its members in the social, political and professional life of the country, by participating in elections, representing the interests of Poles, organising Polish cultural centres, being present in the mass media, establishing contacts with social organisations in Poland, taking part in cultural and touristic exchanges with communities in Poland, and initiating economic activity.

In April 1993, the Second UPB Congress was held, at which amendments to the statute were made that took account of the "spirit of Christian values", which was understandable because the Union had been established during the Soviet era. The Congress issued a proclamation to the government of the Republic of Belarus and to Poles, Belarusians and citizens of other nationalities of the country. In it, the Union requested that the Supreme Council and Government of the Republic should take decisive steps towards implementing the following demands: to build Polish schools in Grodno, Lida and Vawkavysk; to create a Republican "Polish Cultural Centre" in Grodno; to finance the Polish newspaper *Głos znad Niemna* and the periodical *Magazyn Polski*; to grant Home Army soldiers status as veterans of the Second World War[52]; to introduce changes in history textbooks to reflect historical truth. As it turned out, the Belarusian authorities did not help the Polish minority in fully achieving those demands. In the programme established during the 2nd Congress, the Union was defined as an organisation "striving to guarantee Poles living in Belarus that their freedom, personal dignity, equality before the law and participation in public and economic life will be respected" (Giebień, 2014, p.

---

52 This demand was renewed, without effect, at the 4th UPB Congress in 1997.

77). The Union also supported efforts to build an independent Republic of Belarus. At the central level, the Belarusian government took a favourable view of the Polish national renaissance. However, at the local level, the authorities were not so understanding and helpful, especially in education. In Lida, Voranava, Szczuczyn and Navahrudak, they took no decisions in respect of building Polish schools, and even blocked the creation of classes taught in Polish (Giebień, 2014, p. 164).

The first president of the UPB, Tadeusz Gawin, held office for several terms, at the conclusion of which, in October 2000, the 5th UPB Congress was held, during which a new president – Tadeusz Kruczkowski – was elected. The atmosphere at the Congress was tense due to ideological and personal conflicts arising out of different assessments of the political situation in Belarus concerning restrictions of democracy. During his presidency, Gawin had politicised the Union, actively cooperating with the Belarusian opposition and trying to engage it in UPB activities. This political approach was met with criticism and disapproval by some members of the Union, and the conflict deepened when Gawin resigned as president. Most UPB activitists withdrew from the political struggle, as emphasised in nine points of the UPB programme ("neglect of political activity"). Gawin's approach had been a response to the changing policies of the Belarusian government, which at that time had not yet intervened in the UPB's activities, though it did look on its demands with a critical eye. Poles began to be perceived as a threat to the country and its government, as a foreign element embodying the "evil of the West" (Czachor, 2011, p. 230). This is why Gawin was opposed to cooperating with the government and identified with the opposition. He accused some UPB activists of being "a destructive opposition", of having "disloyal connections" with the authorities in Grodno, Brest and Minsk, and even of acting as agents for the KGB, which, in Gawin's opinion, was in order to disrupt the construction of a Polish school in Navahrudak. At the same time, he stated, the internal opposition within the Union was cooperating with the Consul General in Grodno. Polish diplomatic posts in Belarus eventually stopped supporting his activities. Together with the Union, Gawin sought to build up civil society by cooperating with the Belarusian opposition. This meant that the Union itself became an opposition organisation, and failed to take appropriate decisions on key issues for the organisation. Gawin summed up that period as follows: "The Lukashenko governments clearly collided with the Polish renaissance in Belarus. Poles could have successively developed their education and culture if the authorities had been elected, and not appointed from above as the president and his entourage wanted. The UPB leadership was interested in free, democratic elections, particularly for local government, for that would create an opportunity for joint government along with Belarusians in those regions where the number of Poles was significant. There were other regions as well, such as Voranova, Szczuczyn and Lida, where Poles could govern on their own. That's how the political situation in Belarus at the time was understood" (Gawin, 2010, p. 238). The success of Poles in sharing power at the local and regional levels varied, but was most often disappointing[53]. In the opinion of Gawin himself, Lukashenko's policies of changing the constitution, granting Russian the status of a second official language and declaring integration with Russia showed that Lukashenko was heading towards an authoritarian state and an alliance with Russia, which could lead to the loss of Belarus's independence and sovereignty: "Giving the Russian language official status equal to that of Belarusian put the latter in a weaker position. None of the attempts of the Union of Poles in Belarus to coexist peacefully with the authorities met with success, because those in power were fighting with the Belarusian nation and its culture, and had no intention of supporting the development of Polish culture and language among the Polish national minority living in Belarus" (Gawin, 2010, p. 242).

When he was elected to the office of president, Tadeusz Kruczkowski presented a different vision for the Union, and took up a completely different stance towards the Belarusian opposition and the state authorities. He stated that he would not support any political option and would deal only with Polish issues, in cooperation with the Belarusian authorities. Faced with this approach, opposition organisations stopped cooperating with and supporting the Union. Kruczkowski focused on statutory activities. At the Congress he emphasised that the most important goal of the Union continued to be the rebirth of the Polish language and the creation of Polish-language education. In reference to the Union's cessation of political activity,

---

53 For example, in 1995 the UPB introduced to the Belarusian parliament, the Supreme Council, a single representative, to regional councils (in the Grodno and Voranava regions) two, and to district councils none. Union candidates had a chance to win the election in the most numerous constituencies if not for the falsification of results and various types of hindrances on the part of the authorities. It was typical of post-Soviet states to influence election results through the use of the state apparatus at various levels; this is known in Russian as *administrativnyĭ resurs*.

Kruczkowski stated that "the UPB must remain a social and cultural organisation, and get out of politics. Of course, there does exist a certain reason to fight, but to fight for a Polish renaissance, and not to fight with the authorities, for the simple reason that they are the authorities. But this shouldn't be done through some sort of political game in hand with the opposition. We have to talk with the government and demand that our constitutional rights be respected" (Giebień, 2014, p. 83). In order to achieve political goals, Kruczkowski proposed the creation of a Polish political party, separate from the UPB. Its task would be to take care of Polish matters in the political process[54].

Delegates at the 5th Congress sent an appeal to the president of Belarus, Aleksander Lukashenko, in which they emphasised that Poles are fully-fledged, loyal citizens of Belarus who make a contribution to the cultural and economic development of the country. They also emphasised that the state was not living up to its obligations towards national minorities, e.g., pertaining to the construction of Polish schools; this approach on the part of the government did not favour the harmonisation of relations between the authorities and the Union, and further, violated the rights of Poles and the law of Belarus (especially the Constitution). For these reasons, the delegates appealed to Lukashenko to grant his consent to the construction of Polish-language schools in Navahrudak and Grodno, at the cost of the Union. Yet, despite such favourable financial conditions, the government did not consent to the construction of more schools with lessons conducted in Polish.

Under Kruczkowski's leadership, the UPB was loyal as an organisation to the state, and supported the development of an independent, democratic Republic of Belarus. In its programme, the Union avoided ideology, accepted restrictions on human rights and minority rights, assumed that the Belarusian state would abide by the Universal Declaration of Human

---

54 The first attempt to create a Polish political party in Belarus was made in 1993, and was successful. In October of that year, the Polish Democratic Union arose in Minsk. The party's name was taken from the political organisation of Poles in Minsk that existed from 1917 to 1919. The goals of the PDU included representing and defending the interests of Polish citizens of the Republic of Belarus using political means: taking part in local government and parliamentary elections, formulating political principles taking account of the mentality and traditions of the nation, and legally influencing the nature of the political system" (Giebien, 2014, p. 84). In 1994, the party was registered by the authorities, but due to the inexperience of its members, it soon ceased to exist.

Rights, and with Belarusian and international law concerning the rights of national minorities. Poles strove to have their right to develop their culture and religion guaranteed because of the contribution they made to Belarusian society. Yet the UPB did not want to get mixed up in political activism, but sought to ensure that there were Polish representatives at every level of government authority.

The UPB and its structures demanded that the government support and assist it in its statutory activities. Its programme also extended to such issues as: education and schooling, culture, religion, youth and scouting, contacts outside the Union, the press and publishing, UPB financing, and economic activity (Giebień, 2014, p. 87).

At the end of 2004, there was an increasingly clear division within the UPB between supporters and opponents of Tadeusz Kruczkowski and his strategy for the Union. The opponents were led by Andżelika Borys, who was put forward as the new UPB president, and her group began a battle with Kruczkowski's supporters, for whom, as Helena Giebień writes, "loyalty towards the Lukashenko governments and his local authorities was a priority issue for the ideals of the Polish renaissance in Belarus". Thus, there was a potential threat that the activities of Kruczkowski's supporters could lead to greater intervention by the Belarusian authorities and secret services in the internal affairs of the Union, thereby strengthening the influence of that camp and subjugating the organisation to them, which could result in the complete destruction of the UPB (Giebień, 2014, p. 305). In these circumstances, in January 2005 the Main Board of the Union of Poles in Belarus decided to suspend president Kruczkowski from his duties. The Belarusian Minister of Justice overturned that decision on the basis of procedural irregularities. The issue of the leadership of the organisation was left to be resolved at the next, 6th Congress, to be held in March of the same year.

With help from the media, in the period leading up to the Congress the Belarusian authorities began applying pressure on delegates to vote for Kruczkowski. They also managed to prevent the Union's vice president, Józef Porzecki, who might have run for the presidency, from taking part in the Congress.The Polish Ministry of Foreign Affairs assessed these actions as an infringement of bilateral agreements and international standards pertaining to the protection of national minority rights. The Belarusian Ambassador in Warsaw was even summoned to provide an explanation. Because of the strained political situation, high representatives of the Polish authorities (of the Polish Parliament, Ministry of Foreign Affairs and the Polish Ambassador to Belarus) declined to take part in the Congress.

In Grodno on 12-13 March 2005, in an atmosphere of conflict and mutual accusations, the 6th Congress of the Union of Poles in Belarus took place, of which the consequences are still felt today. Against the efforts of the Belarusian authorities, the majority of delegates to the Congress voted for Angelica Borys as the new president (she obtained 152 votes, and Tadeusz Kruczkowski 116). In this way, the existing leadership of the Union, which was loyal to the Lukashenko regime, was replaced by a group of activists who stood in opposition to the government. In her address, the new President declared that the UPB would be an apolitical organisation that would demand that its rights be respected and seek to achieve its goals through lawful means. But the regime was aware that, with the coming to power of Borys, it had lost control over the organisation. For this reason, in May 2005 the Belarusian Ministry of Justice ruled deemed that the 6th UPB Congress had not been binding, justifying its decision by infringements of the statute during the selection of delegates and procedural flaws during meetings. This decision by the government meant that, until such time as a new congress was held, the previous UPB leadership would remain in power. The government of the Republic of Poland supported the new leadership, which had declared itself in opposition to the Lukashenko regime. At the same time, as if in response to the decision of the Belarusian authorities not to recognise the new leadership under Borys, the Polish Ministry of Foreign Affairs banned those persons responsible for the actions against the UPB from entering Poland (Eberhardt, 2006, p. 261). In return, the Belarusian authorities accused Polish diplomats of unlawful interference in the activities of the UPB and of destabilising the situation in Belarus. Polish-Belarusian relations worsened still. In May 2005, the situation led to Marek Bućko, a consultant to the Polish embassy in Minsk, being deemed *persona non grata*[55]. He was depicted on Belarusian television as the initiator of the "upheaval in the UPB", and the Polish

---

55 In response, Poland expelled Maksym Ryżenkow, a consultant at the Belarusian embassy. Despite attempts to resolve the conflict, a series of similar actions were taken by both sides. In July 2005, Belarus forced Andrzej Buczak, head of the Consular Department at the Polish embassy, to leave the country. Poland responded by declaring Mikoła Pietrowicz, a consultant at the Belarusian embassy in Warsaw, persona non grata. Andrzej Olborski, chargé d'affaires and a consultant at the Polish embassy in Minsk, was expelled.

minority as a "fifth column" (*MSZ Białorusi o sprawie Marka Bućki*, 2005). In its efforts, Poland sought to utilise the European Union and other international organisations as well.

On 27 August 2005 in Vawkavysk, the 6th UPB Congress was repeated; it took place with the intervention and support of the government and the KGB. Józef Łucznik was elected as president; a co-founder of the UPB, like Tadeusz Kruczkowski he enjoyed the support of the government in Minsk. He gave his assurances that the UPB would act within Belarusian law. Angelica Borys and her supporters were not permitted to take part in sessions. Poland declared that this Congress had been undemocratic, and refused to recognise the new leadership. The Polish authorities decided that financial support from Poland for the Polish minority in Belarus would be redirected away from the UPB. The result was a division of the Union of Poles in Belarus into two different organisations having the same name but different legal – and political – status. One, led by Angelica Borys, was not recognised by the Belarusian authorities and was subjected to repressions, though it was recognised and supported by the Polish government. The second, led by Józef Łucznik, was recognised by the Belarusian government, but not by Poland[56].

Both Poland and Belarus made efforts to resolve the problem, but none were successful. The proposal most often made by the two sides was to hold another unified congress of both Unions, e.g. with the participation of impartial mediators. It is difficult to assess the conflict categorically, but, when pursuing scientific objectivity rather than political correctness, one should bear in mind the words of Andrzej Drawicz quoted in the introduction, that "relations between states are difficult to assess in terms of the fault of one party. They always result from both objective factors and subjective conditions" (Bieleń, 1997, p. 17). There is no doubt that the conflict over the Union of Poles in Belarus harmed the Polish renaissance in Belarus, and that the division of Poles into "better" and "worse", "correct" and "incorrect" was a contributing factor. Without denying the sincerity and good intentions of Poland in striving for a renaissance in and preservation of Polishness in Belarus, it still seems that the Polish government was guided by an exaggerated faith that, by supporting an organisation that was opposed to the Belarusian regime, the regime would suddenly

---

56 Poland banned UPB activists led by Łucznik, recognised by the Belarusian government, from entering Polish territory for a period of 3 years. A similar decision had been taken previously against Kruczkowski.

change, becoming more democratic and reorienting itself geopolitically towards the West. Mirosław Habowski was certainly correct when he stated that "the Polish government was more interested in opportunities for yet another "democratic revolution" within the Russian sphere of influence than it was in the situation of the Polish national minority in Belarus" (Habowski, 2009, p. 249). This is proved by a statement by the then Minister of Foreign Affairs of the Republic of Poland, Daniel Rotfeld: "Poland is understandably concerned by the state of affairs in Belarus, with which we share a common border. We support the democratic, pro-European aspirations of Belarusian society. Along with our European and trans-Atlantic partners, we are trying to form the policy of the West so that democratic and liberal tendencies in Belarus can count on our full solidarity" (Rotfeld, 2006, p. 21). The same trend was indicated by Tadeusz Kruczkowski: "... since 2004 there has been an adverse political tendency to support one specific political option – the Belarusian nationally-oriented opposition". In Kruczkowski's opinion, the idea that "Poland should build its relations with the Republic of Belarus taking account of the Polish national minority has not been reflected in practice" (Kruchkovskiĭ, 2011, p. 500). Belarus, in turn, sought to exercise complete control over social and political life out of the fear, perhaps ungrounded, that another "Orange Revolution" might break out there. The Belarusian author Petra Rudkoŭski thus described the conflict over the UPB (Rudkoŭski, 2007, p. 210).

Yet, it should be stated that the Belarusian authorities did not so much fight against Polishness in the ethno-cultural sense, or especially against Roman Catholicism[57] (Dzwonkowski, 2005), as they did against the evident aversion of the Polish minority towards the current government, and towards Aleksander Lukashenko in particular. It was a battle against Polishness in the "political" or institutional sense. Information given in the Polish media on discrimination against the Polish minority in Belarus did not concern "ordinary" Poles, but Polish political activists engaged in op-

---

57 Poles in Belarus are identified as Catholics. Catholics in Belarus can celebrate Christmas on 25 December, according to the Gregorian calendar, which is a public holiday in the country, as is 7 January, the Orthodox Christmas. Every Sunday, the Belarus state radio station broadcasts a Roman Catholic mass, and every day there is a Polish-language programme. Belarusian Catholics have religious freedom, though, like every community in the country, they are faced with a number of hurdles.

position activities. Without justifying the actions taken by the Belarusian authorities against Polish activists, it is hard to imagine how similar activities by Belarusian activists in Poland could be accepted by the Polish government. On both sides there was a failure to separate taking care over the growth of the Polish national minority – which was in the interests of both sides – from specific goals of internal and international policy. Moreover, an analysis of the division in the UPB and the involvement of the Polish and Belarusian governments in that issue must also take account of the personal ambitions of Polish activists in Belarus, on both sides of the conflict. The problem of the Polish minority, and specifically the Union of Poles in Belarus, continues to divide the two countries.

Another issue related to the Polish minority in Belarus is the creation of conditions under which the Polish language can be taught. The Republic of Poland finances the development of social infrastructure for Belarusian Poles (schools, culture houses), while the local Belarusian authorities responsible for such matters do not (Waszkiewicz, 2005). For this reason, the Polish authorities believe they should act more decisively to defend the Polish minority in Belarus. This is taken by the Belarusian government as interference in Belarus's internal affairs, and as using the Polish minority instrumentally in a political process supported from the outside. This has resulted in an intensification of the anti-Polish campaign. For several years, there has been a visible tendency to restrict the teaching of Polish in Belarus (*Władze Białorusi ograniczają nauczanie języka polskiego*, 2015). An additional threat to Polish schools in Belarus is an amendment to the Education Code, in accordance with which the majority of subjects must be taught in Russian or Belarusian, and not in the languages of national minorities (*Likwidacja polskich szkół i rusyfikacja. Związek Polaków o reformie edukacji na Białorusi*, 2017)[58]. Polish activists argue that this creates the possibility of eliminating Polish as a language for teaching specific subjects (*Ministerstwo Edukacji Białorusi nie zmienia nastawienia do polskich szkół*, 2017). The Polish language is very rarely treated by people as having autotelic value. When choosing a school in which Polish is taught, people usually approach the matter instrumentally, mainly in order to be able to study in Poland in the future. There are only two schools in Belarus where classes are taught in Polish – in Grodno and in Vawkavysk.

---

58 Activists of the unrecognised UPB issued an appeal to the President Lukashenko in this regard, to which they received an unsatisfactory response from the Ministry of Education.

Both were financed from Polish funds in the 1990s, though today Belarus incurs the costs of maintaining them. In Brest, several schools have been started up that teach in Polish. A total of about 5,000 children and adolescents learn in Polish, while another 5,000 can learn Polish in elective courses. In addition, Polish language courses are run at the Polish Institute in Minsk. All of this, of course, is inadequate for the almost 300,000-strong Polish community, and is in need of change (*Jak uczy się języka polskiego na Białorusi. Liczby i fakty*, 2017).

A third bone of contention in Polish-Belarusian relations in the context of the Polish minority in Belarus is the Polish Card, introduced in September 2007. Its purpose is to facilitate contacts of Poles living in the CIS with the homeland[59]. The Polish Card is a document confirming that its bearer belongs to the Polish nation, and can be issued to anyone who shows their ties to Poland by demonstrating a sufficient command of the language and knowledge of Polish traditions and customs, who signs a relevant declaration in the presence of a consul, and at least one of whose parents, grandparents or great grandparents was of Polish nationality or had Polish citizenship[60].

The Belarusian government has often expressed its doubts over that Act and the implementation thereof, making official accusations that it leads to unequal treatment among Belarusian citizens, and unofficially suggesting that holding a Polish Card undermines loyalty towards Belarus[61], and in November 2011 submitted an amendment to the Act on State Service to the Belarusian parliament which would ban Belarusian officials of Polish origin from holding a Polish Card (*Ustawa z dnia 7 września 2007 r. o Karcie Polaka*, 2007). According to the Belarusian authorities, the Polish

---

59 The Polish Card is similar to the Hungarian Card approved by the Hungarian government in 2001 for persons of Hungarian nationality living in neighbouringcountries. It facilitates studies at Hungarian universities, and provides discounts on public transport within Hungary, a three-month work permit each year, and access to free health care.

60 A holder of a Polsih Card has the right to an exemption from paying for a Polish visa, or to a refund of costs incurred for the issuance of a visa; he or she needs no permit to work or open a business in Poland, can study at university, has free health care in emergencies, and may visit state museums for free. In 2008, a Council for Issues of Poles in the East was established, a body for considering appeals against decisions of consuls concerning the issuance of Polish Cards.

61 In April 2011, the Constitutional Court of Belarus ruled that certain provisions of the Act on the Polish Card are contrary to international legal standards.

Card creates certain obligations towards Poland, and raises doubts as to the loyalty of Belarusian citizens towards Belarus (*Chinovnikam Belorusii zapreshcheno pol'zovat'sia „kartoĭ poliaka"*, 2011). This problem was raised during a visit to Belarus in December 2016 by a delegation of the Speaker of the Polish Senate, Stanisław Karczewski. The head of the Council of the Republic – the upper chamber of the Belarusian parliament, declared that the Polish Card "requires serious study at the expert level. Such a policy encourages young people and highly qualified specialists to emigrate from Belarus to Poland, when it should not harm the interests of my country" (*Będzie porozumienie w sprawie Związku Polaków na Białorusi i Karty Polaka?*, 2017). Time will tell how things turn out in reality. For now, the Polish Card is very popular in Belarus; about half of all Polish Cards issued, that is, about 100,000, have been issued in Belarus (*Polovina „kart poliaka" wydana grazhdanam Belarusi*, 2017). It seems that, as is the case concerning knowledge of the Polish language, the Polish Card is often treated instrumentally for creating an opportunity to travel abroad. Paweł Ładykowski points out that such "national cards" have the effect of creating a division "of the neighbouring society according to an ethnic code, which is inadmissible from the perspective of European legislation". He states that the Card is a "legal instrument that interferes in the interests of foreign states, and must inevitably be met with resistance" (Ładykowski, 2011, pp. 36-39).

The Belarusian government has also acted as one of the apexes of the first version of the "Brubaker triangle", and has indirectly influenced the situation of the Belarusian minority in Poland. It is true that Belarusian organisations in Poland have not shown much interest in politics, but relations with them as leaders in the foreign homeland caused a split in Belarusian circles in Poland. The situation of that community is in many ways better than that of the Polish minority in Belarus, and in principle it would be difficult to accuse it of any breach of the provisions of the bilateral treaty on the protection of minorities. Yet the Belarusian authorities do nothing beyond the undertakings foreseen in the treaty and domestic legislation. They are not, for example, obliged to implement the provisions of the Council of Europe Framework Convention for the Protection of National Minorities, because Belarus does not belong to that organisation and is not a signatory of the Convention.

Belarusian national cultural organisations in Poland function essentially without any legal hindrances. They are all loyal to the Polish state, but differ in their relations with the Belarusian government. Yet this does not affect their relations with the Polish authorities, although certain problematic situations do occur. While they are not perfect, relations between the Belarusian minority in Poland and the Polish authorities have been much more positive than those between some of the Polish minority and the Belarusian authorities. At one point those positive relations were overshadowed by criminal proceedings against eleven members of the editorial board of *Niwa* Weekly[62], including some prominent figures of the Belarusian minority in Poland. The process was initiated in 2003 after the Supreme Audit Office of Poland reported certain violations by *Niwa*, mostly related to bookkeeping. Although in 2006 the trial ended witht he acquittal of all of the *Niwa* editors, the events harmed the image and cultural activities of Belarusian minority organisations (Yeliseyeu, 2017, pp. 164-165).

At the beginning of the 1990s, in what was then Białystok province, the Belarusian minority did have problems in having its presence recognised, and was faced with attempts to marginalize it politically and socially. Belarusians were deliberately marginalised during the post-communist period. In Bielsk Podlaski, for example, following the 1990 election, individuals with Belarusian-sounding surnames were sacked from the administration by the victorious local Solidarity on the basis that, in the United States, a new administration brings in a new team. In a session of council on 8 October 1990, the local Solidarity even questioned the existence of the minority, arguing that the Belarusians were native Poles who had converted to Orthodoxy under duress during the Partitions (Flemming, 2002, p. 540). The largest and most important Belarusian national cultural organisations in Poland include the Belarusian Social and Cultural Association (BSCA), founded in 1956, and the Belarusian Union of the Republic of Poland, which was founded at the beginning of Poland's democratic transformation (Nikitorowicz, 2010, pp. 277-278). Yet these still have problems with financing their activities. The aid they receive from the Polish Ministry of Culture is inadequate, covering only 10-20% of their needs (Łaskiewicz, 2005, p. 160). Nor can Belarusian organisations in Poland count on full support from Belarus, which does not have a systematic policy in place concerning fellow nationals abroad. Other than for education,

---

62 A newspaper for Belarusians in Poland published in Belarussian.

whatever aid is granted from time to time is done so on an *ad hoc* basis[63]. Yet even this limited support has political undertones. In the broader context, the Belarusian authorities do not treat the Belarusian minority in Poland holistically. As noted by Helena Głogowska, they only help those Belarusian organisations in Poland that, despite internal criticism, support Belarusian policy. The BSCA is one such organization. In May 2001, during the 2nd Belarusian National Folk Congress in Minsk, the long-time president of the organisation, Jan Syczewski, spoke critically of the transformation in Poland, but took a favourable view of the social, economic and political situation in Belarus: "In Belarus... the plundering of state assets is not permitted, and income is allocated for the needs of the whole society, and not just a handful of businessmen" (*Jan Syczewski, znany ze swoich kontrowersyjnych wypowiedzi chwalących sytuację na Białorusi, został członkiem zarządu województwa*, 2002). "I'm not particularly in favour of a concept of democracy built at someone's dictate. On this issue, Poland has gone too far... Belarus has become a very unpopular country for the very reason that it is charting its own course of development, and its own path to happiness" (Goliński, 2001). Such statements were not met with enthusiasm in Poland, including by the ruling Democratic Left Alliance government, because in the 1997-2001 term, Syczewski was a Member of Parliament from that group. Syczewski explained that "I spoke out of concern for my two homelands – Poland and Belarus" (*Jan Syczewski, znany ze swoich kontrowersyjnych wypowiedzi chwalących sytuację na Białorusi, został członkiem zarządu województwa*, 2002)[64]. His approval of the Belarusian government was certainly a factor in his being made a member of the Order of Francysk Skaryna, a state award of the Republic of Belarus[65].

---

63 It mainly covers organising cultural events or, say, the creation of the Belarusian Museum and Cultural Centre in Hajnówka by an association of the same name, which received a subsidy from the Ministry of Administration and Digitalisation (previously the Ministry of Internal Affairs and Administration) and financial support from the Belarusian embassy in Poland.

64 For such talk, Syczewski was reprimanded by a DLA party court, and his name did not appear on the list of DLA parliamentary candidates in the 2001 election. Syczewski ran for the Senate as an independent, but unsuccessfully.

65 The ceremony took place in February 2016 in Białystok on the 60th anniversary of the activities of the Belarusian Social and Cultural Association (BSCA). The award was presented by the Belarusian Ambassador to Poland, Aleksander Averyanov.

Yet, despite its efforts, the Belarusian Union of the Republic of Poland, which is critical of the Belarusian regime, is not granted aid (Głogowska, 2009, pp. 197-200). One of its leaders, Eugeniusz Wappa, was even prohibited from entering Belarus. The most important Belarusian-language periodical published in Poland, the weekly *Niwa*, cannot be distributed in Belarus. The Belarusian Union of the Republic of Poland cooperates with the Belarusian opposition and non-governmental organisations. Its leaders appear on *Radio Racja* and *Belsat* TV. Yet they can count on the support of only a small number of the urban Belarusian population, whereas the BSCA is popular among a majority of the Belarusian community in Poland (Barwiński, 2013, p. 18).

Belarusian organisations are legally entitled to represent the interests of the Belarusian minority nationally in the political sphere. However, in spite of the affirmative action of exempting national and ethnic minorities from the 5% election threshold requirement (*Ustawa z dnia 12 kwietnia 2001 r. Ordynacja wyborcza do Sejmu Rzeczypospolitej i do Senatu Rzeczypospolitej*, 2001), a lack of agreement among Belarusian organisations has meant that, rather than forming a joint list of candidates for parliament, candidates from the Belarusian community ran on several different lists; this split the minority vote, with the result that none of those candidates were elected. The role of representing the Belarusian minority in the Polish parliament went to candidates, and later, MPs, from other election committees (e.g. the Orthodox Election Committee, or national political parties). Belarusians in Poland are somewhat more effective in elections at the local level. In elections to the provincial parliament in Podlaskie province, where most Belarusians in Poland live, the community manages to win seats from national party lists, as well as positions as mayors of municipalities and towns, and as district and county councillors in Podlaskie province.

Despite organisational, political and financial problems, Belarusian communities in Poland are actively involved in publishing activities[66], for which they receive state aid. An important role in preserving Belarusian identity is played by the Orthodox Church and its press, because a clear majority of Belarusians identify with Orthodoxy and are loyal to the Pol-

---

66 The best-known magazines are: *Niva, Kharadotskiia naviny*, the bilingual *Czasopis*, and *Belarusian Historical Notebooks*.

ish Autocephalous Orthodox Church[67]. The regional department of Polish Radio and Programme TV Białystok broadcast a weekly programme for minorities, including the Belarusian minority.

For every national minority, an issue of decisive importance to its survival as a distinct group is education, the use of and care for the mother tongue. In fact, a loss thereof does not necessarily mean a loss of identity, but linguistic conversation can be the first step towards total assimilation. Studying the Belarusian language is possible in Poland on the basis of conventions and international agreements accepted by Poland, and is conducted within the school system for national and ethnic minorities in Poland, which provides for the creation of schools: 1) in which the minority language is the language of instruction, 2) that are bilingual (some subjects taught in the minority language and some in Polish), 3) that provide additional courses in a given minority language. In the 2015/2016 academic year, there were 47 schools and outlets in Poland in which Belarusian was taught (2 preschools, 25 elementary schools, 17 middle schools and 3 high schools – in Bielsk Podlaski, Hajnówka and Białystok). Because of the local density of the Belarusian population, all of these schools are located in Podlaskie province in Białystok, Bielsk Podlaski, Hajnówka, Sokolski counties and the city of Białystok. In the 2015/2016 academic year, 3,140 students attended those schools. In a strategy for the development of Belarusian minority education in Poland prepared by the board of trustees in Białystok, numerous problems in education among the Belarusian minority are mentioned, such as: "a deepening demographic trough and increasing assimilation among youth, a lack of textbooks, a lack of didactic assistance, a lack of computer technology for learning one's own language, history and culture, as well as geography and regional education, a limitation of the teaching model to include the minority language only as a supplementary subject, a lack of continuity in Belarusian education from preschool to high school in places inhabited by the Belarusian minority". Solutions to these problems will require appropriate measures to be taken by government and local government administration.

The situations of the Polish minority in Belarus and the Belarusian minority in Poland are comparable, though the conditions under which the latter group functions are somewhat more favourable. A subjective com-

---

67 The monthly *Orthodox Review*, which contains a supplement in Belarusian "Sami pra siabie", co-financed with funds from the Ministry of Interior Affairs and the Prince Konstanty Ostrogski Foundation.

parison can be made on the basis of access to the minority school system, access to the mother tongue in the public arena, access to religious practices and representation in the structures of power. As to schooling for the minority, quantitatively (number of schools per population), Belarusian is taught as a minority language in Poland, but only as a supplementary subject; it is not used as a language of instruction. Whereas there are two schools in Belarus in which Polish, as a minority language, is also the language of instruction. This, of course, has both advantages and drawbacks. The use of a minority language as a language of instruction enables it to be more fully acquired without the need for excess technology. On the other hand, it can limit knowledge of the official state language, and hinder further education and career success. In the case of access to the mother tongue in the public arena, Belarusians in Poland are definitely ahead of Poles in Belarus. The international obligations resulting from Poland's having signed the Council of Europe Framework Convention for the Protection of Minority Rights and the application thereof in domestic law opened up the way for minority languages to be used as auxiliary languages in municipal administration, and as an additional writing system for traditional place names and buildings, as well as for streets, alongside the binding forms in the Polish language. This affects municipalities in which the number of inhabitants belonging to a given minority constitutes at least 20% of the population. In one municipality with a dominant Belarusian population – Orla – at the end of September 2011 bilingual place name signs were introduced (*Lista gmin wpisanych na podstawie art. 12 ustawy z dnia 6 stycznia 2005 r. o mniejszościach narodowych i etnicznych oraz o języku regionalnym (Dz. U. Nr 17, poz. 141, z późn. zm.) do Rejestru gmin, na których obszarze używane są nazwy w języku mniejszości,* 2017). Furthermore, in five municipalities (urban Hajnówka, rural Hajnówka, Czyże, Narewka and Orla) Belarusian has been introduced as an auxiliary language.

In terms of access to religious practices (most Poles in Belarus are Catholic, while most Belarusians in Poland are Orthodox), these are in principle guaranteed to an equal degree in each country. The situation is somewhat more favourable in Belarus, where Roman Catholic holidays (Christmas and Easter) are public holidays for all citizens. Orthodox believers in Poland have the statutory right to leave from work, which must be made up for. In schools and universities in Podlaskie province, as well as in some municipalities, Orthodox Christmas and Easter are usually public holidays.

As concerns the representation of minorities in the structures of power, as described above, the Belarusian minority in Poland has decidedly better conditions than those of the Polish minority in Belarus, and Belarusians in Poland could be even better represented in the legislature if they managed to organise themselves better.

Another significant problem in Polish-Belarusian relations, while not on the same scale as that of national minorities, is border and visa traffic.

3. Border and visa traffic

On the eve of entering the EU, Poland had to introduce short-term national visas for citizens of neighbouring states to the east, including Belarus. The visa requirements were quite simple, and visa fees for Belarusians were not high. When Poland joined the Schengen zone in December 2007, Polish consulates started issuing Schengen visas; the fees went up[68] and the procedures became more burdensome. This resulted in an almost four-fold decrease in the number of visas issued by Polish consulates in 2008 year on year, a "real collapse of the bilateral movement of persons" (Yeliseyeu, 2017, p. 165).

While visa procedures for Belarusian travelers to Poland have become much more costly and complicated in the last decade, in recent years Belarus has introduced a number of measures making travel to Belarus easier for nationals of Poland and other Western countries. One such solution was an understanding on small border traffic signed in 2010 by the Polish and Belarusian diplomatic heads, subsequently ratified by both parliaments and signed by presidents Bronisław Komorowski and Aleksander Lukashenko. In order for the understanding to enter into force, there must be an exchange of diplomatic notes between the two countries, which to date has not happened. Belarus fears the economic effects of the move: an increase in private imports from Poland and a drain of currency from the country. This is a justifiable fear in that Belarusians are interested in visiting Poland. Further, Belarus says that its border infrastructure is inadequate and may not be able to handle the increased flow of people

---

68 As long as Belarus did not have a visa facilitation agreement with the EU – and it still does not — the standard fee for a Schengen visa increased to EUR 60.

(*Białoruś: mały ruch graniczny z Polską bez przygotowania to katastrofa*, 2016)[69].

Within the 50-kilometre zone that should be affected by the small border traffic, about 920,000 people live at present. The Belarusian authorities will open the border to incoming foreign traffic, but are reluctant to open it to traffic of its own citizens going out. In the summer of 2015, visa-free travel was introduced for Polish tourists visiting the Białowieża Forest for up to 3 days. In October 2016, visa-free travel was expanded to include the Augustowski Canal, Grodno, and part of the Grodno region (Petrovskaya, 2017, p. 110). Poland, seeking to get small border traffic with Belarus going, has recently going beyond official channels to make use as well of the potential of civil society[70].

Furthermore, since February 2017 nationals of 80 countries, including all EU Member States, can enter Belarus visa-free through the Minsk airport for up to 5 days. Obviously, arrival by plane through Minsk is not the option of choice for most of the Poles wishing to visit Belarus. However, given that return plane ticket from Warsaw to Minsk can be bought in advance for around EUR 100, this could ease up travel for some Polish nationals who plan to make just a short trip to Belarus (Yeliseyeu, 2017, p. 166).

The existence of "difficult issues" has not entirely ruled out the possibility of economic cooperation, which has been growing, at varying rates, throughout the period considered here. An improvement in the political climate will no doubt favour faster development.

References

Arutiunian, Iu., Drobizheva, L. and Susokolov, A., 1999. *Ètnosotsiologiia*. Moskva: Aspekt-Press.

Barwiński M., 2013. Polish interstate realtions with Ukraine, Belarus and Lithuania after 1990 in the context of the situation of national minorities. *European Spatial Research and Policy*, 1(20), p. 5-26.

---

69 Poland, with EU help, may have to incur some of the costs of modernising Belarusian infrastructure.

70 In the summer of 2016, representatives of Belarus House in Warsaw and Hramadzianskaĭ Hrodzienshchyny ran information campaigns at border crossings, calling on Belarusians to support small border traffic.

Będzie porozumienie w sprawie Związku Polaków na Białorusi i Karty Polaka?, 05.12.2016. [online] Available at: <https://kresy.pl/wydarzenia/bedzie-porozumieni e-w-sprawie-zwiazku-polakow-na-bialorusi-i-karty-polaka/> [Accessed 19 September 2017].

Belorusskim chinovnikam zapreshcheno pol'zovat'sia kartoĭ poliaka, 11.02.2012. [online] Available at: <https://news.tut.by/society/273618.html> [Accessed 21 September 2017].

Białoruś: mały ruch graniczny z Polską bez przygotowania to katastrofa, 09.02.2016. [online] Available at: <http://wiadomosci.onet.pl/swiat/bialorus-maly-ruch-graniczn y-z-polska-bez-przygotowania-to-katastrofa/yw6kng> [Accessed 21 September 2017].

Bieleń S., 1997. Długa droga do przyszłości. *Wiadomości Kulturalne,* 51-52 (187-188), p. 17.

Brubaker, R., 1998. *Nacjonalizm inaczej. Struktura narodowa i kwestie narodowe w nowej Europie.* Warszawa–Kraków: Wydawnictwo Naukowe PWN.

Chałupczak, H., 2006. Liczba mniejszości narodowych i etnicznych w Polsce w świetle powszechnego spisu ludności z 2002 roku oraz badań naukowych. In: E. Michalik and H. Chałupczak, eds. *Mniejsości narodowe i etniczne w procesach transformacji oraz integracji,* Lublin 2006: Wydawnictwo Uniwersytetu Marii Curie-Skłodowskiej, pp. 263-270.

Chodubski, A., 2016. 70 lat do różnorodności. Mniejszości narodowe i etniczne w Polsce, *Studia Gdańskie. Wizje i rzeczywistość*, Vol. 13, pp. 395-408.

Czachor R., 2011. *Polityka zagraniczna Republiki Białoruś w latach 1991-2011. Studium politologiczne.* Polkowice: Wydawnictwo Dolnośląskiej Wyższej Szkoły Przedsiębiorczości i Techniki w Polkowicach.

Dzwonkowski, R., 2005. Sytuacja religijna Polaków na Białorusi. In: H. Chałupczak and E. Michalik,, eds. 2005. *Polska-Białoruś. Problemy sąsiedztwa.* Lublin: Wydawnictwo Uniwersytetu Marii Curie-Skłodowskiej, pp. 91-102.

Eberhardt, A., 2006. Polska a konflikt wokół Związku Polaków na Białorusi. *Rocznik Polskiej Polityki Zagranicznej.* Warszawa: Polski Instytut Spraw Międzynarodowych, pp. 258-266.

Eparkhi. Rimo-Katolicheskaya Cerkov' v Belarusi, 2017. [online] Available at: <http:// old.catholic.by/2/ru/belarus/dioceses.html> [Accessed 19 September 2017].

Flemming, M., 2002. The new minority rights regime in Poland: the experience of the German, Belarussian and Jewish minorities since 1989, *Nations and Nationalism"*, 8 (4), pp. 531-549.

Gawin, T., 2010. *Polskie odrodzenia na Białorusi 1988-2005.* Białystok: Wyższa Szkoła Administracji Publicznej im. Stanisława Staszica.

Giebień, H., 2014. *Działalność Związku Polaków na Białorusi w latach 1987-2005 na tle sytuacji społeczno-politycznej w Białoruskiej Socjalistycznej Republice Radzieckiej/Republice Białoruś.* Wrocław: Oficyna Wydawnicza Arboretum.

Głogowska H., 2009. Mniejszości narodowe w stosunkach polsko-białoruskich po 1989 roku. In: M. Mieczkowska and D. Scholze eds. 2009. *Polityczne wymiary etniczności.* Kraków: Wydawnictwo DANTE, pp. 181-205.

Goliński, C., 18.05. 2001. Poseł SLD gani Polskę na Białorusi, chwali władzę Łukaszenki. [online] Available at: <http://wiadomosci.gazeta.pl/wiadomosci/1,114873,280079.html> [Accessed 22 September 2017].

Gumilow, L., 1997. *Dzieje etnosów Wielkiego Stepu.* Przekład Andrzej Nowak. Kraków: Oficyna Literacka.

Habowski, M., 2009. Stosunki Białorusi z Polską. In: I. Topolski, ed. 2009. *Białoruś w stosunkach międzynarodowych.* Lublin: Wydawnictwo Uniwersytetu Marii Curie-Skłodowskiej, pp. 233-253.

Informacja o ustaleniach końcowych śledztwa S 28/02/Zi w sprawie pozbawienia życia 79 osób – mieszkańców powiatu Bielsk Podlaski w tym 30 osób tzw. furmanów w lesie koło Puchał Starych, dokonanych w okresie od dnia 29 stycznia 1946 r. do dnia 2 lutego 1946. Available at: <http://ipn.gov.pl/pl/dla-mediow/komunikaty/9989,Informacja-o-ustaleniach-koncowych-sledztwa-S-2802Zi-w-sprawie-pozbawienia-zycia.html> [Accessed 23 September 2017].

Iz stenogramy zasedaniia Orgbiuro TsK RKP(b) po voprosu o sostoianii i rabote KP(b) Belorussii, 4 noiabria 1925, 2005. In: L. Gatagova, L. Kosheleva and L. Rogovaia, eds. 2005. *TsK RKP(b)-VKP(b) i natsional'nyi vopros. Kniga 1.* 1918-1933. Moskva: ROSSPEN, pp. 334-346.

Jackson-Preece, J., 2007. *Prawa mniejszości.* Przełożyła Małgorzata Stolarska. Warszawa: Wydawnictwo Sic!

Jak uczy się języka polskiego na Białorusi. Liczby i fakty, 2017. [online] Available at: <http://poland.mfa.gov.by/pl/embassy/news/f5026a6dfa11ae10.html> [Accessed 23 September 2017].

Jan Syczewski, znany ze swoich kontrowersyjnych wypowiedzi chwalących sytuację na Białorusi, został członkiem zarządu województwa, 02.12.2002. [online] Available at: <http://www.wspolczesna.pl/aktualnosci/art/5215490,jan-syczewski-znany-ze-swoich-kontrowersyjnych-wypowiedzi-chwalacych-sytuacje-na-bialorusi-zostal-czlonkiem-zarzadu-wojewodztwa,id,t.html> [Accessed 22 September 2017].

Janusz, G., 2005. Mniejszość białoruska w Polsce i polska na Białorusi. In: H. Chałupczak and E. Michalik, eds. 2005. *Polska-Białoruś. Problemy sąsiedztwa.* Lublin: Wydawnictwo Uniwersytetu Marii Curie Skłodowskiej, pp. 53-78.

Kabzińska, I., 2012. Od euforii do lęku. Polacy w Republice Białorusi. In: M. Głowacka-Grajper and R. Wyszyński, eds. 2012. *20 lat rzeczywistości poradzieckiej. Spojrzenie socjologiczne.* Warszawa: Wydawnictwa Uniwersytetu Warszawskiego, pp. 317-336.

Konwencja Ramowa o ochronie mniejszości narodowych, sporządzona w Strasburgu dnia 1 lutego 1995 r., 2002. Dziennik Ustaw Rzeczypospolitej Polskiej [Journal of Laws], 22, item, 209.

Kruchkovskiĭ, T., 2011. Belorussko-pol'skie otnosheniia: polityko-natsional'nyĭ aspekt. In: *Belorussiia i Ukraina: istoriia i ku'ltura.* Vyp.4. Moskva: TEZAURUS, pp. 472-503.

Liczebność polskiej diaspory, 2017. [online] Available at: <http://www.polskinetwork. org/strona,polacy,31,liczebnosc-polskiej-diaspory.html>http://www.belstat.gov.by/i nformatsiya-dlya-respondenta/perepis-naseleniya/perepis-naseleniya-2009-goda/vy hodnye-reglamentnye-tablitsy/natsionalnyi-sostav-naseleniya-grazhdanstvo/ >[Accessed 19 September 2017]

"Likwidacja polskich szkół i rusyfikacja". *Związek Polaków o reformie edukacji na Białorusi*, 17.03.2017. [online] Available at: <http://www.polsatnews.pl/wiadomosc /2017-03-21/likwidacja-polskich-szkol-i-rusyfikacja-zwiazek-polakow-o-reformie-e dukacji-na-bialorusi/> [Accessed 21 September 2017].

Lista gmin wpisanych na podstawie art. 12 ustawy z dnia 6 stycznia 2005 r. o mniejszościach narodowych i etnicznych oraz o języku regionalnym (Dz. U. Nr 17, poz. 141, z późn. zm.) do Rejestru gmin, na których obszarze używane są nazwy w języku mniejszości, 2017. Available at: <http://mniejszosci.narodowe.mswia.gov.pl/mne/re jestry/rejestr-gmin/6794,Rejestr-gmin-na-ktorych-obszarze-sa-uzywane-nazwy-w-jezyku-mniejszosci.html> [Accessed 23 September 2017].

Ładykowski, P., 2011. Gra w karty. „Karta narodowa" jako stawka w państwowej polityce narodowościowej. In: W. Dohnal and A. Posern-Zieliński, eds. 2011. *Antropologia i polityka. Szkice z badań nad kulturowymi wymiarami władzy*. Warszawa: Wydawnictwo IAE PAN, pp. 15-41.

Łaskiewicz, W., 2005. Tożsamość i kultura w działalności Białoruskiego Towarzystwa Społeczno-Kulturalnego w Polsce. In: H. Chałupczak and E. Michalik, eds. 2005. *Polska-Białoruś. Problemy sąsiedztwa*. Lublin: Wydawnictwo Uniwersytetu Marii Curie Skłodowskiej, pp. 155-160.

Łodziński, S., 2002. *Ochrona praw osób należących do mniejszości narodowych i etnicznych – perspektywa europejska*. Kancelaria Sejmu, Biuro Studiów i Ekspertyz, 208(2002), pp. 1-39.

Łodziński, S., 2004. *Międzynarodowe standardy ochrony i wspierania mniejszości narodowych. Instytucje oraz organizacje powołane do ochrony mniejszości*. Materiał konferencyjny.

Martin, T., 2001. *The Affirmative Action Empire. Nations and Nationalism in the Soviet Union*, 1923-1939. New York: Cornell University Press.

Ministerstwo Edukacji Białorusi nie zmienia nastawienia do polskich szkół, 18.06.2017. Available at: <https://kresy.pl/wydarzenia/kresy/ministerstwo-edukacji-bialorusi-zmienia-nastawienia-wobec-polskich-szkol/> [Accessed 21 September 2017].

MSZ Białorusi o sprawie Marka Bućki, 18.05.2005. [online] Available at: <https://wia domosci.wp.pl/msz-bialorusi-o-sprawie-marka-bucki-6032047141983361a [Accessed 21 September 2017].

Naselenie po natsional'nosti i rodnomu iazyku. Respublika Belarus', 2009. [online]Available at: <http://www.belstat.gov.by/upload-belstat/upload-belstat-pdf/pere pis_2009/5.8-0.pdf> [Accessed 19 September 2017].

Natsional'naia akademiia nauk Belarusi. Institut istorii, 2014. *Rizhskiĭ mir v sud'be belorusskogo naroda 1921-1953 gg*. Minsk: «Belaruskaia navuka», Vol.1.

Natsional'nyĭ sostav naseleniia, grazhdanstvo, 2009. [online] Available at: <http://ww w.belstat.gov.by/informatsiya-dlya-respondenta/perepis-naseleniya/perepis-naseleni ya-2009-goda/vyhodnye-reglamentnye-tablitsy/natsionalnyi-sostav-naseleniya-graz hdanstvo/>[Accessed 19 September 2017].

Nikitorowicz, J., 2010. *Grupy etniczne w wielokulturowym świecie.* Sopot: Gdańskie Wydawnictwo Psychologiczne Sp. z o.o.

Oświadczenie Ministerstwa Spraw Zagranicznych RP ws. uznania przez władze Repu-bliki Białorusi za persona non grata Kierownika Wydziału Konsularnego Ambasady RP w Mińsku, 2005. Available at: <http://bbb.livejournal.com/1310256.html?thread =6167344> [Accessed 3 September 2017].

Polovina „kart poliaka" wydana grazhdanam Belarusi, 20.08.2017. [online] Available at: <https://www.eurointegration.com.ua/rus/news/2017/08/20/7069975/view_print /> [Accessed 3 September 2017].

Polscy i białoruscy historycy rozpoczęli dialog o „sprawach trudnych", 2017. [online] Available at: <http://kresy.pl/wydarzenia/spoleczenstwo/polscy-bialoruscy-historyc y-rozpoczeli-dialog-o-sprawach-trudnych/> [Accessed 3 September 2017].

Raspredelenie naselenia Respubliki Belarus' po natsionalnostiam i iazykam v 1999 go-du, 1999. [online] Available at: <http://www.belstat.gov.by/informatsiya-dlya-respo ndenta/perepis-naseleniya/perepis-naseleniya-1999-goda/tablichnye-dannye/raspred elenie-naseleniya-respubliki-belarus-po-natsionalnostyam-i-yazykam-v-1999-godu/ >[Accessed 19 September 2017].

Rotfield, A.D., 2006. Informacja rządu na temat polskiej polityki zagranicznej w 2005 roku (przedstawiona przez ministra spraw zagranicznych Adama Daniela Rotfelda na posiedzeniu Sejmu w dniu 21 stycznia 2005 roku). In: *Rocznik Polskiej Polityki Zagranicznej*, pp. 9 -21.

Rotschild J., 1981. *Ethnopolitics. A Conceptual Framework.* New York: Columbia University Press.

Rudkoŭski, P., 2007. *Paustan'nie Belarusi.* Vil'nia: Instytut belarusistyki.

Smith, A. D., 2009. *Etniczne źródła narodów.* Przekład Małgorzata Głowacka-Grajper. Kraków: Wydawnictwo Uniwersytetu Jagiellońskiego.

Strategia rozwoju oświaty mniejszości białoruskiej w Polsce, 2014. Białystok. [online] Available at: <http://lozbjn.edu.pl/upload/aktualnosci2013_2014/Strategia_rozwoju _mb.pdf> [Accessed 23 September 2017].

Tishkov, V., Shabaev Iu., 2011. *Ètnopolitologiia. Politicheskie funktsii ètnichnosti.* Moskva: Izdatel'stvo Moskovskogo universiteta.

Ukaz Prezidenta Respubliki Belarus' ot 26 marta 1998 goda Nr 157 O gosudarstven-nykh prazdnikakh prazdnichnykh dniakh i pamiatnykh datakh v Resublike Belarus', 1998. [online] Available at: <https://online.zakon.kz/document/?doc_id=31255067# pos=0;279> [Accessed 18 September 2017].

Urzędowy rejestr gmin, w których używany jest język pomocniczy, 2017. Available at: <https://bip.mswia.gov.pl/bip/wyznania-i-mniejszosci/23923,Urzedowy-Rejestr-Gmin-w-ktorych-jest-uzywany-jezyk-pomocniczy.html >[Accessed 18 September 2017].

Ustawa z dnia 12 kwietnia 2001 r. Ordynacja wyborcza do Sejmu Rzeczypospolitej Polskiej i do Senatu Rzeczypospolitej Polskiej, 2001. Dziennik Ustaw Rzeczypospolitej Polskiej [Journal of Laws],46, item 499. Available at: <http://isap.sejm.g ov.pl/DetailsServlet?id=WDU20010460499>[Accessed 21 September 2017].

Ustawa z dnia 6 stycznia 2005 r. o mniejszościach narodowych i etnicznych oraz o języku regionalnym, 2005. Dziennik Ustaw Rzeczypospolitej Polskiej [Journal of Laws], 17, item 141.

Ustawa z dnia 7 września 2007 r. o Karcie Polaka, 2007. Dziennik Ustaw Rzeczypospolitej Polskiej [Journal of Laws],180, item 1280. Available at: <http://isap.sejm.go v.pl/DetailsServlet?id=WDU20071801280>[Accessed 21 September 2017].

Waszkiewicz, J., 2005. Mniejszość polska w stosunkach polsko-białoruskich. In: H. Chałupczak and E. Michalik, eds. 2005. *Polska Białoruś. Problemy sąsiedztwa.* Lublin: Wydawnictwo Uniwersytetu Marii Curie-Skłodowskiej, pp. 45-52.

Wierzbicki, A., 2008. Mniejszości narodowe i etniczne w Polsce. Status prawno-konstytucyjny. In: W. Jakubowski and T. Słomka, eds. 2008. *Porządek konstytucyjny w Polsce. Wybrane problemy.* Warsaw-Pułtusk: Oficyna Wydawnicza ASPRA-JR, pp. 225-244.

Władze Białorusi ograniczają nauczanie języka polskiego, 2015. [online] Available at: <https://kresy.pl/wydarzenia/wladze-bialorusi-ograniczaja-nauke-jezyka-polskiego-foto/> [Accessed 18 September 2017].

Wyniki Narodowego Spisu Powszechnego Ludności i Mieszkań 2011 Podstawowe informacje o sytuacji demograficzno-społecznej ludności Polski oraz zasobach mieszkaniowych, marzec 2012. [online] Available at: <http://stat.gov.pl/cps/rde/xbcr/gus/l u_nps2011_wyniki_nsp2011_22032012.pdf> [Accessed 18 September 2017].

Yeliseyeu A., 2017. The Poland–Belarus relationship: Geopolitics gave new impetus, but no breakthrough. In: A. Kudors, ed. 2017. *Belarusian Foreign Policy: 360°*. Rīga: University of Latvia Press, The Centre for East European Policy Studies. Available at: <http://appc.lv/wp-content/uploads/2017/05/book_Belarusian_360-w ww-2.pdf> [Accessed 7 September 2017].

Zakon Respubliki Belarus' ot 5 ianvaria 2004 g. Nr 261-3 „O vnesenii izmenenii i dopolnenii v Zakon Respubliki Belarus' „O natsional'nykh men'shinstvakh v Respublike Belarus', 2004. Available at: <http://pravo.levonevsky.org/bazaby09/sbor37/text 37853.htm> [Accessed 19 September 2017].

Żołędowski, C., 2003. *Białorusini i Litwini w Polsce, Polacy na Białorusi i Litwie. Uwarunkowania współczesnych stosunków między większością i mniejszościami narodowymi.* Warszawa: Oficyna Wydawnicza ASPRA-JR.

Chapter 5 Economic relations

Poland and Belarus attach a lot of importance to economic cooperation, which is enhanced by the "recreation" of political relations discussed in the preceding chapters. This is reflected in, for example, the following statement by the Belarusian President Aleksander Lukashenko: "We must work very seriously to develop neighbourly relations with Poland, above all with regard to commercial and economic ties. When there is economy, politics will follow. What is most important today is to increase exports of Belarusian products. With Polish partners, one can reach an agreement and trade normally" (Esin, 2016, p. 183).

1. The legal and treaty foundations of economic cooperation

If Polish-Belarusian political relations had continuously developed at the same rate over the years, economic cooperation between the two states would be even more advanced today than it is. Economic relations between states are normally determined by their political relations, but the proximity of Poland and Belarus and their economic interests have ensured that both countries have striven to keep up economic cooperation. Mention of "mutually beneficial economic cooperation" already appeared in the treaty of 1992, where Article 18 states: "The Parties will foster mutually beneficial economic cooperation, striving to preserve and develop traditional economic and commercial ties, taking account of the needs and real possibilities of the two States, based on market economy principles. The Parties will create suitable economic, financial, fiscal and legal conditions, including for the development of entrepreneurship. They will support and protect investments, will comply with copyright and patent standards, and will facilitate the flow of goods, services, labour and capital across their common border. The Parties will facilitate the development of direct cooperation between state and private enterprises and other economic entities, and will exchange experience and provide each other with training and other assistance in the process of creating a market economy" (*Traktat między Rzecząpospolitą Polską a Republiką Białoruś o dobrym sąsiedztwie i przyjaznej współpracy*, 1992). Apart from the treaty laying out a general framework of cooperation in the 1990s, a series of agreements and understandings were concluded to regulate economic relations, including: inter-governmental agreements on the avoidance of double taxation (18 November 1992) and on mutual support for and protection of investments (24 April 1992).

Since Poland's accession to the EU, the country's economic cooperation with Belarus has been regulated by the Trade Agreement between the EU and the USSR from 1989, whose provisions extended to new EU Member States. An agreement on partnership and cooperation signed by the EU and Belarus was ratified by Belarus, but not by the EU, and so never entered into force.

On 30 April 2004, an Agreement between the Government of the Republic of Poland and the Government of the Republic of Belarus on Economic Cooperation was signed, whose provisions do not conflict with EU competencies. That agreement provided a legal basis for appointing a new Polish-Belarusian Joint Commission for Economic Cooperation. To date, there have been four sessions of the Commission, the first on 14 April 2008 in Warsaw, the second on 14 January 2010 in Minsk, the third on 1 December 2014 in Warsaw, and the fourth in the autumn of 2016. Since July 2010, Belarus has been a member of the Belarus-Russia-Kazakhstan Customs Union, and of the Common Economic Area established by those countries, which began to function on 1 January 2015. On that same date, Belarus entered into the Eurasian Economic Union.

2. Trade

In the first few years after the collapse of the USSR, Belarus was in dire need of highly processed goods from Western countries, and this caused its imports to grow faster than its export, resulting in a negative trade balance. In 1992, Poland became Belarus's main trade partner outside the CIS, and the third largest partner apart from Russia and Ukraine. The two countries's mutual turnover was not impressive, at USD 300 million in total. Poland absorbed 16.5% of Belarusian exports, and provided 20.9% of its imports. Poland exported grain, sugar, potatoes, textiles, dyes, plastics, cosmetics and pharmaceuticals, as well as passenger cars. Its most important imports from Belarus were oil-derived products, textiles, fertilisers, household products, tools, and electric machines. In 1993, the value of mutual trading fell by one third. In trade relations, an important role was played by the Chamber of Commerce, the Polish-Belarusian Association, the Polish-Belarusian Society, and the Polish-Belarusian Mixed Commission for Economic and Commercial Cooperation (Głogowska, 2012, p. 402).

In June 1993, Michaił Miasnikowicz, the Belarusian Vice Premier for the Economy, paid a visit to Poland, as a result of which the two countries signed a letter of intent on cooperation on the construction of the Berlin-Warsaw-Minsk-Moscow motorway. In 1993, the Polish-Belarusian Chamber of Commerce (PBCC) was founded. The PBCC organised an annual "Good Neighbours" Polish-Belarusian Economic Forum, as well as seminars, conferences, trainings, economic missions, volunteer work and work traineeships. Economic relations up to 1994 can be seen as a period of missed opportunities. The economic relations during that time were limited to the signing of a number of understandings and relatively low levels of trade. Yet, it should be emphasised that those first steps in establishing cooperation were very important in that they provided the foundation for later developments.

In the years 1996-2000, during the critical dialogue that Poland conducted towards Belarus, and in view of the latter's internal situation, the level of economic relations between the countries declined drastically, even though mutual turnover increased up to USD 540.8 million (including exports of USD 319.2 million and imports of USD 221.6 million) in 1997. Belarus was Poland's third-largest trading partner among former Soviet states, after Russia and Ukraine, while for Belarus, Poland was its second-largest partner outside the CIS after Germany. Polish exports at that time were dominated by agricultural and food products and electric machines for industry, while imports were dominated by mineral products. Up to 1997, growth in mutual trading was seen. Poland had a positive trade balance with Belarus. The crisis in Russia at the end of the 1990s adversely affected trade between Poland and Belarus, but the situation began to improve in the year 2000. After a number of fluctuations in which the value of Belarusian exports prevailed over imports, which resulted in a negative trade balance for Poland, in the most recent period the situation has again begun to change in favour of Poland. The development of Polish-Belarusian economic relations is to a large extent determined by the countries' complicated political relations. Yet, after the year 2000, trade cooperation has grown much faster than the bilateral relations between the two states. Economic relations in areas near the border are the most significant and of most interest to Polish entrepreneurs and investors. In the period 2008-2013, the economic sphere was characterised by a relative standstill in Polish-Belarusian relations. It is worth emphasising the lack of engagement on both sides at the highest level in establishing inter-state economic regulations, initiating new ideas in trade and the exchange of goods, or implementing innovative economic solutions. In 2016, 40.7% of the total value of bilateral trade constituted Belarusian exports to Poland, and 59.3% imports from Poland (*Struktura vneshneĭ torgovli tovarami Respubliki Belarus' s otdel'nymi stranami v 2016 godu*, 2016).

Poland is a more important trading partner for Belarus than Belarus is for Poland. In terms of Poland's total foreign trade turnover, Belarus stands in 29th place, in terms of export value in 25th place, and in terms of imports in 36th place (*Statistical Yearbook of the Republic of Poland*, 2016, pp. 565-568). Poland's most important export trade partners are Germany, Great Britain and the Czech Republic, and it imports mainly from Germany, China and Russia[71], whereas, in 2015, Poland was in 6th place in Belarus's overall trade balance. Belarusian exports to Poland amounted to USD 767 million, and imports from Poland exceeded USD 1 million. Belarus, then, had a negative trade balance with Poland. The value of trade turnover with Poland was 3.2% of Belarus's total foreign trade (Table 1). Poland was Belarus's 8th-largest partner in terms of exports, and 4th in terms of imports.

Table 1. Value and structure of Belarus foreign trade (in millions of USD) in 2015

Country	Export	Import	Turnover	Balance	Share %
1. Russia	10,389.1	17,144.2	27,533.3	-6,755.1	48.3%
2. Ukraine	2,520.8	950.0	3,470.8	1,570.8	6.1%
3. China	781.6	2,399.6	3,181.2	-1,618.0	5.6%
4. Great Britain	2,981.3	176.2	3,157.5	2,805.1	5.5%
5. Germany	1,086.50	1,385.0	2,471.5	-298.5	4.3%
6. Poland	**767.0**	**1,082.1**	**1,849.1**	**-315.1**	**3.2%**
7. Holland	1,157.5	211.1	1,368.6	946.4	2.4%
8. Lithuania	964.4	277.7	1,242.1	686.7	2.2%

Source: Statisticheskiĭ ezhegodnik, 2016, p. 476.

---

71 By current prices in millions of zlotys.

Table 2. Value and structure of Belarus exports (in millions of USD) in 2015

Country	Export	Share %
1. Russia	10,389.1	38.9%
2. Great Britain	2,981.3	11.2%
3. Ukraine	2,520.8	9.4%
4. Holland	1,157.5	4.3%
5. Germany	1,086.50	4.1%
6. Lithuania	964.4	3.6%
7. China	781.6	2.9%
8. Poland	**767.0**	**2.9%**

Source: Statisticheskiĭ ezhegodnik, 2016, p. 476.

Table 3. Value and structure of Belarus imports (in millions of USD) in 2015

Country	Import	Share %
1. Russia	17,144.2	56.6%
2. China	2,399.6	7.9%
3 .Germany	1,385.0	4.6%
4. Poland	**1,082.1**	**3.6%**
5. Ukraine	950.0	3.1%
6. Italy	636.6	2.1%
7. Turkey	487.8	1.6%
8. USA	445.6	1.5%

Source: Statisticheskiĭ ezhegodnik, 2016, p. 476.

One positive tendency is the systematic growth in the value of trade between the two countries despite short-term fluctuations[72] (Table 4) such as usually occur when political relations worsen, e.g. in connection with the Belarusian elections in 2010 and the initial problems relating to the implementation of Eurasian integration.

---

72 Even in the year 2000, the value of trade turnover between the two countries was slightly over USD 500 million.

Table 4. Growth rate of Belarusian exports to Poland in the years
2000-2016 (in millions of USD)

Year	2000	2002	2005	2007	2008	2010	2011	2012	2013	2014	2015	2016
Value	276.8	273.3	847.3	1,226.2	1,798.4	885.8	1,124.8	949.7	781.8	843.9	766.3	814.5

Source: Èksport iz Respubliki Belarus' po otdel'nym stranam vne SNG, 2017.

Table 5. Growth rate of Belarusian imports from Poland in the years
2000-2016 (in millions of USD)

Year	2000	2002	2005	2007	2008	2010	2011	2012	2013	2014	2015	2016
Value	223.8	221.8	578.9	819.1	1,154.9	1,079.8	1,289.2	1,349.2	1,581.5	1,535.0	1,085.8	1 185,2

Source: Import tovarov v Respubliku Belarus' po otdel'nym stranam vne SNG, 2017.

In the structure of Polish exports to Belarus, machines and tools, electric and electrotechnical equipment, and agricultural and food products (meat, fruit, vegetables) dominate, while in the structure of Polish imports from Belarus, fuels, electricity and chemical products are at the fore (*Potencjał MSP w handlu ze Wschodem – szanse na dynamiczny rozwój współpracy handlowej z krajami post-radzieckimi*, 2006, pp. 33-37). In the years 2014-2016, as a result of economic sanctions imposed by the European Union on Russia and ensuing sanctions by Russia against the EU (in response to the events in Ukraine), exports of Polish agricultural products (particularly fruit, vegetables and milk) to Belarus increased. After the EU countries, Belarus became Poland's largest market for farming products.

Alongisde these positive aspects of the economic relations between the two countries, certain adverse phenomena also exist. During a visit to Belarus in March 2016, the Polish Foreign Minister, Witold Waszczykowski, expressed his dismay at the ban on imports of pork from Poland. Polish pork producers are interested in having access to the Belarusian market (*Pol'skiĭ agrarnyĭ biznes gotov investirovat' v Belarus', no ozhidaet garantiĭ*, 2016). Moreover, infrastructural barriers exist, such as the poor condition of border crossings, which severely limits trade and transport in both directions. In order to solve this problem, Poland invested in building a terminal in Horoszczyce and in expanding the border crossing in Bobrowniki. Yet Belarus made no investments at all on its side of the border, which to a large extent put a halt to any increase in the economy and bilateral trade turnover. The weakness of local government authorities in Belarus poses a serious barrier, for they are able to enter into cooperation with neighbouring regions solely upon the consent of the central powers in Minsk.

3. Investment and capital cooperation

Poland and Belarus are mutually attractive economic partners, for a number of reasons. Firstly, investments in the Polish or Belarusian markets open the door to the market of the European Union (500 million consumers), and the countries of the Joint Economic Zone (Belarus, Russia, Kazakhstan and Armenia – 180 million consumers), as well as to other countries of the CIS and Ukraine (280 million consumers in total). Secondly, investments in Belarus encourage an investment and taxation climate that is competition-friendly, including customs and tax relief for businesses run within six special economic zones, a High Technology Park and the Chinese-Belarusian "Great Stone" Industrial Park. An additional incentive is the possibility of locating foreign investments in small and medium-sized businesses. Thirdly, as a nexus between the countries of the CIS and those of the EU, Belarus has a well-developed transport infrastructure, which is of enormous importance to foreign investors. A similar role is played by Poland. And fourthly, both countries have highly-qualified managers who are able to work in various branches of the economy.

As early as 1992, about 300 joint ventures with the participation of Polish capital were registered in Belarus. They constituted about 20% of foreign investment in Belarus, and about 40% of businesses with a share of foreign capital. Near the end of 1992, the Belarusian government decided to privatise state companies; according to the plan, this was to take from 5 to 10 years to accomplish. However, economic reform in Belarus moved more slowly than in Poland, due to difficulties during the transition period and the need to maintain ties with the countries of the CIS. These different paces of reform hindered economic cooperation between the two countries, which remained below expectations. The total direct Polish investment in Belarus from the beginning of 1991 is estimated as being about USD 360 million. In terms of quantity, in 2015 Poland was in 9th place in foreign investments in Belarus (in 2014 – 10th place). In 2015, USD 136.9 million of Polish investments flowed into Belarus.

In 1998, there was a weakening in economic cooperation. This was caused by the economic crisis in Belarus and by the growing difficulties the uncompetitive Belarusian economy was having with payments. In the second half of the year, Polish companies began withdrawing from the Belarusian market because they were increasingly fearful of the lack of stability, the high level of risk on the market, and the above-mentioned payment difficulties. These adverse tendencies could be halted only by radical changes in the rules of how the Belarusian economy operated, and such changes did not seem realistic in the foreseeable future. In 1999, there was a further drop in trade of 30%, and more Polish companies withdrew from the Belarusian market. The only office of a Polish bank in Belarus was closed down. The sole positive development in that year was when the National Bank of Belarus recognised the Polish zloty as an exchangeable currency; this made it easier to settle transactions between economic entities in Poland and Belarus. In the year 2000, the two sides made serious efforts to establish bilateral cooperation. In June, the municipal authorities of Białystok and Grodno signed an Agreement on Direction for Economic Cooperation to 2003, and in Minsk the Polish-Belarusian Agricultural and Food Cooperation Forum was established. The Belarusian and Polish authorities began implementing an understanding concerning the main directions for cooperation as agreed at one of the sessions of a bilateral special commission. In Brest in November, the seventh annual "Good Neighbours" economic seminar was organised, attended by 350 representatives from Poland, Belarus, Ukraine and Russia. In December, a session of the Polish-Belarusian Mixed Commission for Economic and Trade Cooperation was held.

In 2001, about 250 production and trading companies were active in Belarus, as well as 137 companies with 100% Polish capital, at a level of USD 14 million. In 2002, the number of Polish-Belarusian production and trading companies remained the same. Belarus became Poland's 4th-largest partner (after Russia, Ukraine and Lithuania) in terms of trade turnover among post-Soviet countries.

After Poland's accession to the EU in 2004, economic cooperation between Poland and Belarus began to be largely regulated by the standards and provisions of EU law. This resulted in restrictions on certain types of Belarusian production, regulations on customs tariffs, requirements concerning production standards, etc. In the Agreement between the Government of the Republic of Poland and the Government of the Republic of Belarus on Economic Cooperation, it was stipulated that "The Parties will foster mutually beneficial economic cooperation in all areas and sectors of the economy on the principles of equality, mutual benefit and in compliance with the law binding in the States of the Parties. The goals of the cooperation undertaken within the framework of this agreement are: 1) to use economic potential to strengthen bilateral economic relations, 2) to intensify bilateral economic relations, particularly within the sphere of investing in and financing economic enterprises, 3) to expand transport and industrial infrastructure, 4) to develop inter-regional economic cooperation" (*Umowa między Rządem Rzeczypospolitej Polskiej a Rządem Republiki Białoruś o współpracy gospodarczej*, 2004). On the basis of the Agreement, a Joint Polish-Belarusian Commission for Economic Cooperation was established. Its tasks include: "1) to conduct periodic reviews and evaluations of economic cooperation, 2) to prepared proposals aimed at the further development of economic cooperation, 3) to identify organisational problems hindering the development of economic cooperation and to propose appropriate measures to eliminate these, 4) to discuss contentious issues concerning the application or interpretation of this agreement" (*Umowa między Rządem Rzeczypospolitej Polskiej a Rządem Republiki Białorusi o współpracy gospodarczej*, 2004). The Commission should assemble at least once per year, and is composed of representatives of both sides. Polish companies are most active in the construction industry, medicinal products, rail modernisation, and bulk trade (construction materials). The value of direct Polish investments in Belarus in 2015 was about USD 195 million. Poland is in 7th place in terms of investment quantity in the Belarusian economy. Well over 300 businesses with Polish capital exist in Belarus (including more than 200 joint ventures)[73], while in Poland there are 17 offices representing Belarusian businesses[74]. In 2014, in Plonsk, Poland, the official opening was held of an assembly plant for trucks of the MAZ brand (*Minskiĭ avtomobil'nyĭ zavod. Sborochnoe proizvodstvo tekhniki MAZ otkryto v Pol'she*, 2016), while in Podlaskie province, the distributor MTZ Belarus Traktor sp. z o.o. was registered (*MTZ Belarus Traktor sp. z o.o.*, 2016).

Cross-border cooperation has a beneficial effect not only on economic relations, but also on Polish-Belarusian relations in general.

---

73 Among the largest companies with Polish capital active in Belarus are: VOX, Atlas, Getin Holding, Idea Bank, and Black Red White.

74 Including Bielneftechim, BielAZ, Belarus Potassium Company, Belavia Belarusian Airlines, and Belarusian Rail.

4. Cross-border cooperation

The goal of cooperation is "to bring local communities closer together through joint activities aimed at supporting economic, social and cultural development, initiating contacts among various types of institutions – centres of local government, education, sports, culture, environmental protection, and others" (Iwanow, 2008, p. 131). Provinces that are active in promoting bilateral cross-border cooperation are Lubelski province with the Brest region, and Podlaskie province with the Grodno region. Cross-border cooperation between Poland and Belarus is based on the European Outline Convention for Transfrontier Cooperation between Territorial Communities or Authorities of 21 May 1980, signed in Madrid and later ratified by the Polish government. In order to effectively develop standards pertaining to cross-border cooperation, bilateral international commissions are created to regulate cross-border activities. International documents have made it possible to revitalise bilateral contacts, including through the creation and functioning of the Polish-Belarusian Intergovernmental Coordination Commission for Cross-border Cooperation. On 25-26 November 1998, the second session of that commission was held in Białystok, during which the following tasks were established:

– to coordinate work on agreeing the water balance of the Narew river in connection with the construction of the Siemianówka water reservoir
– to efficiently circulate information on depots of hazardous substances and waste and on environmental threats that arise
– to identify trans-border areas that are under protection and to improve the state of the natural environment in border areas
– to develop an effective methodology for providing information on binding regulations in cross-border trade on either side of the border, and for providing assistance in organising fairs, exhibitions and other promotional events, as well as seminars and trainings
– to support coordination among schools and educational outlets organising school and youth exchanges and sports and cultural events" (Kraska, 2006, pp. 7-8).

In order to expand bilateral cross-border cooperation, what are known as Euroregions were created. Three Euroregions are located across the Polish-Belarusian border: the Bug, the Neman, and the Białowieża Forest.

Euroregion Bug was created in September 1995 in Lutsk, Ukraine, and includes terrain in Poland (Lubelski province), Belarus (the Brest Region since 1998) and Ukraine (Volyn Oblast and two areas of Lviv Oblast). The purpose of the Euroregion is to enhance cooperation in areas near the borders of the three states in the areas of transport, communication, the construction of new border crossings, zoning, healthcare, education, culture, sports and tourism, the prevention and remedy of natural disasters, protection and improvement of the natural environment, and the development of cooperation among economic entities near the border. In spite of the work put in by the parties involved in the Euroregion Bug and the initial assumptions for developing cooperation at an equal level, there is no doubt that Poland has cooperated more intensively with Ukraine than with Belarus. This is because of differences in the political situations in those countries, undoubtedly affected by geopolitics.

Euroregion Neman was created under a trilaterial understanding between Poland, Belarus and Lithuania signed in June 1997 in Augustów. The goal was to integrate communities near the borders, to catch up economically, socially and politically in relation to EU countries, and to develop local democracy. This Euroregion includes: on the Polish side – local governments of Podlaskie and Warmian-Masurian Provinces; on the Lithuanian side – the regions of Alytus, Mariampol and Vilnius; on the Belarusian side – Grodno Region; and on the Russian side – Kaliningrad Oblast (since 2002). Cross-border cooperation within Euroregion Neman is conducted mainly within the scope of the economy and trade, creating links between Western and Eastern countries to facilitate trade; exchanging goods and services; developing public infrastructure, forestry and agriculture; environmental protection and waste management; cooperation on culture, sports and tourism; science and education; cooperation on combating and remedying natural disasters; using areas near the border creatively; and improving cross-border infrastructure.

Euroregion Białowieża Forest was established on the basis of an agreement signed on 25 May 2002. It includes, on the Polish side – Hajnówka County, the Municipality of Hajnówka, the rural districts of Hajnówka, Białowieża, Dubicze Cerkiewne, Czyże, Narew, Narewka, Czeremcha, Bielsk Polaski and Orla, and the rural-urban district of Kleszczele; and on the Belarusian side – the Pruzhany, Kamenets and Svislach Districts. The goal of Euroregion Białowieża Forest is to develop friendly, beneficial cross-border cooperation in adjacent areas of Poland and Belarus, and:
– to engage in cooperative activities aimed at supporting economic, social and cultural development in order to bring local communities closer together

- to initiate contacts among different types of institutions – local governments, and educational, sports, cultural and other outlets.

An important purpose of a Euroregion, particularly in the case of Białowieża Forest, is to protect the natural environment in border areas by conducting activities to prevent natural hazards and disasters. Polish-Belarusian cross-border cooperation could certainly develop more effectively if barriers were removed, such as the internal policy of the Belarusian regime, problems over visas, the inhospitable attitude of the Polish and Belarusian border services towards people crossing the border, corruption at border crossings, and high customs tariffs (Iwanow, 2008).

Energy has become another important area of Polish-Belarusian cooperation that has been conditioned by geopolitics and geoeconomics.

5. Energy

The construction of the Nord Stream gas pipeline, which began in 2007, provided a serious impetus for a reactivation of dialogue between Belarus and Poland. The project involved building a pipeline that would circumvent the transit countries of Belarus and Poland, and was a blow to their political interests. The Nord Stream was to run from Russia to Germany, through the Baltic Sea. In discussions at the highest level, the issue was raised again of building a second pipeline, the Yamal Europe, planned as a cheap alternative to the Nord Stream for all interested countries. Although in the end this idea was not carried through and the Nord Stream began delivering in 2011 (the first thread), the situation provided a strong impulse for a renewal and thaw in Polish-Belarusian relations. It also showed that, when faced with common economic problems, the two countries are able to unite and work out a common position. These events caused a significant reactivation of Polish-Belarusian relations in the field of energy. In 2009, the Belarusian Ambassador to Poland, Wiktar Hajsionak, stated that both Belarus and Poland were interested in connected a network of pipelines in order to achieve energy security. Further, in 2008, an understanding was signed between the Belarusian Energy Minister and the Polish company Kulczyk Investments. It contained an investment project for the construction of a combined heat and power plant in Zelva, in Grodno Region. However, the project remained on paper only due to a lack of consensus among the parties involved concerning issues of distribution and how the energy generated would be shared. In the near future, the prospects for partnership and cooperation between Poland and Belarus in the field of energy seem to be good, and such activities could boost bilateral relations to a new, higher level. The positive signs in this area of the economy after the bilateral crisis in 2005-2006 made the Belarusian authorities realise that they can achieve more when Poland is seen not as a threat to national security, but as a strategic partner and ally (Shevchenko, 2015, p. 3).

6. Other areas, prospects for and barriers to cooperation

In October 2008, the Polish-Belarusian Commission for Economic Cooperation established in 2004 set up a working group for cooperation in the area of agriculture. This type of cooperation with Belarus is carried out on the basis of bilateral meetings at various levels, including between the Polish and Belarusian Vice Ministers of agriculture, and through participation by administrative officials in fairs, seminars and economic forums. In 2009, an important event in Polish-Belarusian economic relations was the Polish-Belarusian Economic Summit organised in Warsaw. There were numerous activities aimed at improving economic cooperation through various types of national exhibitions held in both Poland and Belarus, and through bilateral talks at the level of ministers and vice ministers of agriculture.

Despite fears to the contrary, Poland's access to the EU had a beneficial effect on bilateral cooperation. It motivated Belarus to expand its border crossings, and to make use of Polish experience and assistance in organising cross-border projects, including on environmental protection.

In December 2013, Warsaw was host to a meeting between Undersecretary of State Katarzyna Kacperczyk and the Belarusian Vice Minister of Foreign Affairs, Aleksander Gurianow. The subject of the meeting was economic cooperation, mainly in the areas of trade and investments. The issues of the detainment of Polish trucks at the border and Belarus's potential membership in the World Trade Organisation were discussed. Vice Minister Gurianow also met with Vice Minister Katarzyna Pełczyńska-Nałęcz. Both European and Polish-Belarusian bilateral issued were raised.

Yet such positive developments in Polish-Belarusian relations are not free of barriers. The Belarusian economy is one of the most regulated and closed on the continent, and this has an adverse effect on foreign investments and export growth. Since 2010, Belarus has been a member of the

Belarus-Russia-Kazakhstan Customs Union; it also belongs to the Joint Economic Area created by those countries that began functioning on 1 January 2015, and is a member of the Eurasian Economic Union. The Customs Union has introduced many barriers protecting those markets. The Belarusian authorities have introduced a series of customs tariffs and restrictions such as quotas, administrative formalities and sanitary, social and technical standards. At present, Belarus is bound by the Common Customs Tariff and the Common Customs Code. The barriers to economic cooperation most commonly cited are: an expensive, complicated procedure for certifying goods, the need to renew certification if even the name of a product is changed, but not its properties, the refusal to recognise Polish and EU certificates even in cases of identical requirements, a lack of willingness of Belarusian certification institutes to cooperate with their Polish counterparts in order to gradually introduce reciprocal recognition of certificates, frequent changes in the binding provisions, a complicated, time-consuming procedure for registering companies in Belarus, and a complicated, time-consuming procedure for approving construction projects and inspecting existing projects for future production and services activities (*Białoruś. Informator Ekonomiczny Ministerstwa Spraw Zagranicznych*, 2017).

In the years 2014-2016, a number of activities were undertaken for developing bilateral economic cooperation. In 2014, after a 5-year break, cooperation was renewed at the level of the Polish-Belarusian Commission for Economic Cooperation. On 1 December of that year, a Memorandum on Cooperation was signed between the Polish Agency for Information and Foreign Investments (PAIiIZ S.A.) and the Belarusian National Agency for Investments and Privatisation (NAIP). On 15 June 2015, the 4th session of a permanent Polish-Belarusian working group for trade and investments was held in Minsk, within the activities of the Polish-Belarusian Joint Commission for Economic Cooperation. Important areas of economic cooperation were discussed, particularly in respect of trade and investments, where intensive contacts were maintained at the level of businesses. In 2014, more than 80 delegations took part in various types of economic events in Belarus. On 3 April, Minsk hosted a Polish-Belarusian Business Forum, attended by representatives of Polish and Belarusian enterprises.

The renewal of political relations in 2016 created a climate that was conducive to deepening economic cooperation. On 24 October 2016, a meeting was held in Minsk between the Polish Vice Premier Mateusz

Morawiecki and the Belarusian President, Aleksander Lukashenko. Morawiecki also met with Prime Minister Andrej Kobiakow and Vice Minister Michaił Rusym, and opened the 20th Good Neighbours Polish-Belarusian Economic Forum for 2016. The forum was attended by a record number of more than 500 participants. During his meeting with Lukashenko, Morawiecki said that "trade and economic relations with Belarus are the best way to deepen cooperation in other areas as well. Poland is a gateway to the East for the European Union, and Belarus a gateway to the West for the Eurasian Union. We must take advantage of this... We definitely want our cooperation to be under conditions of partnership and mutual benefit. For me personally, cooperation with the Belarusian nation is very important" (*Morawiecki w Mińsku: Polska bramą na Wschód dla UE*, 2016). Lukashenko in turn emphasised that "turnover between the two countries isn't bad at all, and Poland is one of Belarus's main partners. We want to increase cooperation and trade. The economy can be a pillar of our cooperation... If there is also willingness on the Polish side, we will guarantee assistance in creating Polish businesses, both those with purely Polish capital and those that are mixed" (*Morawiecki w Mińsku: Polska bramą na Wschód dla UE*, 2016).

During the 20th Good Neighbours Polish-Belarusian Economic Forum for 2016, a letter of intent was signed concerning the creation of a Polish-Belarusian Initial Public Offering Centre. The aim of the understanding is to provide a professional education centre, consultations and legal advice for Belarusian businesses. The Polish-Belarusian IPO Centre will conduct activities to make it easier for Belarusian companies to access modern sources of financing using the Polish capital market. The document was signed by representatives of the Warsaw Stock Exchange, the Polish-Belarusian Chamber of Commerce and Industry, and the Belarusian State University, in the presence of Vice Premier Morawiecki and the Belarusian Prime Minister Mikhaił Rusy. "The Polish government has taken steps favouring a tightening of Polish-Belarusian relations. This goes along with the process of improving relations between Minsk and the EU, and more broadly, between Belarus and the West. Both sides see this process as something positive, that opens up many opportunities in various fields, including economic cooperation. According to data for the first half of 2016, today Poland is Belarus's third-biggest trading partner, the third-largest exporter to Belarus, and the 9th-biggest investor. Poland is also Belarus's 6th-largest export market. This is a good starting point for developing cooperation, trade and investments that can help deepen and stabilise mutual relations" (*Wizyta wicepremiera RP Mateusza Morawieckiego w Mińsku*, 2016).

The most promising areas for economic cooperation are energy, including renewable sources and the effectiveness thereof, construction, transport, environmental protection, banking, and insurance. The main regions for developing tourism on either side of the border are Białowieża Forest and the Augustowski Canal. Belarus is decided on expanding economic and trade cooperation with Poland, and sees Poland as an important strategic partner. Interest in attracting large investors and trading partners from Poland, and in opening Belarus up to Polish business, is evident in proposals to take part in Belarusian privatisation, and in the trend to establish personal contacts among businessmen (*Morawiecki Mateusz. Prywatyzacja na Białorusi z polskimi firmami*, 2016). In response, Poland has stepped up its participation in Belarusian economic forums. Another important goal is to restore and increase trade between the two countries. Minsk counts on Warsaw's support in Belarus's bid to accede to the WTO, as well as on the issue of building a nuclear power plant in Astravyets and distributing electricity to Europe. These depend on the will of both sides.

Mateusz Morawiecki's visit to Minsk showed that, while previous Polish-Belarusian economic contacts had been made without the official involvement of the Polish authorities, today those authorities not only support Polish business in Belarus, but are also ready to stimulate its development. Poland agrees with the Belarusian conception of mutual relations, under which the basis of those relations should be the economy. Poland has declared its readiness to resolve common problems.

One development that is unprecedented is today's Polish-Belarusian cooperation in the field of transport. Belarus and Poland see each other as partners in developing transit. In March 2016, the 4th session of the Polish-Belarusian Carriers Commission was held in Warsaw, during which it was decided to lift administrative barriers, increase the number of permits for irregular and free shipments. Container shipments from China to Europe are increasing rapidly.

Poland and Belarus are also interested in taking an active part in transport-communication projects initiated by the People's Republic of China. They would like to become a hub connecting not only East and West, but North and South. This could be accomplished by cooperation in the field of road, rail, air and maritime transport, and by Belarus using river ports. Poland intends to simplify the movement of goods through its territory and to make Belarus part of the Via Carpathia transport corridor connecting the nine countries of the Three Seas Initiative (Romanova, 2016). In October 2016, Belarusian Minister of Transport and Communication Anatoliĭ Sivak and Polish Minister of Infrastructure and Construction Andrzej Adamczyk, as well as the Polish Minister of Martime Economy and Inland Navigation, signed a memorandum on cooperation in the sphere of revitalising the waterway along the Dnieper-Vistula section (*Ministerstwo Gospodarki Morskiej i Żeglugi Śródlądowej Mińsk. Memorandum dotyczące odtworzenia drogi wodnej Dniepr-Wisła*, 2016)[75]. Both sides also plan to sign an understanding on the construction of a new road bridge at the Domaczewo-Sławatycze border crossing, which was closed down for being technically unfit.

Without doubt, the development of economic cooperation will benefit both countries and bring about a rapprochement not only among politicians and businessmen, but also among the two societies, through joint projects and the creation of new jobs – in which people in both Poland and Belarus have a keen interest. In this way, conditions will be created that favour intensified cultural exchanges as well.

References

Białoruś. Informator Ekonomiczny Ministerstwa Spraw Zagranicznych, 2017. [online] Available at: <http://www.informatorekonomiczny.msz.gov.pl/pl/europa/bialorus/bialorus ;jsessionid=F1ECBA9DD1E006F0B6F5E710055E9BC8.cmsap6p >[Accessed 24 May 2017].

Èksport iz Respubliki Belarus' po otdel'nym stranam vne SNG. [online] Available at: <http://www.belstat.gov.by/ofitsialnaya-statistika/makroekonomika-i-okruzhayushc haya-sreda/vneshnyaya-torgovlya_2/osnovnye-pokazateli-za-period-s-__-po-___ g ody_10/eksport-tovarov-respubliki-belarus-po-stranam-s_2/>[Accessed at 25 September 2017].

Esin, R., 2016. Belorusskiĭ èksport i investitsionnaia privlekatel'nost': segodnia i zavtra. In: J. Tymanowski, A. Daniluk and J. Bryll., eds. 2015. *Polska i Białoruś we współczesnej Europie*. Warsaw: Wydział Dziennikarstwa i Nauk Politycznych, pp. 183-189.

---

75 Pursuant to the European Understanding on the most important internal waterways having international significance, the E-40 waterway, which passes through the territory of Belarus, Poland and Ukraine (from Gdańsk to Warsaw, up the Narew and Bug to Brest, and then through Polesie to the Dnieper), should become a new trade route between ports on the Baltic and Black Seas. A technical and economic justification for the Polish-Belarusian Dnieper-Vistula section has already been prepared using European Union funds, and a working group to make the project a reality has been set up.

Europejska Konwencja ramowa o współpracy transgranicznej między wspólnotami i władzami terytorialnymi, sporządzona w Madrycie dnia 21 maja 1980 roku, 1993. Dziennik Ustaw Rzeczypospolitej Polskiej [Journal of Laws], 61, item 287.

Głogowska H., 2012. *Stosunki polsko-białoruskie w XX wieku. Od Imperium Rosyjskiego do Unii Europejskiej*. Białystok: Wydawnictwo Uniwersytetu w Białymstoku.

Import tovarov v Respubliku Belarus' po po otdel'nym stranam vne SNG. [online] Available at: <http://www.belstat.gov.by/ofitsialnaya-statistika/makroekonomika-i-okruzhayushchaya-sreda/vneshnyaya-torgovlya_2/osnovnye-pokazateli-za-period-s -_-po-____gody_10/import-tovarov-v-respubliku-belarus-po-osnovnym-stranam-v ne-sng/> [Accessed 25 September 2017].

Iwanow, T., 2008. Wyzwania współpracy transgranicznej Polska-Białoruś (transgraniczny region województwo lubelskie i obwód brzeski). *Studenckie Prace Prawnicze, Administratywistyczne i Ekonomiczne*, 5(2008), pp. 131-141.

Kraska, B., 2006. Polsko-białoruska współpraca transgraniczna jako nowy model więzi międzynarodowych. *Zeszyty Naukowe Ostrołęckiego Towarzystwa Naukowego*, 20 2006) pp. 241-260. [online] Available at: <http://mazowsze.hist.pl/28/Zeszyt y_Naukowe_Ostroleckiego_Towarzystwa_Naukowego/649/2006/23147/> [Accessed 20 May 2017].

Ministerstwo Gospodarki Morskiej i Żeglugi Śródlądowej. Memorandum dotyczące odtworzenia drogi wodnej Dniepr-Wisła, 03.10.2016. [online] Available at: <www.mgm.gov.pl/321-minsk-memorandum-dotyczace-odtworzenia-drogi-wodnej-dnieprwisla-podpisane> [Accessed 25 November 2016].

Minskiĭ avtomobil'nyĭ zavod. Sborochnoe proizvodstvo techniki MAZ otkryto v Pol'she, 13.09.2016. [online] Available at: http://maz.by/ru/news/general/2014/9/sp_maz_po land/> [Accessed 13 September 2016].

Morawiecki Mateusz. Prywatyzacja na Białorusi z polskimi firmami, 24.10.2016. [online] Available at: <http://www.rp.pl/Prywatyzacja/310249888-Mateusz-Morawieck i-Prywatyzacja-na-Bialorusi-z-polskimi-firmami.html> [Accessed 25 November 2016].

Morawiecki w Mińsku: Polska bramą na Wschód dla UE, 24.10.2016. [online] Available at: <http://www.tvp.info/27458219/morawiecki-w-minsku-polska-brama-na-w schod-dla-ue> [Accessed 22 May 2017].

MTZ Belarus Traktor sp. z o.o., 25.11.2016. [online] Available at: http://mtzbelarus.pl /> [Accessed 25 November 2017].

Pol'skiĭ agrarnyĭ biznes gotov investirovat' v Belarus', no ozhidaet garantiĭ, 08.11.2016. [online] Available at: <http://naviny.by/new/20161108/1478628479pol skiy-agrarnyy-biznes-gotov-investirovat-v-belarus-no-ozhidaet-garantiy> [Accessed 27 November 2016].

Potencjał MSP w handlu ze Wschodem – szanse na dynamiczny rozwój współpracy handlowej z krajami post-radzieckimi, 2006. [online] Available at: <https://www.pa rp.gov.pl/images/PARP_publications/pdf/2006_msp_wschod_europy.pdf> [Accessed 25 September 2017].

Rocznik Statystyczny Rzeczypospolitej Polskiej. Statistical Yearbook of the Republic of Poland, 2016. Warsaw: Główny Urząd Statystyczny.

Romanova, N., 04.10.2016. Bol'shie i konkretnye biznes-plany. *Sovetskaya Belorussiia*. № 190 (25072). [online] Available at: <http://www.sb.by/belarus/article/bolshi e-ikonkretnye-biznes-plany.html> [Accessed 1 November 2016].

Shevchenko, A.N., 2015. Analiz i tendetsii pol'sko belorusskikh otnosheniĭ v nachale XXI veka. *Pravova derzhava*. 19/2015. [online] Available at: <http://dspace.onu.ed u.ua:8080/bitstream/123456789/6754/1/175-182.pdf> [Accessed 25 May 2017].

Statisticheskiĭ ezhegodnik, 2016. Minsk: Natsional'nyĭ Statisticheskiĭ Komitet Respubliki Belarus'.

Struktura vneshneĭ torgovli tovarami Respubliki Belarus' s otdel'nymi stranami v 2016 godu, 2016. [online] Available at: <http://www.belstat.gov.by/ofitsialnaya-statistika /makroekonomika-i-okruzhayushchaya-sreda/vneshnyaya-torgovlya_2/dannye-o-vn eshnei-torgovle-respubliki-belarus-p_2/vneshnetorgovyi-oborot-tovarami-respubliki -belarus-so-stranami-vne-sng/> [Accessed 25 September 2017].

Traktat między Rzecząpospolitą Polską a Republiką Białoruś o dobrym sąsiedztwie i przyjaznej współpracy, podpisany w Warszawie dnia 23 czerwca 1992 r, 1993. Dziennik Ustaw Rzeczypospolitej Polskiej [Journal of Laws], 118, item 527. Available at: <http://dziennikustaw.gov.pl/du/1993/s/118/527> [Accessed 5 September 2017].

Umowa między Rządem Rzeczypospolitej Polskiej a Rządem Republiki Białoruś w sprawie unikania podwójnego opodatkowania w zakresie podatków od dochodu i majątku, sporządzona w Mińsku dnia 18 listopada 1992 r, 1993. Dziennik Ustaw Rzeczypospolitej Polskiej [Journal of Laws], 120, item 534. Available at: <www.dziennikustaw.gov.pl/D1993120053401.pdf> [Accessed 5 September 2017].

Umowa między Rządem Rzeczypospolitej Polskiej a Rządem Republiki Białorusi o współpracy gospodarczej, sporządzona w Warszawie dnia 30 kwietnia 2004 r., 2006. Monitor Polski, 26, item 286. Available at: <http://isap.sejm.gov.pl/DetailsSe rvlet?id=WMP20060260286> [Accessed 5 September 2017].

Wizyta wicepremiera RP Mateusza Morawieckiego w Mińsku, 25.10.2016. [online] Available at: <http://www.minsk.msz.gov.pl/pl/aktualnosci/wizyta_wicepremiera_r p_mateusza_morawieckiego_w_minsku> [Accessed 5 September 2017].

Chapter 6 Cultural cooperation

1. Cultural contacts

The foundations of Polish-Belarusian cooperation in the sciences and culture are provided by the Treaty on Neighbourly Relations and Friendly Cooperation of 1992, the Agreement between the Government of the Republic of Belarus and the Republic of Poland on Cooperation in the Fields of Culture, Science and Education of 27 November 1995, and relevant understandings concluded in the second half of the 1990s.

Pursuant to Article 22 of the treaty, both sides refer to the positive values of centuries of cultural heritage and agree to foster further cooperation in the fields of culture, science, education and information. In order to reciprocally disseminate knowledge of national achievements in those areas, each side is to create cultural centres within the territory of the other state. The parties are to cooperate through the mass media, to facilitate the distribution of books, press and audiovisual productions of the other side, to expand cultural exchanges, to support cooperation between cultural institutions and organisations and artistic associations at the national, regional and local levels. They should also support direct contacts between cultural and artistic creators, expand cooperation in the fields of education, science and technology, and foster the development of cooperation between universities, schools and other academic institutions within the scope of student exchanges, scholarships and academic personnel. Each side is to guarantee appropriate legal, material and other protection of historical sites, values and artefacts associated with the historical and cultural heritage of the other party or common to both sides located within its territory, and should act to discover, save and preserve them, put them into cultural circulation, and provide access to them. In accordance with international standards and norms, and on the basis of bilateral agreements, the parties are to initiate and support activities aimed at the identification and return of cultural and historical objects that have been lost, were unlawfully removed or have otherwise illegally found themselves in the territory of the other party. Article 25 of the treaty also contains a provision on the protection of cemeteries within the territory of both parties (*Traktat między Rzecząpospolitą Polską a Republiką Białoruś o dobrym sąsiedztwie i przyjaznej współpracy*, 1992).

In the field of culture, the development of Polish-Belarusian relations in the years 1990-1994 was mainly directed towards a renaissance of Polish culture in Belarus and Belarusian culture in Poland, as discussed in the previous chapter. Bilateral cultural cooperation was addressed mainly to national minorities, and to a lesser extent concerned the entire population of a state.

After 1995, two important understandings were signed that defined Polish-Belarusian cultural relations. These were the Understanding between the Government of the Republic of Belarus and the Government of the Republic of Poland on Cooperation on the Protection of Cultural Hertiage of 25 March 1995, and the Agreement between the Government of the Republic of Poland and the Government of the Republic of Belarus on Cooperation in the Fields of Culture, Science and Education of 27 November 1995. In the first of these, the parties undertook to conduct joint notification, inventory and research work to determine the number, value and condition of movable and immovable cultural goods located within the territory of each state that are connected with the culture and history of the other state and were unlawfully moved or appropriated. It was decided that cultural goods within the territory of one state that are significant to the other state will be returned to the latter on a reciprocal basis (*Porozumienie między Rządem Republiki Białorusi a Rządem Rzeczypospolitej Polskiej o współpracy w dziedzinie ochrony dziedzictwa kulturalnego*, 1995).

The Agreement on Cooperation in the Fields of Culture, Science and Education lays out in detail the forms and rules of cooperation in these areas. It provides for, among other measures, exchanges of academic personnel; joint research; traineeships; exchange visits of academics, teachers and other specialists; the recruitment of lecturers; upgrading the qualifications of academic staff (doctoral studies, habilitation internships, language courses, etc.); full- and part-time studies; student exchanges for traineeships during holidays; the creation of joint academic centres; the exchange of academic information, publications and documents; access to archival materials, library collections and other source materials; the organisation of joint academic events (congresses, conferences, symposia, academic excursions, etc.); and other specific forms of cooperation foreseen in interministerial understandings (*Umowa między Rządem Rzeczypospolitej Polskiej a Rządem Republiki Białoruś o współpracy w dziedzinie kultury,*

159

nauki i oświaty, 1995). Some of those provisions – studies, exchanges and joint academic events (congresses, conferences, symposia and academic excursions) are in principle being implemented[76].

In 1995, an Agreement between the Government of the Republic of Poland and the Government of the Republic of Belarus on the protection of Graves and Places of Commemoration of Victims of War and Repression was concluded (*Umowa między Rządem Rzeczypospolitej Polskiej a Rządem Republiki Białoruś o ochronie grobów i miejsc pamięci ofiar represji*, 1995), as was an Agreement between the Government of the Republic of Poland and the Government of the Republic of Belarus on Recognising the Equivalence of Higher Education, Academic and Artistic Degrees (*Umowa między Rządem Rzeczypospolitej Polskiej a Rządem Republiki Białorusi o uznaniu ekwiwalencji w szkolnictwie wyższym, równoważności stopni naukowych i stopni w zakresie sztuki*, 1995). Both of those touch on very important issues for the two states and nations.

In 1994, at the Polish embassy in Minsk, the Polish Institute was opened. It has status as a diplomatic mission, and belongs to a series of Polish institutions that promote Polish culture in more than 20 countries worldwide, but especially in Europe. In its work in Belarus, the Polish Institute has significantly expanded the scope of Polish-Belarusian cultural cooperation. Its goal is to popularise achievements in Polish culture and science and knowledge of Polish culture among Belarusians, and to develop relations between the two countries by exchanging experience and supporting dialogue between Polish and Belarusian representatives of literature, science, art, music, cinema and theatre (*Instytut Polski w Mińsku*, 2017).

In 1995, in connection with the conflict in the Main Board of the Union of Poles in Belarus over staffing in the first Polish school in Grodno, some UPB activists, led by Teresa Kryszy and Stanisław Sienkiewicz, left the organisation and founded the Polish School Matrix. It is still active today in the educational community, teaching Polish language and history in local clubs and outlets, helping teachers with methodology, supporting young people in their Polish education, organising various types of competitions, and recruiting for Polish universities. The opening of Consulates

---

76 Examples are the academic conferences at the Faculty of Political Sciences and International Studies at Warsaw University (formerly the Faculty of Journalism and Political Science) entitled *Poland and Belarus in Contemporary Europe 2015-2016.*

General of the Republic of Poland in Brest and Grodno in 1995, the construction of the first Polish school in Grodno in 1996, and of another in Vawkavysk in 1999, where Polish is the language of instruction, and the construction of 17 Polish Houses in cooperation with the Polish School Matrix, have strengthened Poles in Belarus and have stepped up the pace of the development of Polish culture.

In 1997, a Chair of Belarusian Culture was opened at Białystok University, while at Belarusian State University in Minsk, a Department of Polish Language functions at the Faculty of Philology. At the state universities in Grodno and Brest, there are Polish departments that train teachers of Polish.

An important event in the cultural relations between the two states was the announcement by the Belarusian opposition that 1996 was the "Year of Tadeusz Kościuszko". A series of events commemorating the 250th anniversary of his birth concluded in May with the unveiling of a monument to him. The Belarusian opposition considers Kościuszko to be a Belarusian "the whole world knows". One year later, in Poland, the first Belarusian Cultural Days were held, and in 1999, Polish Cultural Days in Belarus (Malak, 2003, p. 104).

The year 1998 was declared the Year of Adam Mickiewicz in Belarus, in connection with the 200th anniversary of his birth. At the Mickiewicz Museum in Navrahudak, the Museum of Literature in Warsaw organised a special exhibition accompanied by concerts and meetings. In Zaosie, near Navrahudak, where Mickiewicz was born, a manor farm was created. Mickiewicz's masterpiece *Sir Thaddeus* was translated into Belarusian, and a monument to the poet was erected in Grodno. The anniversary was given official state status, emphasising Polish-Belarusian connections (Głogowska, 2012, pp. 417-418), which was particularly significant given the worsening political atmosphere.

Though the degree to which it is implemented varies, an important field of cooperation in Poland's and Belarus's support of their nationals living abroad is education. In the Białystok region in 1994, a Polish-Belarusian commission met to deal with the problem of Belarusian education in Poland and Polish education in Belarus. Both countries undertook to cooperation on organising schooling, and jointly preparing textbooks in geography, history and the mother tongues of both nations (Głogowska, 2012, p. 437). Under a cooperation agreement between the Polish and Belarusian Education Ministers, on 30 March 1994 a Joint Consultation Commission for Polish Education in Belarus and Belarusian Education in Poland was

formed. Its tasks were to develop a conception of Polish schools and prepare textbooks. Since its inception, despite internal conflicts within its
Board and conflicts with the Belarusian authorities, the Union of Poles in
Belarus fought for the development of Polish education in Belarus. Its
main achievements in this area include the opening of two Polish general
schools in Grodno and Vawkavysk, the organisation of part-time studies at
Białystok University for foreign students of Polish background, and the
organisation since 1992 of the Polish Language and Literature Olympics.
One of the UPB's fundamental goals was to create Polish Houses to foster
integration among Poles and the development of Polish culture in Belarus.
There are 17 Polish Houses in the country, of which 15 operate officially,
though after the crisis in 2005 described in Chapter 5, only 2 really function – in Lida and Baranavichy. The Polish Houses in Grodno, Vitebsk,
Shchuchyn and Mogilev limit their activities to a handful of closed events
each year. The development of Polish culture in Belarus began with a
movement among the Polish minority and the teaching of the Polish language. Choirs were formed, which often performed along with an orchestra and national dance troupes. In November 1998, in the Grodno region, a
delegation led by Tadeusz Kopacz arrived from the Polish Senate; it presented Polish folk costumes to Polish groups in Radun and Słonim. Gradually, adaptations of Polish national culture appeared that were previously
unknown to Poles in Belarus. Along with this Polish renaissance, people
were recruited to Polish groups (e.g. *Voice from the Neman* in Grodno,
Home Country in Baranavichy, *Flame* in Shchuchyn, and *Red Poppies* in
Minsk). In 1998, there were 66 Polish choirs and groups in Belarus. They
appeared at various types of special events within the Polish minority
community – most often at the UPB and in schools. They were supported
by theatre, choreography and singing workshops organised in Belarus and
Poland. Festivals were organised of Polish singing, Polish scouting; there
was an international festival of Polish stage singing. In 1994, festivals of
carol singing groups began, organised in cooperation with the Podlaski
Branch of the Polish Community organisation. In the newspaper *Voice
from the Neman*, literary works by members of the Polish minority began
to appear. In 1998, an evening of the poetry of Maria Walentyna Osipowa
was held in Minsk. Unfortunately, however, the artistic activities of Polish
authors were not active enough for a Polish literary community to form in
Belarus. An important aspect worth mentioning here is that, apart from talent, a mastery of the Polish language was necessary, and this was general-
ly lacking among the younger generation. Recital competitions were also

held, such as Borderlands, the Adam Mickiewicz Poetry Recital Competition, and the Maria Konopnicka Poetry Festival; at all of these classics of Polish literature were presented. Unfortunately, no Polish theatre was created in Belarus, though numerous theatre clubs and school cabarets appeared. As early as 1992, there arose a Polish Society of Artists, and the first exhibition of Polish artists took place on 14 May 1998 at the Polish Consulate General in Grodno. In the same city, since 1997 there have been Republican Festivals of National Cultures in which Polish artists and groups have taken part (Głogowska, 2012, pp. 500-502). In the broader context, bilateral cultural relations involve regional cross-border cooperation, most developed within Euroregions. Within Euroregion Bug, in 2002 16 different cultural projects were implemented, of which the 5 most interesting were carried off with flair: the world-class "International Poleskie Summer with Folklore" organised in Włodawa, the 1st Eurofolk International Folklore Festival in Zamość, the International Festival of Artistic Works by Disabled Persons, also in Zamość, the International Borderlands Outdoor Art Workshop in Wola Uhruwska, the Trans-border Roztocz festival with outdoor painting, and border crossing improvement projects (Kraska, 2006). In Poland, the most frequent events organised in cooperation with Brest Oblast are: the January Music Nights international festival, the Peasant's Homeland international folklore festival, the With a Song to Europe festival, the international Music, Theatre and Folklore on the Bug festival, the Biała Wieża theatre festival, the Youth Together youth meetings, the Brest Sprouts sports competition, exchanges of sports delegations in boxing, running, weightlifting, judo, rowing, archery and swimming. Within Euroregion Neman, the following cultural events are organised: the Euroregion Neman Summer Festival, at which the Augustowski Canal has been promoted as a waterway of the region, the International Rescue Seminar Białystok 2001, the 6th Suwalki Theatre Explorations, the Polish-Lithuanian Commonwealth in baroque music, initiated by the Suwalki Music Society, and the Hajnówka 2001 cross-border youth meetings as a way of promoting the national cultures of Poland and Belarus. Active cooperation in Euroregion Białowieża Forest has resulted in numerous projects, including: Białowieża Forest – the spirit of nature and human talent at the crossroads of cultures, run in 2003 in Dubicze Cerkiewne, "Let's Get to Know Each Other", which focuses on cultural education of Polish and Belarusian youth within the Białowieża Forest, and a series of concerts entitled "Euroregion Białowieża Forest 3 Years Later", organised on 26-29 May 2005 and celebrating the third anniversary of the creation of the Euroregion (Kraska, 2006). In summary, it can be noted that the most active areas of Polish-Belarusian cultural cooperation are in the border areas, where the Belarusian community has a greater affinity with things Polish, and where the people speak or understand the Polish language, at least at a basic level. Poles who live in areas of Belarus near the Polish border tend to be interested to a certain degree in Polish history and culture.

Since 2008, the promotion of Belarusian culture in Poland has accelerated, because in July of that year the Belarusian Cultural centre was established at the Belarusian embassy in Warsaw. The goals of the centre are to present and promote the cultural heritage and contemporary art and culture of Belarus, to provide information on the social, political and economic life of Belarus, and to support the development of Polish-Belarusian cooperation in the fields of culture, education, information and tourism by expanding contacts and cooperation between creative centres, institutions and educational and cultural organisations in the two countries. Its main areas of activity are: promoting and ensuring a cultural presence within the Republic of Poland by implementing various cultural, educational, academic, sports and other programmes; creating its own library and making resources available to interested organisations and person in Poland; creating databases on the culture, science, education, scientific research, technological and economic development of both states in order to organise conferences, seminars and consultations on cultural, scientific, humanitarian and economic cooperation; publishing and disseminating its own programme of activities and other materials on Polish and Belarusian culture, science, education, tourism and humanitarian cooperation; supporting comprehensive cooperation between public organisations and non-governmental organisations; and inter-regional cooperation" (*Centrum Kulturalne Białorusi w Warszawie*, 2017). The Centre organises exhibitions from the collections of Belarusian museums, memorial complexes, and exhibitions of known and young Belarusian artists. Painters from Belarus take an active part in outdoor art workshops and symposia in Poland.

In 2013, for the first time after a break of close to 20 years, Belarusian Cultural Days were held in Poland, and included a series of cultural events such as: appearances by the National Academic Grand Opera and Ballet Theatre of the Republic of Belarus, the Belarusian State Group Pesnyary, the Żynowicz National Academic Orchestra, the folk group of the Belarusian State Philharmonic, Kupalinka, an exhibition on the palaces in Nieśwież and Mir, and a presentation of Belarusian cuisine. In 2015, a new project began – a concert by groups from various national minorities living in Belarus, run in cooperation with the Office of the Plenipotentiary for Religion and Nationalities of the Republic of Belarus. The goal of the project is to present the inter-ethnic harmony, agreement, hospitality and tolerance of Belarus, where various nationalities maintain friendly relations, developing and preserving their own culture and traditions. In intercultural dialogue, an important role is played by Belarusian music and dance groups, which often perform in Poland. These are folk music and dance ensembles from all regions of Belarus, as well as symphonic orchestras, orchestras playing national instruments, classical music groups, and above all, student ensembles from the Belarusian State Academy of Music and the Belarusian State University of Culture and Art. A series of traditional projects for children continues, for example, the Get to Know Belarus national competition, which attracts more than 200 children to take part each year. Cooperation has also been established with the Cyril and Metody Orthodox Cultural Centre in Warsaw and the Orthodox Cultural Centre in Białystok, where presentations are made of the Orthodox heritage and Belarusian traditions. A Polish-Belarusian consultation commission for historical and cultural heritage has been created in order to discuss current issues concerning the preservation of the historical and cultural heritage. Joint projects are implemented in the following areas of the commission's mandate: library sciences, movable and immovable historical and cultural monuments, museum sciences, and archival materials and collections. At present, Polish-Belarusian cultural contacts take place at the level of cooperation between individual organisations and performers. Understandings between 16 Polish and Belarusian cultural institutions are being implemented, with another 2 agreements in preparation. In order to enhance the preservation of the cultural heritage of the country and of national traditions and to foster love of country, 2016 was declared the Year of Belarusian Culture.

Popularising Polish culture in Belarus takes place through various types of projects, some with the participation of the Union of Poles in Belarus. Every year, numerous workshops, concerts, festivals, fairs, etc. are organised. The Polish ambassador in Minsk and the Consulates General in Grodno and Brest play an important role. In Grodno each year, the Koziuki fair is held, as is the Eurydyka Anna German Song Festival in Minsk, the Mallow Flowers Festival of Polish Stage Songs in Grodno, the Brasławskie Zarnice Traditional Culture Festival in Brasław, and the Borderlands Culture Festival in Mrągowo. In 2016, the first Rakowiecki Fest was held in Rakowo. Other events include the "Colourful Notes" Festival of Polish Songs for Children and Youth in Grodno, the Polonaise Festival in Słonim and, since 2012, the Ejsmontowski Fest of Polish Culture and Life in the village of Wielkie Ejsmonty in Grodno Oblast.

In May 2017, the Polish consulate in Grodno celebrated Polonia and Poles Abroad Days, with the participation of the vice speaker of the Polish Senate, Maria Koc. In many Belarusian towns and villages, Polish cultural festivals are held, as are art exhibitions, song and dance competitions, and literary soirees, with the participation of members of the Polish minority, the Belarusian community, and various song and dance groups, and painters and artists from Poland.

2. *Cooperation in the field of education*

Polish-Belarusian cooperation in the field of education is also developing, based on an Understanding between the Government of the Republic of Poland and the Government of Belarus on Cooperation in the Field of Education of 20 July 2016, and on the Agreement between the Government of the Republic of Poland and the Government of the Republic of Belarus on Recognising the Equivalence of Higher Education, Academic and Artistic Degrees from 2005. In accordance with the Understanding, a joint consultation commission was established to coordinate the work of schools for the Polish minority in Belarus and the Belarusian minority in Poland. The Understanding also provides a legal basis for mobility in the spheres of science and education, and regulates the conditions for exchanges of students and academic personnel.

Cooperation is developing actively towards strengthening direct contacts between universities in the two countries. Almost all Belarusian universities maintain contacts with universities and other academic institutions in Poland. At present, 52 Belarusian universities have concluded 156 cooperation agreements with 133 Polish universities.

A measurable effect of this policy is the growing number of Belarusian students in Poland. According to data for 2015 from the Polish Central Statistical office, 4,165 Belarusian students studied at Polish universities (4,118 in academic year 2014/2015), including 1,453 in their first year. It is worth noting that ethnic Polish students having additional students privileges and relief, including holders of a Polish Card, comprised 46.5% of that group, which means that a small majority of Belarusian students in

Poland never had previous connections with Poland (*Szkolnictwo wyższe, stan w dniu 30.XI.2015 r. — dane wstępne*, 2016). Belarusians are the second-largest groups of foreign students at Polish universities, after Ukrainians. Importantly, the current Polish government has changed the format of the Konstanty Kalinowski Scholarship Programme for Belarusian students created in the autumn of 2006. As from 2016, it is allocated not so much towards supporting students involved in opposition politics as towards all graduates of Belarusian universities who wish to study in Poland (*Program im. Kalinowskiego zmienia format: stypendia będą wypłacane tylko przez rok*, 2016). It is true that the number of scholarships under the programme is growing, but their share in the growing number of Belarusian students is diminishing. This shows how attractive Poland is for Belarusians as a place to study, since they are ready to pay to do so.

Polish-Belarusian cultural, scientific and educational relations are rapidly being transformed, partly due to the current political rapprochement. It is worth emphasising that many cultural events in which Polish artists participate are now taking place not only near the border, but throughout Belarus. An important contribution to the development of Polish-Belarusian cultural relations is made by national minorities – the Polish minority in Belarus and the Belarusian minority in Poland. They act as 'ambassadors' of their two homelands – political and historical.

References

Centrum Kulturalne Białorusi w Warszawie, 2017. [online] Available at: <http://poland.mfa.gov.by/pl/bilateral_relations/cultural/centrum/>[Accessed 24 May 2017].

Głogowska, H., 2012. *Stosunki polsko-białoruskie w XX wieku. Od Imperium Rosyjskiego do Unii Europejskiej*. Białystok: Wydawnictwo Uniwersytetu w Białymstoku.

Kraska, B. Polsko-białoruska współpraca transgraniczna jako nowy model więzi międzynarodowych. *Zeszyty Naukowe Ostrołęckiego Towarzystwa Naukowego* 20/2006. [online] Available at: <http://mazowsze.hist.pl/28/Zeszyty_Naukowe_Ostr oleckiego_Towarzystwa_Naukowego/6 49/2006/23147/> [Accessed 24 May 2017].

Instytut Polski w Mińsku, 24.09.2017. [online] Available at: <http://www.minsk.msz.g ov.pl/pl/ambasada/instytut_polski/> [Accessed 24 September 2017].

Malak, K., 2003. *Polityka zagraniczna i bezpieczeństwa Białorusi, Akademia Obrony Narodowej*. Warsaw: Akademia Obrony Narodowej.

Porozumienie między Rządem Republiki Białorusi a Rządem Rzeczypospolitej Polskiej o współpracy w dziedzinie ochrony dziedzictwa kulturalnego z dnia 25 marca 1995 roku, 20.05.2017. Available at: <https://traktaty.msz.gov.pl/bap.php> [Accessed 20 May 2017].

Program im. Kalinowskiego zmienia format: stypendia będą wypłacane tylko przez rok, 06.03.2016. [online] Available at: <http://belsat.eu/pl/news/program-im-kalino wskiegozmienia-format-stypendia-beda-wyplacane-tylko-przez-rok/> [Accessed 27 October 2016].

Szkolnictwo wyższe, stan w dniu 30.XI.2015 r. — dane wstępne. [online] Available at: 06.04.2016. <http://stat.gov.pl/obszary-tematyczne/ edukacja/edukacja/szkolnict-wo-wyzsze-stan-w-dniu-30-xi-2015-r-dane-wstepne,8,3.html> [Accessed 27 October 2016].

Traktat między Rzecząpospolitą Polską a Republiką Białoruś o dobrym sąsiedztwie i przyjaznej współpracy, podpisany w Warszawie dnia 23 czerwca 1992 r., 1993. *Dziennik Ustaw Rzeczypospolitej Polskiej* [Journal of Laws],118, item 527. Available at: <http://dziennikustaw.gov.pl/du/1993/s/118/527> [Accessed 5 September 2017].

Umowa między Rządem Rzeczypospolitej Polskiej a Rządem Republiki Białoruś o ochronie grobów i miejsc pamięci ofiar represji, sporządzona w Brześciu 21 stycznia 1995 r., 1997. Dziennik Ustaw Rzeczypospolitej Polskiej [Journal of Laws], 32, item 185. Available at: <http://isap.sejm.gov.pl/DetailsServlet?id=WDU199703201 85>[Accessed 24 September 2017].

Umowa między Rządem Rzeczypospolitej Polskiej a Rządem Republiki Białorusi o uznaniu ekwiwalencji w szkolnictwie wyższym, równoważności stopni naukowych i stopni w zakresie sztuki, sporządzona w Warszawie w dniu 28 kwietnia 1995 r. Available at: <http://www.nauka.gov.pl/g2/oryginal/2013_05/a323bf3a52a5961eba 4f2a44f261ae4a.pdf> [Accessed 24 September 2017].

Umowa między Rządem Rzeczypospolitej Polskiej a Rządem Republiki Białoruś o współpracy w dziedzinie kultury, nauki i oświaty, sporządzona w Warszawie dnia 27 listopada 1995 r. Available at: <http://www.infor.pl/akt-prawny/DZU.1996.076.000 0365 ,umowa-miedzy-rzadem-rzeczypospolitej-polskiej-a-rzadem-republiki-bialo-rus-o-wspolpracy-w-dziedzinie-kultury-nauki-i-oswiaty.html> [Accessed 15 September 2017].

Conclusions

In recent times, that is, over the past 30 years or so, three factors have formed Polish-Belarusian relations since the collapse of the USSR and the system of socialist states, as stated in the Introduction: history and culture, identity, and geopolitics. These have been and continue to be affected by Polish-Russian relations. There is no doubt that in this period they have gone through a tempestuous evolution – a transformation from a good start, to missed opportunities, to critical dialogue, to problems arising in connection with the expansion of the European Union, to a "honeymoon". What is important now is that both countries adeptly and prudently draw conclusions from the past – both distant and recent – and above all, that they overcome complexes they have about each other. As Piotra Rudkoŭski has written: "Between Poland and Belarus there is a certain lack of symmetry. Both during the times of the First Republic and during the national liberation movements of the 19th century, Poland outweighed Belarus considerably, and the influence of Polish culture on Belarus was (and is) greater than that of Belarusian culture on Poland. Poles can forge a historical narrative in which Belarus is not even mentioned, while for Belarusians it would be extremely difficult, if not impossible, for them to recount their history without mentioning Poland. Historical narratives often sharpen the problem of identity: in certain Polish texts, Belarus is presented as a radically dependent entity, as an embryo in the womb of Mother Poland, culturally (and even materially) dependent on her. Belarusians must "get their own back for this", for example, by appropriating the biggest Polish heroes such as Tadeusz Kościuszko, Adam Mickiewicz and others. Both nations often fall prey to their own complexes: inferiority for the Belarusians, and superiority for the Poles" (Rudkoŭski, 2007, p. 185). The "recreation" – to use the term employed by the Polish Foreign Minister Witold Waszczykowski – of Polish-Belarusian relations seems to show that an attempt is being made to overcome those complexes. As to whether it is lasting, time will tell. For now, we can state that both countries realise they should be guided in their reciprocal contacts above all by pragmatism, and not sentiment.

The Belarusian authorities see potential economic problems that could weaken or even destroy the social paternalism established in the country as a greater threat even than territorial integrity, the inviolability of the borders or a strengthening of the eastern flank of NATO. They start from the assumption that having strict economic ties with only one partner – Russia – loses its priority in times of crisis. Economic benefits increase in importance at the expense of other factors. This diversification is served by an improvement in relations with Poland, with whom cooperation mainly concerns trade and the economy. Belarus views Poland as an important partner, and hopes to implement the idea of "integrating integration" (of the European Union and the Eurasian Union), as a result of which both it and Poland will strengthen their position in Europe.

Poland's new policy towards Belarus does not mean a total or partial withdrawal from influencing culture, promoting European values or 'pulling Belarus out' of the Russian sphere of influence. Scholarship programmes for Belarusian students, support for the Polish minority and the Catholic Church in Belarus, the conservation of the historical and cultural heritage, and the transmission of information through their own media or through cooperation with Polish and Belarusian non-governmental organisations all remain important. The basis of the Polish conception for a renewal in Polish-Belarusian relations is the conviction that this should be a comprehensive process covering all spheres of activity. There has been a noticeable reduction in Poland's activity pertaining to the democratisation of Belarus. Supporting the Belarusian opposition to achieve political success in the form of unification and an election victory can only make sense when, taking account of the historical and cultural conditions, and of the identity and geopolitics of Belarus and Belarusians, the conception ceases to be "romantic" and becomes pragmatic. For this to happen, that conception must be less enthusiastically pro-Western, less "rabidly" anti-Russian and less zealously Belarus-centric. This last aspect, while it may seem paradoxical, is vital in conditions where Belarusian identity is more socio-political and civil than it is ethno-cultural. It is based on the sovereignty of the state and the rights of its citizens, together with limitations thereof deriving from the country's authoritarian government. The Belarusian sociologist Oleg Manaev points out that everyone living in Belarus can be considered a Belarusian: "The problem of whether you live in a Belarusian village or the asphalt jungle, what language you use in your daily contacts... is secondary in nature" (Bulgakov, 2006, p. 145). Politicians of the ruling Law and Justice Party have begun to realise that it is impossible to bring about a quick internal and external reorientation in Belarus. They are beginning to count more of gradual concessions in the political sphere in exchange for economic advantages offered by the EU.

No change in the character of Polish-Belarusian relations would be possible without willingness and openness on both sides. This is all the more surprising in that it would seem contrary to the potential forecasts relating to the strengthening of NATO's eastern flank. Poland wants to have a real, and not just a strategic, "beachhead" in the east, while Belarus treats Poland similarly, as its closest western neighbour. For now, it would be unwise to overestimate the progress made in Polish-Belarusian relations; to a large extent they remain declared intentions more than concrete results, which is understandable given the short period of time in which the two countries have been sovereign. Hopefully, the two sides will not repeat the mistakes of the past, for a "recreation" of mutual relations brings benefits to both. It reinforces the international status of each. From the Polish perspective, bringing Belarus closer to Poland, and through it to the West, means pulling it away from Russia, though it is clear that this shift will not be total. On the other hand, it can become a solid bridgehead in normalising Poland's own relations with Russia. From the Belarusian perspective, it means maintaining the country's position internationally and the autonomy of its foreign policy, which, contrary to public opinion, is not completely dependent on Russia, as attested to, for example, by Belarus's refusal to recognise the independence of Abkhazia, South Ossetia or the annexation of Crimea, and by Belarus acting as mediator in the conflict in Donbass.

References

Bulgakov, V., ed. 2006. Belarus': ni Evropa, ni Rossiia. Mneniia belorusskikh èlit. Warsaw: Izdatel'stvo „ARCHE"

Rudkoŭski, P., 2007. Paŭstan'nie Belarusi. Vilnius: Instytut belarusistyki.

Bibliography

DOCUMENTS AND LEGAL ACTS

Akademiia upravleniia pri Prezidente Respubliki Belarus', 2004. *Osnovy ideologii belarusskogo gosudarstva.* Minsk: Redaktsionno-izdatel'skiĭ tsentr Akademii upravleniia pri Prezidente Respubliki Belarus'.

Average Salary in European Union, 2017. [online] Available at: <https://www.reinisfis cher.com/average-salary-european-union-2017> [Accessed 24 August 2017].

Białoruś. Informator Ekonomiczny Ministerstwa Spraw Zagranicznych, 2017. [online] Available at: <http://www.informatorekonomiczny.msz.gov.pl/pl/europa/bialorus/bi alorus;jsessionid=F1ECBA9DD1E006F0B6F5E710055E9BC8.cmsap6p> [Accessed 24 May 2017].

Deklaracja o dobrym sąsiedztwie, wzajemnym zrozumieniu i współpracy między Rzeczypospolitą Polską i Republiką Białoruś, 10 października 1991, *Zbiór dokumentów,* 2(48).

Èksport iz Respubliki Belarus' po otdel'nym stranam vne SNG. [online] Available at: <http://www.belstat.gov.by/ofitsialnaya-statistika/makroekonomika-i-okruzhayushc haya-sreda/vneshnyaya-torgovlya_2/osnovnye-pokazateli-za-period-s-__-po-___g ody_10/eksport-tovarov-respubliki-belarus-po-stranam-s_2/> [Accessed 25 September 2017].

Europejska Konwencja ramowa o współpracy transgranicznej między wspólnotami i władzami terytorialnymi, sporządzona w Madrycie dnia 21 maja 1980 roku, 1993. Dziennik Ustaw Rzeczypospolitej Polskiej [Journal of Laws], 61, item 287.

Human Development Report 2016. Human Development for Everyone, 2016. [online] Available at: <http://hdr.undp.org/sites/default/files/2016_human_development_rep ort.pdf> [Accessed 25 September 2017].

Import tovarov v Respubliku Belarus' po po otdel'nym stranam vne SNG. [online] Available at: <http://www.belstat.gov.by/ofitsialnaya-statistika/makroekonomika-i-okruzhayushchaya-sreda/vneshnyaya-torgovlya_2/osnovnye-pokazateli-za-period-s -__-po-____gody_10/import-tovarov-v-respubliku-belarus-po-osnovnym-stranam-v ne-sng/> [Accessed 25 September 2017].

Informacja o ustaleniach końcowych śledztwa S 28/02/Zi w sprawie pozbawienia życia 79 osób – mieszkańców powiatu Bielsk Podlaski w tym 30 osób tzw. furmanów w lesie koło Puchał Starych, dokonanych w okresie od dnia 29 stycznia 1946 r. do dnia 2 lutego 1946. [online] Available at: <http://ipn.gov.pl/pl/dla-mediow/komunik aty/9989,Informacja-o-ustaleniach-koncowych-sledztwa-S-2802Zi-w-sprawie-pozb awienia-zycia.html> [Accessed 23 September 2017].

Iz stenogramy zasedaniia Orgbiuro TsK RKP(b) po voprosu o sostoianii i rabote KP(b) Belorussii, 4 noiabria 1925, 2005. In: L. Gatagova, L. Kosheleva and L. Rogovaia, eds. 2005. *TsK RKP(b)-VKP(b) i natsional'nyi vopros. Kniga 1.* 1918-1933. Moskva: ROSSPEN, pp. 334-346.

Bibliography

Konstitutsiia Respubliki Belarus' 1994 goda (s izmeneniiami i dopolneniiami, priniaty-mi na respublikanskikh referendumakh 24 noiabria 1996 g. i 17 oktiabria 2004 g.), 2006. Minsk: Amalfeia.

Konstytucja Rzeczypospolitej Polskiej z dnia 2 kwietnia 1997 r., 1997, 2001, 2006. Dziennik Ustaw Rzeczypospolitej Polskiej [Journal of Laws], 78, item 483; 28, item 319; 200, item 1471; 114, item 946.

Konwencja ramowa o ochronie mniejszości narodowych, sporządzona w Strasburgu dnia 1 lutego 1995 r., 2002. Dziennik Ustaw Rzeczypospolitej Polskiej [Journal of Laws], 22, item 209.

Liczebność polskiej diaspory, 2017. [online] Available at: <http://www.polskiinternet.c om/poland/polonializba.shtml> [Accessed 23 September 2017].

Lista gmin wpisanych na podstawie art. 12 ustawy z dnia 6 stycznia 2005 r. o mniejs-zościach narodowych i etnicznych oraz o języku regionalnym (Dz. U. Nr 17, poz. 141, z późn. zm.) do Rejestru gmin, na których obszarze używane są nazwy w języku mniejszości, 2017. [online] Available at: <http://mniejszosci.narodowe.mswia.gov.p l/mne/rejestry/rejestr-gmin/6794,Rejestr-gmin-na-ktorych-obszarze-sa-uzywane-na zwy-w-jezyku-mniejszosci.html> [Accessed 23 September 2017].

Lukashenko, A.G., 2004. *Vystuplenie Prezidenta Respubliki Belarus A.G. Lukashenko „Vneshniaia politika Respubliki Belarus' v novom mire" na soveshchanii s rukovo-diteliami zagranuchrezhdeniĭ Respubliki Belarus'.* [online] Available at: < http://pre sident.gov.by/ru/news_ru/view/vystuplenie-prezidenta-respubliki-belarus-aglukashe nko-vneshnjaja-politika-respubliki-belarus-v-novom-mire-na-5837/> [Accessed 10 April 2017].

Łodziński, S., 2002. *Ochrona praw osób należących do mniejszości narodowych i et-nicznych – perspektywa europejska.* Kancelaria Sejmu, Biuro Studiów i Ekspertyz, 208(2002), pp. 1-39.

Ministerstwo Gospodarki Morskiej i Żeglugi Śródlądowej. Memorandum dotyczące odtworzenia drogi wodnej Dniepr-Wisła, 03.10.2016. [online] Available at: <www.mgm.gov.pl/321-minsk-memorandum-dotyczace-odtworzenia-drogi-wodnej -dnieprwisla-podpisane> [Accessed 25 November 2016].

Naselenie po natsional'nosti i rodnomu iazyku. Respublika Belarus', 2009. [online] Available at: <http://www.belstat.gov.by/upload-belstat/upload-belstat-pdf/perepis_ 2009/5.8-0.pdf >[Accessed 19 September 2017].

Natsional'nyĭ sostav naseleniia, grazhdanstvo, 2009. [online] Available at: <http://ww w.belstat.gov.by/informatsiya-dlya-respondenta/perepis-naseleniya/perepis-naseleni ya-2009-goda/vyhodnye-reglamentnye-tablitsy/natsionalnyi-sostav-naseleniya-graz hdanstvo/> [Accessed 19 September 2017].

Oświadczenie Ministerstwa Spraw Zagranicznych RP ws. uznania przez władze Repu-bliki Białorusi za persona non grata Kierownika Wydziału Konsularnego Ambasady RP w Mińsku, 2005. [online] Available at: <http://bbb.livejournal.com/1310256.htm l?thread=6167344> [Accessed 3 September 2017].

Porozumienie między Rządem Republiki Białorusi a Rządem Rzeczypospolitej Polskiej o współpracy w dziedzinie ochrony dziedzictwa kulturalnego z dnia 25 marca 1995 roku, 20.05.2017. Available at: <https://traktaty.msz.gov.pl/bap.php> [Accessed 20 May 2017].

Poslanie Prezidenta Respubliki Belarus' A.G. Lukashenko belorusskomu narodu i Natsional'nomu sobraniiu Respubliki Belarus' „Blagopoluchie rodnoĭ zemli – delo vsekh i kazhdogo", 23 aprelia 2009 g. [online] Available at: <http://pravo.by/document/?guid=3871&p0=P009p0001> [Accessed 7 September 2017].

Posłanie Sejmu Rzeczypospolitej Polskiej do Narodu Białoruskiego, 1999. Available at: <http://orka.sejm.gov.pl/proc3.nsf/uchwaly/780_u.htm> [Accessed 7 September 2017].

Potencjał MSP w handlu ze Wschodem – szanse na dynamiczny rozwój współpracy handlowej z krajami post-radzieckimi, 2006. [online] Available at: <https://www.pa rp.gov.pl/images/PARP_publications/pdf/2006_msp_wschod_europy.pf >[Accessed 25 September 2017].

Priorytety polskiej polityki zagranicznej 2012-2016, 2012. Warszawa: Ministerstwo Spraw Zagranicznych.

Przemówienie prezydenta RP Lecha Wałęsy wygłoszone na spotkaniu noworocznym z korpusem dyplomatycznym, Warszawa, 14 stycznia 1993 r. *Rocznik Polskiej Polityki Zagranicznej 1993.*

Rachunki kwartalne produktu krajowego brutto w latach 2012-2016, 2017. [online] Available at: <https://stat.gov.pl/obszary-tematyczne/rachunki-narodowe/kwartalne-rachunki-narodowe/rachunki-kwartalne-produktu-krajowego-brutto-w-latach-2012-2016,6,11.html> [Accessed 19 September 2017].

Raport dla Sekretarza Generalnego Rady Europy z realizacji przez Rzeczpospolitą Polską postanowień Konwencji ramowej Rady Europy o ochronie mniejszości narodowych, 2002. Warszawa.

Raspredelenie naselenia Respubliki Belarus' po natsionalnostiam i iazykam v 1999 godu, 1999. [online] Available at: <http://www.belstat.gov.by/informatsiya-dlya-respo ndenta/perepis-naseleniya/perepis-naseleniya-1999-goda/tablichnye-dannye/raspred elenie-naseleniya-respubliki-belarus-po-natsionalnostyam-i-yazykam-v-1999-godu /> [Accessed 19 September 2017].

Rocznik Statystyczny Rzeczypospolitej Polskiej. Statistical Yearbook of the Republic of Poland, 2016. Warsaw: Główny Urząd Statystyczny.

Rotfeld, A.D., 2006. Informacja rządu na temat polskiej polityki zagranicznej w 2005 roku (przedstawiona przez ministra spraw zagranicznych Adama Daniela Rotfelda na posiedzeniu Sejmu w dniu 21 stycznia 2005 roku). In: *Rocznik Polskiej Polityki Zagranicznej*, pp. 9 -21.

Rudzutak, Ia., 1924. Tsyrkuliarnoe pis'mo TsK RKP(b) o meropiiatiakh po realizatsii postanovleniĭ po natsional'nomu voprosu, priniatykh XII s"ezdom RKP(b) i IV soveshchaniem TsK RKP(b) s otvestvennymi rabotnikami natsional'nykh republik i oblasteĭ, 2005. In: L. Gatagova, L. Kosheleva and L. Rogovaia, eds. *TsK RKP(b) i natsional'nyĭ vopros. Kniga I. 1918-1933*. Moskva: Rossiĭkaia politicheskaia èntsiklopediia, pp. 169-175.

Sejmowe exposé ministra spraw zagranicznych RP Krzysztofa Skubiszewskiego, 26 kwietnia 1990 r. Available at: <http://www.msz.gov.pl/resource/ 432b9164-91e5-4ef7-8c7a-3e0656cc48d9:JCR> [Accessed 5 September 2017].

Statisticheskiĭ ezhegodnik, 2016. Minsk: Natsional'nyĭ Statisticheskiĭ Komitet Respubliki Belarus'.

Bibliography

Strategia rozwoju oświaty mniejszości białoruskiej w Polsce, 2014. Białystok. [online] Available at: <http://lozbjn.edu.pl/upload/aktualnosci2013_2014/Strategia_rozwoju _mb.pdf> [Accessed 23 September 2017].

Struktura vneshneĭ torgovli tovarami Respubliki Belarus' s otdel'nymi stranami v 2016 godu, 2016. [online] Available at: <http://www.belstat.gov.by/ofitsialnaya-statistika /makroekonomika-i-okruzhayushchaya-sreda/vneshnyaya-torgovlya_2/dannye-o-vn eshnei-torgovle-respubliki-belarus-p_2/vneshnetorgovyi-oborot-tovarami-respubliki -belarus-so-stranami-vne-sng/> [Accessed 25 September 2017].

Szkolnictwo wyższe, stan w dniu 30.XI.2015 r. — dane wstępne, 06.04.2016. [online] Available at: <http://stat.gov.pl/obszary-tematyczne/ edukacja/edukacja/szkolnict-wo-wyzsze-stan-w-dniu-30-xi-2015-r-dane-wstepne,8,3.html> [Accessed 27 October 2016].

Traktat między Rzecząpospolitą Polską a Republiką Białoruś o dobrym sąsiedztwie i przyjaznej współpracy, podpisany w Warszawie dnia 23 czerwca 1992 r., 1993. Dziennik Ustaw Rzeczypospolitej Polskiej [Journal of Laws], 118, item 527. Available at: <http://dziennikustaw.gov.pl/du/1993/s/118/527> [Accessed 5 September 2017].

Uchwała Sejmu Rzeczypospolitej Polskiej z dnia 31 sierpnia 1991 r. w sprawie ogłoszenia niepodległości Białorusi. Available at: <isap.sejm.gov.pl/DetailsServlet? id=WMP19910290206 [Accessed 12 January 2017].

Uchwała Sejmu Rzeczypospolitej Polskiej z dnia 22 stycznia 1999 r. Posłanie Sejmu Rzeczypospolitej Polskiej do Narodu Białoruskiego, 1999. Monitor Polski, 4, item 15, 16 i 17. Available at: <http://dziennikustaw.gov.pl/mp/1999/s/4/16/1> [Accessed 7 September 2017].

Uchwała Senatu Rzeczypospolitej Polskiej z dnia 3 sierpnia 1990 r. Do narodu Białoruskiego z okazji proklamowania suwerenności państwowej Białorusi. Available at: <https://www.senat.gov.pl/prace/senat/uchwaly/> [Accessed 12 January 2017].

Ukaz Prezidenta Respubliki Belarus' ot 26 marta 1998 goda Nr 157 O gosudarstvennykh prazdnikakh prazdnichnykh dniakh i pamiatnykh datakh v Resublike Belarus', 1998. Available at: <https://online.zakon.kz/document/?doc_id=31255067#pos=0;2 79> [Accessed 18 September 2017].

Umowa między Rządem Rzeczypospolitej Polskiej a Rządem Republiki Białoruś o ochronie grobów i miejsc pamięci ofiar represji, sporządzona w Brześciu 21 stycznia 1995 r., 1997. Dziennik Ustaw Rzeczypospolitej Polskiej [Journal of Laws], 32, item 185. Available at: <http://isap.sejm.gov.pl/DetailsServlet?id=WDU199703201 85> [Accessed 24 September 2017].

Umowa między Rządem Rzeczypospolitej Polskiej a Rządem Republiki Białoruś o współpracy w dziedzinie kultury, nauki i oświaty, sporządzona w Warszawie dnia 27 listopada 1995 r. Available at: <http://www.infor.pl/akt-prawny/DZU.1996.076.000 0365,umowa-miedzy-rzadem-rzeczypospolitej-polskiej-a-rzadem-republiki-bialorus -o-wspolpracy-w-dziedzinie-kultury-nauki-i-oswiaty.html> [Accessed 15 September 2017].

Umowa między Rządem Rzeczypospolitej Polskiej a Rządem Republiki Białorusi o uznaniu ekwiwalencji w szkolnictwie wyższym, równoważności stopni naukowych i stopni w zakresie sztuki, sporządzona w Warszawie w dniu 28 kwietnia 1995 r. Available at: <http://www.nauka.gov.pl/g2/oryginal/2013_05/a323bf3a52a5961eba 4f2a44f261ae4a.pdf> [Accessed 24 September 2017].

Umowa między Rządem Rzeczypospolitej Polskiej a Rządem Republiki Białoruś w sprawie unikania podwójnego opodatkowania w zakresie podatków od dochodu i majątku, sporządzona w Mińsku dnia 18 listopada 1992 r., 1993. Dziennik Ustaw Rzeczypospolitej Polskiej [Journal of Laws], 120, item 534. Available at: <www.dz iennikustaw.gov.pl/D1993120053401.pdf> [Accessed 5 September 2017].

Umowa między Rządem Rzeczypospolitej Polskiej a Rządem Republiki Białorusi o współpracy gospodarczej, sporządzona w Warszawie dnia 30 kwietnia 2004 r., 2006. Monitor Polski, 26 item 286. Available at: <http://isap.sejm.gov.pl/DetailsSer vlet?id=WMP20060260286> [Accessed 5 September 2017].

Urzędowy rejestr gmin, w których używany jest język pomocniczy, 2017. Available at: <https://bip.mswia.gov.pl/bip/wyznania-i-mniejszosci/23923,Urzedowy-Rejestr-G min-w-ktorych-jest-uzywany-jezyk-pomocniczy.html> [Accessed 18 September 2017].

Ustawa z dnia 12 kwietnia 2001 r. Ordynacja wyborcza do Sejmu Rzeczypospolitej Polskiej i do Senatu Rzeczypospolitej Polskiej, 2001. Dziennik Ustaw Rzeczypospolitej Polskiej [Journal of Laws],46, item 499. Available at: <http://isap.sejm.g ov.pl/DetailsServlet?id=WDU20010460499> [Accessed 21 September 2017].

Ustawa z dnia 6 stycznia 2005 r. o mniejszościach narodowych i etnicznych oraz o języku regionalnym, 2005. Dziennik Ustaw Rzeczypospolitej Polskiej [Journal of Laws],17, item 141.

Ustawa z dnia 7 września 2007 r. o Karcie Polaka, 2007. Dziennik Ustaw Rzeczypospolitej Polskiej [Journal of Laws],180, 1280. Available at: <http://isap.sejm.gov.pl/ DetailsServlet?id=WDU20071801280> [Accessed 21 September 2017].

Wyniki Narodowego Spisu Powszechnego Ludności i Mieszkań 2011 Podstawowe informacje o sytuacji demograficzno-społecznej ludności Polski oraz zasobach mieszkaniowych, marzec 2012. Available at: <http://stat.gov.pl/cps/rde/xbcr/gus/lu_nps20 11_wyniki_nsp2011_22032012.pdf> [Accessed 18 September 2017].

*Zakon Respubliki Belarus' ot 5 ianvaria 2004 g. Nr 261-3 „O vnesenii izmeneniĭ i dopolneniĭ v Zakon Respubliki Belarus' „O natsional'nykh men'shinstvakh v Respubli-ke Belaru*s'. Available at: <http://pravo.levonevsky.org/bazaby09/sbor37/text37853. htm> [Accessed 19 September 2017].

BOOKS AND MONOGRAPHIES

Arutiunian, Iu., Drobizheva, L. and Susokolov, A., 1999. *Ėtnosotsiologiia*. Moskva: Aspekt-Press.

Bieleń S. ed., 2011. *Poland's Foreign Policy in the 21st Century*. Warsaw: Difin SA.

Bieleń, S., 2017. *Czas próby w stosunkach międzynarodowych*. Miscellanea. Warszawa: Oficyna Wydawnicza ASPRA-JR.

Bodio, T., 2001. *Między romantyzmem i pragmatyzmem. Psychopolityczne aspekty transformacji w Polsce.* Warszawa: Dom Wydawniczy ELIPSA.

Brubaker, R., 1998. *Nacjonalizm inaczej. Struktura narodowa i kwestie narodowe w nowej Europie.* Warszawa–Kraków: Wydawnictwo Naukowe PWN.

Chałupczak, H. and Michalik, E. eds. 2006. *Mniejszości narodowe i etniczne w procesach transformacji oraz integracji.* Lublin: Wydawnictwo Uniwersytetu Marii Curie-Skłodowskiej.

Czachor, R., 2011. *Polityka zagraniczna Republiki Białoruś w latach 1991-2011. Studium politologiczne.* Polkowice: Wydawnictwo Dolnośląskiej Wyższej Szkoły Przedsiębiorczości i Techniki w Polkowicach.

Dolbilov, M. and Miller, A., eds., 2008. *Zapadnye okrainy Rossiĭskoĭ Imperii.* Moskva: Novoe literaturnoe obozrenie.

Eberhardt, A. and Ułachowicz, U. eds., 2003. *Belarus' i Pol'shcha. Polska i Białoruś.* Warszawa: Polski Instytut Spraw Międzynarodowych.

Evstigneev, Iu., 2005. *Ishcheznyvshie ètnosy (Kratkiĭ ètno-istoricheskiĭ spravochnik).* St Petersburg: Asterion.

Gawin, T., 2010. *Polskie odrodzenie na Białorusi 1988-2005.* Białystok: Wyższa Szkoła Administracji Publicznej im. Stanisława Staszica.

Giebień, H., 2014. *Działalność Związku Polaków na Białorusi w latach 1987-2005 na tle sytuacji społeczno-politycznej w Białoruskiej Socjalistycznej Republice Radzieckiej/Republice Białoruś.* Wrocław: Oficyna Wydawnicza Arboretum.

Głogowska, H., 2012. *Stosunki polsko-białoruskie w XX wieku. Od Imperium Rosyjskiego do Unii Europejskiej.* Białystok: Wydawnictwo Uniwersytetu w Białymstoku.

Gumilow, L., 1997. *Dzieje etnosów Wielkiego Stepu.* Przekład Andrzej Nowak. Kraków: Oficyna Literacka.

Hroch, M., 2008. *Małe narody Europy. Perspektywa historyczna.* Wrocław – Warszawa – Kraków: Zakład Narodowy imienia Ossolińskich Wydawnictwo.

Jackson-Preece, J., 2007. *Prawa mniejszości.* Przełożyła Małgorzata Stolarska. Warszawa: Wydawnictwo Sic!

Jaczyński, S. and Pęksa, R., eds., 2009. *Stosunki polsko-białoruskie.* Siedlce: Wydawnictwo Akademii Podlaskiej, Vol.1 Historia i polityka, Vol.2. Społeczeństwo i polityka.

Jaśkiewicz, L., 2001. *Carat i sprawy polskie na przełomie XIX i XX wieku.* Pułtusk: Wyższa Szkoła Humanistyczna w Pułtusku.

Jedlicki, J., 1988. *Jakiej cywilizacji Polacy potrzebują. Studia z dziejów idei i wyobraźni XIX wieku.* Warszawa: Państwowe Wydawnictwo Naukowe.

Kappeler, A., 2014. *Russische Geschichte.* Munich: Verlag C.H. Beck.

Kosman, M., 1979. *Historia Białorusi.* Wrocław-Warszawa-Kraków-Gdańsk: Zakład Narodowy imienia Ossolińskich.

Kudors A., ed., 2017. *Belarusian Foreign Policy: 360°.* Rīga: University of Latvia Press, The Centre for East European Policy Studies. Available at: <http://appc.lv/wp-content/uploads/2017/05/book_Belarusian_360-www-2.pdf> [Accessed 7 September 2017].

Kukułka, J., 1998. *Traktaty sąsiedzkie Polski odrodzonej*. Wrocław – Warszawa – Kraków: Zakład Narodowy Imienia Ossolińskich – Wydawnictwo.

Lazarevich, A. and Leviash, I., 2014. *Belarus': kul'turno-tsivilizatsionnyĭ vybor*. Minsk: Belarusskaia navuka.

Łagowski, B., 2016. Parcie na Wschód. In: Łagowski B., 2016. *Polska chora na Rosję*. Warszawa: Fundacja Oratio Recta.

Łodziński, S., 2004. *Międzynarodowe standardy ochrony i wspierania mniejszości narodowych. Instytucje oraz organizacje powołane do ochrony mniejszości*. Materiał konferencyjny.

Malak, K., 2003. *Polityka zagraniczna i bezpieczeństwa Białorusi, Akademia Obrony Narodowej*. Warszawa: Akademia Obrony Narodowej.

Malinovskiĭ, V., 2003. *Istoriia belorusskoĭ gosudarstvennosti*. Minsk: Belarus'.

Martin, T., 2001. *The Affirmative Action Empire. Nations and Nationalism in the Soviet Union*, 1923-1939. New York: Cornell University Press.

Mironowicz, A., 2001. *Kościół prawosławny w dziejach dawnej Rzeczypospolitej*. Białystok: Wydawnictwo Uniwersytetu w Białymstoku.

Mironowicz, E., 2001. *Historia Białorusi*. Białystok: Orthdruk.

Natsional'naia akademiia nauk Belarusi. Institut istorii, 2014. *Rizhskiĭ mir v sud'be belorusskogo naroda 1921-1953 gg*. Minsk: «Belarusskaia navuka», Vol.1.

Nikitorowicz, J., 2010. *Grupy etniczne w wielokulturowym świecie*. Sopot: Gdańskie Wydawnictwo Psychologiczne Sp. z o.o.

Nowak A., 1999. *Jak rozbić Rosyjskie Imperium? Idee polskiej polityki wschodniej (1733–1921)*. Kraków: Wydawnictwo ARCANA.

Picheta, V., 2003. *Istoriia beloruskogo naroda*. Minsk: Izdatel'skiĭ centr BGU.

Pypin, A., 2005. *Istoriia russkoĭ ètnografii*. Minsk: Belarusskaia Èntsyklopedyia.

Radzik, R., 2012. *Białoruś. Między Wschodem a Zachodem*. Lublin: Wydawnictwo Uniwersytetu Marii Curie-Skłodowskiej.

Rotfeld, A., 2012. *Myśli o Rosji ...i nie tylko*. Warszawa: Świat Książki.

Rotschild, J., 1981. *Ethnopolitics. A Conceptual Framework*. New York: Columbia University Press.

Rudkoŭski, P., 2007. *Paŭstan'nie Belarusi*. Vil'nia: Instytut belarusistyki.

Rypiński, A., 1840. *Białoruś. Kilka słów o poezji prostego ludu téj naszéj polskiej prowincji; o jego muzyce, śpiéwie, tańcach, etc. przez Alexandra Rypińskiego, członka akademii przemysłu, rolnictwa, rękodzieł i handlu francuzkiego*. Paryż. W księgotłoczni J. Marylskiego.

Sahanowicz, H., 2001. *Historia Białorusi. Od czasów najdawniejszych do końca XVIII wieku*. Lublin: Instytut Europy Środkowo-Wschodniej.

Smith, A. D., 2009. *Etniczne źródła narodów*. Przekład Małgorzata Głowacka-Grajper. Kraków: Wydawnictwo Uniwersytetu Jagiellońskiego.

Snapkoŭski, V., 2013. *Belaruska-pol'skiia adnosiny (1918-1989 gg.): dasledavanni, dokumenty, iliustratsi i karty*. Minsk: Èntsyklapedyks.

Bibliography

Szybieka, Z., 2002. *Historia Białorusi 1795-2000*. Przeł. Hubert Łaszkiewicz. Lublin: Instytut Europy Środkowo-Wschodniej.

Tishkov, V. and Shabaev, Iu., 2011. *Ètnopolitologiia. Politicheskie funktsii ètnichnosti*. Moskva: Izdatel'stvo Moskovskogo universiteta.

Topolski I., ed. 2009. *Białoruś w stosunkach międzynarodowych*. Lublin: Wydawnictwo Uniwersytetu Marii Curie-Skłodowskiej.

Tymanowski J., Daniluk, A. and Bryll. J. eds., 2015. *Polska i Białoruś we współczesnej Europie*. Warszawa: Wydział Dziennikarstwa i Nauk Politycznych.

Tymanowski, J., 2017. *Rola i znaczenie Republiki Białoruś we współczesnej Europie*. Toruń: Adam Marszałek.

Vonsovich, L., 2005. *Belorusovedenie*. Minsk: TetraSistems.

Walicki, A., 2009. *Naród. Nacjonalizm. Polska*. Prace wybrane. Vol. I. Kraków: UNIVERSITAS. Vol. 1.

Wyszyński, R., 2010. *Narodziny czy śmierć narodu. Narodotwórcze działania elit białoruskich i buriackich po upadku ZSRR*. Warszawa: Wydawnictwo Naukowe Scholar.

Zięba R., 2010. *Główne kierunki polityki zagranicznej Polski po zimnej wojnie*. Warszawa: Wydawnictwa Akademickie i Profesjonalne.

Zięba R., Bieleń, S. and Zając, J. eds., 2015. *Teorie i podejścia badawcze w nauce o stosunkach międzynarodowych*. Warszawa: Wydawnictwo Wydziału Dziennikarstwa i Nauk Politycznych Uniwersytet Warszawski.

Żarnowski, J., 1973. *Społeczeństwo Drugiej Rzeczypospolitej 1918-1939*. Warszawa: Państwowy Instytut Wydawniczy.

Żołędowski, C., 2003. *Białorusini i Litwini w Polsce, Polacy na Białorusi i Litwie. Uwarunkowania współczesnych stosunków między większością i mniejszościami narodowymi*. Warszawa: Oficyna Wydawnicza ASPRA-JR.

PAPERS

Antoszewski, A., 2010. Instytucjonalne uwarunkowania rywalizacji politycznej w państwach poradzieckich. In: T. Bodio, ed. 2010. *Przywództwo, elity i transformacje w krajach WNP. Problemy metodologii badań*, Warszawa: Oficyna Wydawnicza ASPRA-JR, Vol.1, pp. 91-110.

Barwiński M., 2013. Polish interstate relations with Ukraine, Belarus and Lithuania after 1990 in the context of the situation of national minorities. *European Spatial Research and Policy*, 1(20), p. 5-26.

Bieleń, S., 1997. Długa droga do przyszłości. *Wiadomości Kulturalne*, 51-52 (187-188), p.17.

Bieleń, S., 2008. Deficyt realizmu w polskiej polityce zagranicznej. *Stosunki Międzynarodowe – International Relations*, 38(3-4), pp. 9-29.

Bieleń, S., 2012. O polskiej polityce wschodniej. *Polityka Wschodnia*, 1(10), pp. 11-33.

Bieleń, S., 2015. Tożsamość uczestników stosunków międzynarodowych. In: R. Zięba, S. Bieleń and J. Zając, eds. 2015. *Teorie i podejścia badawcze w nauce o stosunkach międzynarodowych.* Warszawa: Wydawnictwo Wydziału Dziennikarstwa i Nauk Politycznych Uniwersytet Warszawski, pp. 153-176.

Bodio, T., Wojnicki, J. and Załęski, P., 2007. Transformacja ustrojowa państw postsocjalistycznych. In: K.A.Wojtaszczyk, W. Jakubowski, eds. 2007. *Społeczeństwo i polityka. Podstawy nauk politycznych.* Warszawa: Oficyna Wydawnicza ASPRA-JR, pp. 468-485.

Bukhovets, O., 2010. Istoriopisanie sovetskoĭ Belarusi. In: F. Bomsdorf and G. Bordiugov, eds., 2010. *Natsional'nye istorii na postsovetskom prostranstve – II. Desiat' let spustia.* Moskva: Fond Friedrikha Naumanna, AIRO-XXI. pp. 15-44.

Chałupczak, H., 2006. Liczba mniejszości narodowych i etnicznych w Polsce w świetle powszechnego spisu ludności z 2002 roku oraz badań naukowych. In: E. Michalik and H. Chałupczak, eds. 2006. *Mniejszości narodowe i etniczne w procesach transformacji oraz integracji,* Lublin: Wydawnictwo Uniwersytetu Marii Curie-Skłodowskiej, pp. 263-270.

Chasnouski, M., 2015. Belarus' i regional'naia integractsiia v Tsentralnoĭ i Vostochnoĭ Evrope: vyzovy XXI v. In: J. Tymanowski, A. Daniluk and J. Bryll., eds. 2015. *Polska i Białoruś we współczesnej Europie.* Warszawa: Wydawnictwo Wydziału Dziennikarstwa i Nauk Politycznych Uniwersytet Warszawski, pp. 71-89.

Chodubski, A., 2016. 70 lat do różnorodności. Mniejszości narodowe i etniczne w Polsce, *Studia Gdańskie. Wizje i rzeczywistość,* Vol. 13, pp. 395-408.

Dmowski, R., 1901. Narodowiec. W naszym obozie. Listy do przyjaciół politycznych. *Przegląd Wielkopolski,* 10(7), pp. 609-625.

Dmowski, R.,1926. Na przełomie stuleci. Odrodzenie myśli politycznej w Polsce. In: R. Dmowski, 1926. *Polityka Polska i odbudowanie państwa z dodaniem memorjału „Zagadnienia Środkowo- i Wschodnioeuropejskie" i innych dokumentów polityki polskiej z lat 1914-1918.* Wydanie drugie. Warszawa: Nakładem Księgarni Perzyński, Niklewicz i Ska, pp. 3-35.

Dmowski, R.,1926. Memorjał o terytorium państwa polskiego złożony przez R. Dmowskiego prezydentowi Wilsonowi w Waszyngtonie d. 8 października 1918 r. In: R. Dmowski, 1926. *Polityka Polska i odbudowanie państwa z dodaniem memorjału „Zagadnienia Środkowo- i Wschodnioeuropejskie" i innych dokumentów polityki polskiej z lat 1914-1918.* Wydanie drugie. Warszawa: Nakładem Księgarni Perzyński, Niklewicz i Ska, pp. 506-520.

Dziemidok-Olszewska, B., 2009. Konstytucyjne ośrodki decyzyjne Republiki Białoruś. In: I. Topolski, ed. 2009. *Białoruś w stosunkach międzynarodowych.* Lublin: Wydawnictwo Uniwersytetu Marii Curie-Skłodowskiej, pp. 17-38.

Dzwonkowski, R., 2005. Sytuacja religijna Polaków na Białorusi. In: H. Chałupczak E. Michalik, eds. 2005. *Polska Białoruś. Problemy sąsiedztwa.* Lublin: Wydawnictwo Uniwersytetu Marii Curie-Skłodowskiej, pp. 91-102.

Eberhardt, A., 2003. Integracja białorusko-rosyjska a stosunki Białorusi z Unią Europejską. In: A. Eberhardt and U. Ułachowicz, eds. 2003. *Belarus' i Pol'shcha. Polska i Białoruś.* Warszawa: Polski Instytut Spraw Międzynarodowych, pp. 41-47.

Eberhardt, A., 2006. Polska a konflikt wokół Związku Polaków na Białorusi. *Rocznik Polskiej Polityki Zagranicznej*. Warszawa: Polski Instytut Spraw Międzynarodowych, pp. 258-266.

Esin, R., 2016. Belorusskiĭ ėksport i investitsionnaia privlekatel'nost': segodnia i zavtra. In: J. Tymanowski, A. Daniluk and J. Bryll., eds. 2015. *Polska i Białoruś we współczesnej Europie*. Warszawa: Wydział Dziennikarstwa i Nauk Politycznych, pp. 183-189.

Fedorowicz K., 2009. Białoruś w polskiej polityce wschodniej w latach 1990-1996. In: S. Jaczyński and R. Pęksa, eds. 2009. *Stosunki polsko-białoruskie. Tom I. Historia i polityka*. Siedlce: Wydawnictwo Akademii Podlaskiej, pp. 85-100.

Flemming, M., 2002. The new minority rights regime in Poland: the experience of the German, Belarussian and Jewish minorities since 1989, *Nations and Nationalism*, 8(4), pp. 531-549.

Glybinny U., 2012. Dolia belaruskae kul'tury pad Savetami 1920-1957. In: A.Taras, 2012. *Dolia belaruskae kul'tury pad savetami 1920-1991 gg*. Minsk: Kharvest, pp. 3-17.

Głogowska H., 2009. Mniejszości narodowe w stosunkach polsko-białoruskich po 1989 roku. In: M. Mieczkowska and D. Scholze eds. 2009. *Polityczne wymiary etniczności*. Kraków: Wydawnictwo DANTE, pp. 181-205.

Habowski, M., 2009. Stosunki Białorusi z Polską. In: I. Topolski, ed. 2009. *Białoruś w stosunkach międzynarodowych*. Lublin: Wydawnictwo Uniwersytetu Marii Curie-Skłodowskiej, pp. 233-253.

Ioffe, G., 2016. Belarus charts course between Russia and Poland. *Eurasia Daily Monitor*, 13(166). [online] Available at: <https://jamestown.org/program/belarus-charts -course-russia-poland/> [Accessed 16 September 2017].

Iwanow, T., 2008. Wyzwania współpracy transgranicznej Polska-Białoruś (transgraniczny region województwo lubelskie i obwód brzeski). *Studenckie Prace Prawnicze, Administratywistyczne i Ekonomiczne*, 5, pp. 131-141.

Iwańczuk K., 2009. Pozycja geopolityczna Białorusi. In: I. Topolski, ed. 2009. *Białoruś w stosunkach międzynarodowych*. Lublin: Wydawnictwo Uniwersytetu Marii Curie-Skłodowskiej, pp. 129-135.

Janusz, G., 2005. Mniejszość białoruska w Polsce i polska na Białorusi. In: H. Chałupczak and E. Michalik, eds. 2005. *Polska-Białoruś. Problemy sąsiedztwa*. Lublin: Wydawnictwo Uniwersytetu Marii Curie Skłodowskiej, pp. 53-78.

Kabzińska, I., 2012. Od euforii do lęku. Polacy w Republice Białorusi. In: M. Głowacka-Grajper and R. Wyszyński, eds. 2012. *20 lat rzeczywistości poradzieckiej. Spojrzenie socjologiczne*. Warszawa: Wydawnictwa Uniwersytetu Warszawskiego, pp. 317-336.

Kornat, M., 2008. Ruch prometejski – ważne doświadczenie polityki zagranicznej II Rzeczypospolitej, *Nowa Europa Wschodnia*, 2, pp. 76-86.

Kosmarskaya, N., 2011. Russia and Post-Soviet '"Russian Diaspora"': Contrasting Visions, Conflicting Projects, *Nationalism and Ethnic Politics*, 17(1), pp. 54-74.

Kraska, B., 2006. Polsko-białoruska współpraca transgraniczna jako nowy model więzi międzynarodowych. *Zeszyty Naukowe Ostrołęckiego Towarzystwa Naukowego*, 20 2006) pp. 241-260. [online] Available at: <http://mazowsze.hist.pl/28/Zeszyt y_Naukowe_Ostroleckiego_Towarzystwa_Naukowego/649/2006/23147/> [Accessed 20 May 2017].

Kravtsevich, A., 2011. Pogranich'e kak sud'ba (VI-XVIII vv.). Mezhdu Vostokom i Zapadom Evropy. In: A. Kravtsevich, and A. Smolenchuk, and S. Tokt'. *Belorusy natsiia pogranich'ia*. Vilnius: Evropeĭskiĭ gummanitarnyĭ universitet, pp. 7-84.

Kruchkovskiĭ, T., 2011. Belorussko-pol'skie otnosheniia: politiko-natsional'nyĭ aspekt. In: *Belorussiia i Ukraina: istoriia i ku'ltura*. Vyp.4. Moskva: TEZAURUS, pp. 472-503.

Krzysztofowicz, M., 2003. Wpływ rozszerzenia Unii Europejskiej na stosunki polsko-białoruskie. In: A. Eberhardt and U. Ułachowicz, eds. 2003. *Belarus' i Pol'shcha. Polska i Białoruś*. Warszawa: Polski Instytut Spraw Międzynarodowych, pp. 27-32.

Kuzio, T., 2001. Nationalising states or nation-building? A critical review of the theoretical and empirical evidence. *Nations and Nationalism*, 7(2), pp. 135-154.

Leshchenko, N., 2004. A fine instrument: two nation-building strategies in post-Soviet Belarus. *Nations and Nationalism*, 10(3), pp. 333–352.

Ładykowski, P., 2011. Gra w karty. „Karta narodowa" jako stawka w państwowej polityce narodowościowej. In: W. Dohnal and A. Posern-Zieliński, eds. 2011. *Antropologia i polityka. Szkice z badań nad kulturowymi wymiarami władzy*. Warszawa: Wydawnictwo IAE PAN, pp. 15-41.

Łaskiewicz, W., 2005. Tożsamość i kultura w działalności Białoruskiego Towarzystwa Społeczno-Kulturalnego w Polsce. In: H. Chałupczak and E. Michalik, eds. 2005. *Polska-Białoruś. Problemy sąsiedztwa*. Lublin: Wydawnictwo Uniwersytetu Marii Curie Skłodowskiej, pp. 155-160.

Łatyszonek, O., 2010. Białorusini. In: M. Kopczyński and W. Tygielski, eds. 2010. *Pod wspólnym niebem. Narody dawnej Rzeczypospolitej*. Warszawa: Muzeum Historii Polski, Bellona, pp. 39-54.

Mieroszewski, J., 1974. Rosyjski „kompleks polski" i obszar ULB. *Kultura*, 9(324), pp. 3-14.

Nemenskiĭ, O., 2012. Politika Pol'shi v otnoshenii Belarusi v kontse nulevykh – nachale desiatykh godov: glubokiĭ krizis i ego prichiny. In: Informatsionno-analiticheskiĭ tsentr pri Administratsii Prezidenta Respubliki Belarus', 2012. *Politika Evropeĭskogo soiuza v otnoshenii Soiuznogo gosudarstva Belarusi i Rossii*. Minsk: Biznesofset, pp. 117-127.

Nemenski, O., 2015. Politika Pol'shi v otnoshenii Belorusii v sisteme belorussko-evropeĭskikh otnosheniĭ. [online] Available at: <http://geo-politica.info/politika-polshi-v -otnoshenii-belorussii-v-sisteme-belorussko-evropeyskikh-otnosheniy.html> [Accessed 16 September 2017].

Nowak-Far A., 2011. Conflicts powers in the realm of Poland's foreign Policy decisions. In: S. Bieleń, ed. 2011. *Poland's foreign Policy in the 21 st century*. Warsaw: Difin SA, pp. 185-196.

Parzymies S., 2011. Successes and failures in building Poland's Western identity. In: S. Bieleń, ed. 2011. *Poland's foreign Policy in the 21st century*. Warsaw: Difin SA, pp. 21-38.

Pawluczuk, W., 2012. W poszukiwaniu tożsamości. Kształtowanie się idei narodowej Białorusinów. In: M., Głowacka-Grajper R., Wyszyński, eds. 2012. *20 lat rzeczywistości poradzieckiej. Spojrzenie socjologiczne*. Warszawa: Wydawnictwa Uniwersytetu Warszawskiego, pp. 155-167.

Pawluczuk, W., 2015. U źródeł idei narodu białoruskiego. In: M. Bieńkowska and W. Żelazny, eds. 2015. *Pogranicza. Księga Jubileuszowa Profesora Andrzeja Sadowskiego*. Białystok: Wydawnictwo Uniwersytetu w Białymstoku, pp. 33-44.

Petrovskaya, O., 2017. Povorot v pol'sko-belorusskikh otnosheniiakh: faktory sblizheniia, mekhanizmy vzaimodeĭstviia. *Problemy natsional'noĭ strategii*, 1(40), pp. 95-127.

Radzik, R., 2009. Kulturowo-cywilizacyjna tożsamość społeczeństwa Białorusi. In: I. Topolski, eds. 2009. *Białoruś w stosunkach międzynarodowych*. Lublin: Wydawnictwo Uniwersytetu Marii Curie-Skłodowskiej, pp. 39-75.

Rudzutak, Ia., 1924. Tsyrkuliarnoe pis'mo CK RKP(b) o meropiiatiakh po realizatsii postanovleniĭ po natsional'nomu voprosu, priniatykh XII s"ezdom RKP(b) i IV soveshchaniem CK RKP(b) s otvestvennymi rabotnikami natsional'nykh republik i oblasteĭ, 2005. In: L. Gatagova, L. Kosheleva and I. Rogovaia, eds. *CK RKP(b) i natsional'nyĭ vopros. Kniga I. 1918-1933*. Moskva: Rossiĭkaia politicheskaia ėntsiklopedia, pp. 169-175.

Shevchenko, A.N., 2015. Analiz i tendetsii pol'sko belorusskikh otnosheniĭ v nachale XXI veka. *Pravova derzhava*. 19/2015. [online] Available at: <http://dspace.onu.ed u.ua:8080/bitstream/123456789/6754/1/175-182.pdf [Accessed 25 May 2017].

Snapkouski, U., 2003. Stosunki polsko-białoruskie (1990-2003). In: A. Eberhardt and, U. Ułachowicz, eds. 2003. *Belarus' i Pol'shcha. Polska i Białoruś*. Warszawa: Polski Instytut Spraw Międzynarodowych, pp. 17-25.

Sulowski S., 2007. Transformacja polskiej polityki zagranicznej. In: J. Błuszkowski, ed., 2007. *Dylematy polskiej transformacji*. Warszawa: Dom Wydawniczy ELIPSA, pp. 282-293.

Szeptycki A., 2011. A new phase of the Polish messianism in the East?. In: S. Bieleń, ed. 2011. *Poland's Foreign Policy in the 21st Century*. Warsaw: Difin SA., pp. 292-316.

Tokt', S., 2011. Belorusy v epokhu formirovaniia modernykh evropeĭskikh natsiĭ. In: A. Kravtsevich, A. Smolenchuk, and S. Tokt', eds. 2011. *Belorusy: natsiia pogranich'ia*. Vilnius: Evropeĭskiĭ gummanitarnyĭ universitet, pp. 85-158.

Vezhbitski A., 2015. Paradigmy pol'skoĭ vostochnoĭ polityki po otnosheniiu k stranam byvshego SSSR. *Memlekettik Zhoene Qyzmet. Gosudarstvennoe upravlenie i gosudarstvennaia sluzhba. Public administration and civil service*. Available at: <http://www.pa-academy.kz/index.php?lang=ru> [Accessed 15 November 2015].

Waszkiewicz, J., 2005. Mniejszość polska w stosunkach polsko-białoruskich. In: H. Chałupczak and E. Michalik, eds. 2005. *Polska Białoruś. Problemy sąsiedztwa*. Lublin: Wydawnictwo Uniwersytetu Marii Curie-Skłodowskiej, pp. 45-52.

Wierzbicki, A., 2008. Mniejszości narodowe i etniczne w Polsce. Status prawno-konstytucyjny. In: W. Jakubowski and T. Słomka, eds. 2008. *Porządek konstytucyjny w Polsce. Wybrane problemy*. Warszawa-Pułtusk: Oficyna Wydawnicza ASPRA-JR, pp. 225-244.

Wierzbicki A., 2012. Nacjonalizm i geopolityka w Europie Wschodniej. In: S. Bieleń, A. Skrzypek, eds. 2012. *Geopolityka w stosunkach polsko-rosyjskich*. Warszawa: Oficyna Wydawnicza ASPRA-JR, pp 87-121.

Winnicki Z.J., 2015. Cywilizacyjno-kulturowe uwarunkowania współczesnych relacji polsko-białoruskich. In: J. Tymanowski, A. Daniluk, J. Bryll, eds. 2015. *Polska i Białoruś we współczesnej Europie*. Warszawa: Wydział Dziennikarstwa i Nauk Politycznych, pp. 227-257.

Włodkowska-Bagan, A., 2015. Kategoria rywalizacji. In: R. Zięba, S. Bieleń and J. Zając, eds. 2015. *Teorie i podejścia badawcze w nauce o stosunkach międzynarodowych*. Warszawa: Wydawnictwo Wydziału Dziennikarstwa i Nauk Politycznych Uniwersytet Warszawski, pp. 241-259.

Wojtaszczyk K.A., 1996. Transformacja ustrojowa w krajach Europy Wschodniej, Środkowej i Południowej. In: E. Zieliński, ed. 1996. *Transformacja ustrojowa państw Europy Środkowej i Wschodniej*. Warszawa: Dom Wydawniczy ELIPSA, pp. 9-20.

Yeliseyeu, A., 2017. The Poland–Belarus relationship: geopolitics gave new impetus, but no breakthrough. In: A. Kudors, ed. 2017. *Belarusian Foreign Policy: 360°*. Rīga: University of Latvia Press, The Centre for East European Policy Studies. Available at: <http://appc.lv/wp-content/uploads/2017/05/book_Belarusian_360-www-2.pdf> [Accessed 7 September 2017].

Zając J., 2015. Teoria ról międzynarodowych. In: R. Zięba, S. Bieleń, S. and J. Zając, eds. 2015. *Teorie i podejścia badawcze w nauce o stosunkach międzynarodowych*. Warszawa: Wydawnictwo Wydziału Dziennikarstwa i Nauk Politycznych Uniwersytet Warszawski, pp. 127-151.

Zięba R., 2011. The search for an international role for Poland: conceptualizing the role of a „middle-ranking" state. In: S. Bieleń, ed. 2011. *Poland's Foreign Policy in the 21st Century*. Warszawa: Difin SA. pp. 61-79.

NEWSPAPERS

Anna Dyner: „Iz Varshavy Minsku podadut ruku", 2016. [online] Available at: <https://www.bsblog.info/anna-dyner-iz-varshavy-minsku-podadut-ruku/> [Accessed 17 September 2017].

Belorusskim chinovnikom zapreshcheno pol'zovat'sia kartoĭ poliaka, 11.02.2012. [online] Available at: <https://news.tut.by/society/273618.html> [Accessed 21 September 2017].

Będzie porozumienie w sprawie Związku Polaków na Białorusi i Karty Polaka?, 05.12.2016. [online] Available at: <https://kresy.pl/wydarzenia/bedzie-porozumienie-w-sprawie-zwiazku-polakow-na-bialorusi-i-karty-polaka/> [Accessed 19 September 2017].

Bibliography

Białoruski klucz do geopolityki polskiej, 2016. [online] Available at: <http://www.grze gorzbraun.pl/2016/05/01/bialoruski-klucz-do-geopolityki-polskiej/> [Accessed 28 June 2017].

Białoruś: mały ruch graniczny z Polską bez przygotowania to katastrofa, 09.02.2016. [online] Available at: <http://wiadomosci.onet.pl/swiat/bialorus-maly-ruch-graniczn y-z-polska-bez-przygotowania-to-katastrofa/yw6kng> [Accessed 21 September 2017].

Centrum Kulturalne Białorusi w Warszawie, 2017. [online] Available at: http://poland. mfa.gov.by/pl/bilateral_relations/cultural/centrum/> [Accessed 24 May 2017].

Dotacje dla TV Biełsat obcięte o 2/3? Romaszewska: to oznacza likwidację stacji, 2016. [online] Available at: <http://kresy.pl/wydarzenia/dotacje-dla-tv-bielsat-obcie te-o-2-3-romaszewska-to-oznacza-likwidacje-stacji/> [Accessed 17 September 2017].

Dr Zapałowski: nie warto odwracać się od Białorusi, 2017. [online] Available at: <http://kresy.pl/wydarzenia/dr-zapalowski-nie-warto-odwracac-sie-od-bialorusi/> [Accessed at 26 June 2017].

Eparkhi. Rimo-Katolicheskaya Cerkov' v Belarusi, 2017. [online] Available at: <http:// old.catholic.by/2/ru/belarus/dioceses.html> [Accessed 19 September 2017].

„Èto nenormal'no, kogda bliskie sosedi ne obshchaiutsia i ne vstrechaiutsia", 2016. [online] Available at: <https://gazetaby.com/cont/art.php?sn_nid=111151> [Accessed 17 September 2017].

Glava MID Pol'shi planiruet 22 marta posetit' Belarus', 2016. [online] Available at: <http://www.belaruspartisan.org/politic/336738/> [Accessed 17 September 2017].

Goliński, C., 18.05. 2001. Poseł SLD gani Polskę na Białorusi, chwali władzę Łukas-zenki. [online] Available at: <http://wiadomosci.gazeta.pl/wiadomosci/1,114873,28 0079.html> [Accessed 22 September 2017].

Instytut Polski w Mińsku, 24.09.2017. [online] Available at: <http://www.minsk.msz.g ov.pl/pl/ambasada/instytut_polski/> [Accessed 24 September 2017].

Jak uczy się języka polskiego na Białorusi. Liczby i fakty, 2017. [online] Available at: <http://poland.mfa.gov.by/pl/embassy/news/f5026a6dfa11ae10.html> [Accessed 23 September 2017].

Jan Syczewski, znany ze swoich kontrowersyjnych wypowiedzi chwalących sytuację na Białorusi, został członkiem zarządu województwa, 02.12.2002. [online] Available at: <http://www.wspolczesna.pl/aktualnosci/art/5215490,jan-syczewski-znany-ze-s woich-kontrowersyjnych-wypowiedzi-chwalacych-sytuacje-na-bialorusi-zostal-czlo nkiem-zarzadu-wojewodztwa,id,t.html> [Accessed 22 September 2017].

"Likwidacja polskich szkół i rusyfikacja". Związek Polaków o reformie edukacji na Białorusi, 17.03.2017. [online] Available at: <http://www.polsatnews.pl/wiadomosc /2017-03-21/likwidacja-polskich-szkol-i-rusyfikacja-zwiazek-polakow-o-reformie-e dukacji-na-bialorusi/> [Accessed 21 September 2017].

Lukashenko budet ubezhdat' èlektorat, chto v krizise vinovata Rossia. [online] Available at: <naviny.by/rubrics/politic/2015/01/17/ic_articles_112_188014/> [Accessed 22 February 2015].

186

Makeĭ v Polshe: My khotim uĭti ot sil'noĭ zavisimosti ot Rossii, 17 oktiabria 2016. [online] Available at: <https://news.tut.by/politics/515492.html> [Accessed 16 September 2017].://Ne

Ministerstwo Edukacji Białorusi nie zmienia nastawienia do polskich szkół, 18.06.2017. [online] Available at: <https://kresy.pl/wydarzenia/kresy/ministerstwo-edukacji-bialorusi-zmienia-nastawienia-wobec-polskich-szkol/> [Accessed 21 September 2017].

Ministerstwo Spraw Zagranicznych RP, 2016. *#Dobry Rok w MSZ – minister Witold Waszczykowski podsumował rok w polskiej polityce zagranicznej*, 17.11.2016. [online] Available at: <http://www.msz.gov.pl/pl/aktualnosci/wiadomosci/0_dobryrok_w_msz___minister_witold_waszczykowski_podsumowal_rok_w_polskiej_polityce_zagranicznej [Accessed 16 September 2017].

Minskiĭ avtomobil'nyĭ zavod. Sborochnoe proizvodstvo tekhniki MAZ otkryto v Pol'she, 13.09.2016. [online] Available at: <http://maz.by/ru/news/general/2014/9/sp_maz_poland/> [Accessed 13 September 2016].

Morawiecki Mateusz. Prywatyzacja na Białorusi z polskimi firmami, 24.10.2016. [online] Available at: <http://www.rp.pl/Prywatyzacja/310249888-Mateusz-Morawiecki-Prywatyzacja-na-Bialorusi-z-polskimi-firmami.html> [Accessed 25 November 2016].

Morawiecki w Mińsku: Polska bramą na Wschód dla UE, 24.10.2016. [online] Available at: <http://www.tvp.info/27458219/morawiecki-w-minsku-polska-brama-na-wschod-dla-ue> [Accessed 22 May 2017].

MSZ Białorusi o sprawie Marka Bućki, 18.05.2005. [online] Available at: <https://wiadomosci.wp.pl/msz-bialorusi-o-sprawie-marka-bucki-6032047141983361a> [Accessed 21 September 2017].

MTZ Belarus Traktor sp. z o.o., 25.11.2016. [online] Available at: <http://mtzbelarus.pl/> [Accessed 25 November 2017].

Nemenski O., 2010. *Poliaki i russkie: narody raznykh vremen i raznykh sudeb*. [online] Available at: http://www.apn.ru/publications/article22387.htm> [Accessed 2 September 2017].

Okolo 70 chelovek proshli shestviem v Varshave po sluchaiu Dnia Voli, 2016. [online] Available at: <http://www.belaruspartisan.org/m/politic/337245/> [Accessed 17 September 2017].

Pełczyńska-Nałęcz, K., 2016. Ostrożnie z graczem Łukaszenką. *Gazeta Wyborcza*. [online] Available at: <http://wyborcza.pl/1,75968,20896047,ostroznie-z-graczem-lukaszenka.html?disableRedirects=true> [Accessed 17 September 2017].

Pełczyńska-Nałęcz K., 2017. *Pożegnanie z Giedroyciem*. Warszawa: Fundacja im. Stefana Batorego, styczeń 2017. [online] Available at: <http://www.batory.org.pl/upload/files/pdf/rap_otw_eu/Pozegnanie%20z%20Giedroyciem.pdf >[Accessed 26 June 2017].

Polovina „kart poliaka" wydana grazhdanam Belarusi, 20.08.2017. [online] Available at: <https://www.eurointegration.com.ua/rus/news/2017/08/20/7069975/view_print/> [Accessed 3 September 2017].

Polscy i białoruscy historycy rozpoczęli dialog o „sprawach trudnych", 2017. [online] Available at: <http://kresy.pl/wydarzenia/spoleczenstwo/polscy-bialoruscy-historyc y-rozpoczeli-dialog-o-sprawach-trudnych/> [Accessed 3 September 2017].

Pol'skiĭ agrarnyĭ biznes gotov investirovat' v Belarus', no ozhidaet garantiĭ, 08.11.2016. [online] Available at: <http://naviny.by/new/20161108/1478628479pol skiy-agrarnyy-biznes-gotov-investirovat-v-belarus-no-ozhidaet-garantiy> [Accessed 27 November 2016].

Program im. Kalinowskiego zmienia format: stypendia będą wypłacane tylko przez rok, 06.03.2016. [online] Available at: <http://belsat.eu/pl/news/program-im-kalino wskiegozmienia-format-stypendia-beda-wyplacane-tylko-przez-rok/> [Accessed 27 October 2016].

Robert Winnitskiĭ: „Politika Pol'shi v otnoshenii Belarusi prosto uzhasna", 2016. [online] Available at: <https://www.bsblog.info/robert-vinnickij-politika-polshi-v-otno shenii-belarusi-prosto-uzhasna/> [Accessed 17 September 2017].

Robiński A., 2010. OBWE: wybory na Białorusi nie były wolne. *Rzeczpospolita*. [online] Available at: <http://www.rp.pl/artykul/581806-OBWE--wybory-na-Bialorusi-nie-byly-wolne.html#ap-1>[Accessed 16 September 2017].

Romanova, N., 04.10.2016. Bol'shie i konkretnye biznes-plany. *Sovetskaya Belorussiia*. № 190 (25072). [online] Available at: <http://www.sb.by/belarus/article/bolshi e-ikonkretnye-biznes-plany.html> [Accessed 1 November 2016].

Wizyta wicepremiera RP Mateusza Morawieckiego w Mińsku, 25.10.2016. [online] Available at: <http://www.minsk.msz.gov.pl/pl/aktualnosci/wizyta_wicepremiera_r p_mateusza_morawieckiego_w_minsku> [Accessed 5 September 2017].

Władze Białorusi ograniczają nauczanie języka polskiego, 2005. [online] Available at: <https://kresy.pl/wydarzenia/wladze-bialorusi-ograniczaja-nauke-jezyka-polskiego-foto/> [Accessed 18 September 2017].

Appendix

TREATY

between the Republic of Poland and the Republic of Belarus on Neighbourly Relations and Friendly Cooperation, signed in Warsaw on 23 June 1992

In the name of the Republic of Poland

THE PRESIDENT OF THE REPUBLIC OF POLAND

makes it known that:

On 23 June 1992 in Warsaw, a Treaty between the Republic of Poland and the Republic of Belarus on Neighbourly Relations and Friendly Cooperation was signed, worded as follows:

TREATY

between the Republic of Poland and the Republic of Belarus on neighbourly relations and friendly cooperation

The Republic of Poland and the Republic of Belarus, hereinafter referred to as the "Parties",

guided by the goals and principles of the United Nations Charter, the Final Act of the Conference on Security and Cooperation in Europe, the Charter of Paris for a New Europe, and other documents on European cooperation,

aware of their responsibility for peace and security in the world,

seeking to contribute to the construction of a just and peaceful order in Europe,

confirming their respect for human rights and fundamental freedoms, and for the principles of democracy, justice and tolerance that constitute an essential element of the European heritage,

appreciating the importance of friendly relations between Poland and Belarus to strengthening trust and cooperation on the European continent, and in particular in Central and Eastern Europe,

considering that Poland and Belarus have, to a large, extent, a shared history, of which the best tradition is the coexistence and mutual enrichment of cultures,

taking account of the ethnic and cultural closeness of the Polish and Belarusian nations,

considering the fact that Poles and Belarusians living within the territories of the two Parties make an important contribution to the development of both Parties and the cultures of both nations,
seeking to strengthen the foundations of neighbourly relations between the Republic of Poland and the Republic of Belarus,
and seeking to deepen mutual understanding between the Polish and Belarusian nations,
hereby agree as follows:

Article 1

The Parties shall form their relations as friendly neighbouring States, in a spirit of mutual respect and partnership. They are guided by the principles of sovereignty, equality, the absence of the use of force or the threat thereof, the inviolability of borders, territorial integrity, the peaceful resolution of disputes, non-intervention in internal affairs, respect for human rights and fundamental freedoms, and the right of nations to self-determination.

Article 2

The Parties confirm the existence of the border between them, recognise that border as inviolable, and declare that they neither have nor will have in the future any territorial claims against each other.

Article 3

The Parties undertake to strengthen the European mechanisms of security, stability and cooperation on the basis of the Final Act of the Conference on Security and Cooperation in Europe, the Charter of Paris for a New Europe, other documents of the Conference on Security and Cooperation in Europe, and the Treaty on Conventional Armed Forces in Europe.

Article 4

The Parties shall support the process of disarmament in the fields of nuclear weapons, chemical weapons and other types of weapons of mass destruction, as well as of conventional weapons. They shall also strive to further limit armed forces and arms in Europe to a degree sufficient for defence, and to strengthen means of building trust and security in the military sphere.

Article 5

In accordance with the Treaty on the Non-Proliferation of Nuclear Weapons, the Parties shall cooperate to work towards the non-proliferation of such weapons, particularly in Central and Eastern Europe. They will co-operate in order to guarantee control over exports of goods and technologies that serve peaceful purposes but could be used in the production of weapons of mass destruction.

Article 6

In accordance with the United Nations Charter and relevant documents of the Conference on Security and Cooperation in Europe, the Parties undertake to settle any disputes that may arise between them solely through peaceful means.

Article 7
1. The Parties repudiate the use of force or the threat thereof in their mutual relations.
2. Neither Party shall allow its territory to be used by any third state or third states for purposes of armed aggression or hostile activities against the other Party.
3. If any third state or third states engage in an armed invasion of one of the Parties, the other Party shall not provide any military assistance or any other aid whatsoever to such third state or third states throughout the duration of the armed conflict, and will act to resolve that conflict in accordance with the rules of the United Nations Charter and documents of the Conference on Security and Cooperation in Europe.
4. The above obligations do not infringe the rights and obligations of the Parties resulting from the United Nations Charter.

Article 8

The Parties shall engage in consultations on matters concerning international security. If one of the Parties deems that a situation or conflict threatens or violates international peace or European security, the Parties shall promptly hold consultations on possible means of overcoming the existing situation or resolving the conflict. Such consultations shall be conducted in accordance with documents of the Conference on Security and Cooperation in Europe.

Article 9

As necessary, the Parties shall hold consultations in the field of defence on matters of common interest.

Article 10
1. The Parties shall develop regularly contacts between government bodies and state administration. The Parties attach particular importance to mutual contacts between their respective parliaments.
2. Meetings and consultations at the highest level will be held in order to ensure the development of bilateral relations and harmonised positions on issues of common interest.
3. The Ministers of Foreign Affairs shall hold regular consultations, at least once per year.
4. Depending on need and on the basis of a mutual understanding, the Parties may establish appropriate joint commissions.

Article 11
1. The Parties shall foster the establishment and development of direct contacts and cooperation between regions, cities and other administrative or territorial units of the Republic of Poland and the Republic of Belarus. Particular attention will be paid to cooperation in border areas. In such matters, separate understandings will be concluded and an intergovernmental commission for regional and border cooperation will be concluded.
2. The Parties shall increase the number of border crossings, modernising them in accordance with international standards and improving the efficiency of border and customs controls, including by taking appropriate measures to simplify procedures in border and customs control cases involving citizens of both Parties.

Article 12
1. The Parties shall strongly foster activities aimed at furthering the positive tradition of relations between the two nations. They shall create conditions for the free exchange of reliable information in all spheres of social and cultural life.
2. The Parties shall actively foster the expansion of contacts between their citizens. They shall create conditions suitable for the development of relations between political parties, social movements, trade unions,

academic and artistic societies, other social organisations, religious organisations, foundations, and mass media.

3. The Parties acknowledge the important role played by the young generation in forming new relations between the two nations, and shall support the development of friendly relations between the youth of both States.

4. The Parties shall foster the development of cooperation in the field of sport and tourism.

Article 13

The Parties undertake to respect international principles and standards concerning the protection of national minorities, in particular those contained in international pacts on human rights, the Final Act of the Conference on Security and Cooperation in Europe, the Document of the Copenhagen Meeting on the Conference of the Human Dimension, and the Charter of Paris for a New Europe.

Article 14

1. The Parties confirm that persons belonging to the Polish minority in the Republic of Belarus or to the Belarusian minority in the Republic of Poland have the right, individually or collectively with other members of their group, to freely preserve, develop and express their ethnic, cultural, linguistic and religious identity, without facing any discrimination whatsoever and in conditions of full equality before the law.

2. The Parties confirm that adherence to a national minority is an individual matter of choice made by such persons, from which no adverse consequences may result.

Article 15

The Parties guarantee that persons as mentioned in Article 14 have, in particular, the right, individually or collectively with other members of their group:
– to freely use their mother tongue in private and public life, to access, disseminate and exchange information in that language, and to use their first and last name in the wording accepting in the mother tongue
– to establish and maintain their own educational, cultural and other institutions, organisations or societies, which may seek voluntary financial or other assistance, as well as state aid, in accordance with domes-

tic law, and may access mass media and take part in the activities of international non-governmental organisations
- to profess and practice their religion, including by acquiring and using religious materials and by conducting religious educational activities in their mother tongue
- to establish and maintain undisrupted contacts among themselves within the territory of their own state, as well as with citizens of other states with whom they share ethnic or national origins, cultural heritage or religious convictions
- to use legal means provided in the domestic legislation of their state of residence in order to actualise and protect their rights.

Article 16
1. The Parties shall develop constructive cooperation within the scope of protecting the rights of persons belonging to national minorities, treating these as a factor in strengthening mutual understanding and neighbourly relations between the Polish and Belarusian nations.
2. When implementing regional development, the Parties shall take account of the social and economic interests of persons as referred to in Article 14 and of their organisations or societies.
3. The Parties shall strive to ensure that persons as referred to in Article 14 have the opportunity to learn their mother tongue or learn in that language in educational outlets, and, where possible and necessary, to use their mother tongue before public authorities. In educational outlets in which such persons learn, account must be taken of a broad scope of the history and culture of national minorities.
4. The Parties shall respect the rights of persons as referred to in Article 14 to take part in public affairs, in particular concerning the protection and strengthening of their identity, and, as necessary, shall hold consultations with organisations and societies of such persons.

Article 17

The Parties agree that persons as referred to in Article 14 should comply with the legislation of their state of residence.

Article 18
1. The Parties shall support mutually beneficial economic cooperation, striving to maintain and develop traditional economic and commercial

ties between them, taking account of the needs and real capabilities of both states, based on the principles of the market economy.

2. The Parties shall create economic, financial, fiscal and legal conditions suitable for economic activity, including the development of entrepreneurship. They shall support and protect investments, comply with copyright and patent standards, and facilitate the flow of goods, services, labour and capital across their common border.

3. The Parties shall facilitate the development of direct cooperation between state enterprises, private enterprises and other economic entities, and shall exchange experience and provide each other with training and other assistance in the process of building the market economy.

Article 19

The Parties shall expand cooperation in order to enhance direct and transit connections and infrastructure related thereto, in all areas of transport, including pipelines and power transmission lines. These matters will be the subject of separate agreements.

Article 20

The Parties shall take appropriate measures, including concluding relevant understandings, in order to modernise and ensure the compatibility of telephone, telegraph and postal connections, and to develop cooperation in the field of electronic data processing.

Article 21

1. The Parties shall expand cooperation in the field of protecting and improving the natural environment, preventing trans-border pollution, in particular in the Bug river basin, reducing and eliminating the effects of natural emergencies and disasters, expanding organic production, and implementing the most effecting measures pertaining to protecting and restoring the environment to its proper condition. The relevant bodies of both Parties shall, in particular, exchange information through regular consultations.

2. The Parties, aware of the consequences of the Chernobyl disaster, shall make particular efforts to minimise and remedy those consequences. The Parties undertake to promptly notify each other in the case of any radioactive, chemical or biological hazard or threat thereof.

3. The Parties shall conclude separate understandings on ecological security and cooperation, in accordance with international standards.
4. The Parties shall take part in creating a coordinated international strategy in the field of environmental protection, and shall cooperate in resolving global, and especially European, ecological problems.

Article 22

1. Invoking the positive values of the centuries-old cultural heritage of the Polish and Belarusian nations and their contributions to European civilization, the Parties shall foster further cooperation in the fields of culture, science, education and information. They shall take account of the provisions of the Document of the Kraków Symposium of the Conference on Security and Cooperation in Europe on the European cultural heritage.
2. In order to reciprocally disseminate knowledge on the national legacy in the fields of culture, science, education and information, each of the Parties shall establish cultural centres within the territory of the other Party, which shall receive broad support from the state in which they are registered.
3. The Parties shall cooperate in the area of mass media, and shall facilitate the dissemination of books, press and audiovisual materials of the other Party.
4. The Parties shall expand cultural exchanges in various forms, fostering cooperation among cultural institutions and organisations, including unions, at the national, regional and local levels, and shall support direct contacts between creators of culture and art.
5. Each of the Parties shall ensure appropriate legal, material and other protection for the values, monuments and objects located within its territory related to the cultural and historical heritage of the other party or to their common heritage, and shall act to identify, preserve and save them, and admit them to cultural circulation, including by making them freely accessible.
6. In accordance with international norms and standards, and on the basis of bilateral understandings, the Parties shall engage in and support activities aimed at identifying and returning cultural and historical goods that have been lost, unlawfully removed or in some other illegal way are now located within the territory of the other Party.
7. The Parties shall expand cooperation in the fields of science, technology and education. They shall foster the development of cooperation

among schools, universities and other academic institutions, including within the scope of exchanges of students, academic personnel and scholarship holders, and shall support the teaching of the Polish language in the Republic of Belarus and the Belarusian language in the Republic of Poland.

Article 23

1. The Parties shall support comprehensive cooperation in the field of healthcare and hygiene, in particular within the scope of preventing and combating contagious diseases and illnesses associated with modern civilization.
2. The Parties shall strive to cooperate closely in the fields of labour, insurance and social welfare. To this end they shall conclude separate agreements.

Article 24

1. The Parties shall enhance consular relations and, on the basis of separate agreements, shall implement the legal order in civil, family, penal and administrative cases.
2. The Parties shall cooperate in combating organised crime, terrorism, economic crime, illegal trading in arms, narcotics and works of art, illegal acts aimed against civil air and maritime security, smuggling, illegal migration, the creation and admitting to trade of counterfeit means of payment, as well as other types of crime. The conditions for such cooperation will be set out in separate understandings that shall contain, in particular, provisions on exchanging experience and information in these areas.

Article 25

1. Each of the Parties undertakes to extend and uphold legal protection, in accordance with international legal standards, including humanitarian, national and religious standards, to military and civil cemeteries, graves and burial places currently located or discovered in the future to be located within its territory.
2. The citizens of each of the Parties will have guaranteed access to the burial places of their relatives and will be entitles to care for them.
3. Each Party shall cooperate in identifying and registering burial places of citizens of the other Party within its territory.

Article 26

The provisions of this treaty do not violate the rights and obligations resulting from bilateral and multilateral agreements binding in the relations of each of the Parties with other states.

Article 27

This treaty is subject to ratification, and enters into force on the day the ratification documents are exchanged, which is to take place in Minsk.

Article 28

This treaty has been concluded for a period of 15 years. After the lapse of that period, the treaty is subject to automatic renewal for further 5-year periods if neither of the Parties provides notification of its withdrawal from the treaty at least one year before the end of a given period.

Article 29

After entering into force, this treaty will be registered at the Secretarial office of the United Nations in accordance with Article 102 of the United Nations Charter.

Drawn up in Warsaw on 23 June 1992 in two counterparts, each in the Polish and Belarusian languages, where each language version has equal force.

For the Republic of Poland, L. Wałęsa For the Republic of Belarus, S. Szuszkiewicz

Having familiarised myself with the above treaty, on behalf of the Republic of Poland, I declare that:

- it has been deemed correct in its entirety and in each of the provisions it contains
- it is accepted, ratified and confirmed
- it will be preserved unchanged.

In witness thereof, this act has been issued and affixed with the seal of the Republic of Poland.

Issued in Warsaw on 29 October 1992.

President of the Republic of Poland: L. Wałęsa

Source: Treaty between the Republic of Poland and the Republic of Belarus on Neighhbourly Relations and Friendly Cooperation, signed in Warsaw on 23 June 1992, *Journal of Laws* 118 item 527.

Index of names